The International Library of Sociology

THE NATIONALITIES PROBLEM AND SOVIET ADMINISTRATION

Founded by KARL MANNHEIM

The International Library of Sociology

THE SOCIOLOGY OF THE SOVIET UNION
In 8 Volumes

I	Chekhov and His Russia	*Bruford*
II	Educational Psychology in the USSR	*Simon and Simon*
III	Family in the USSR	*Schlesinger*
IV	History of a Soviet Collective Farm	*Belov*
	(The above title is not available through Routledge in North America)	
V	The Nationalities Problem and Soviet Administration	*Schlesinger*
VI	Psychology in the Soviet Union	*Simon*
VII	Soviet Legal Theory	*Schlesinger*
VIII	Soviet Youth	*Meek*

THE NATIONALITIES PROBLEM AND SOVIET ADMINISTRATION

Selected Readings on the Development of
Soviet Nationalites Policies

Selected, Edited and Introduced by
RUDOLF SCHLESINGER

Translated by
W. W. GOTTLIEB

LONDON AND NEW YORK

First published in 1956 by
Routledge

Published in 1998, 2002
by Routledge
2 Park Square, Milton Park, Abingdon, Oxfordshire OX14 4RN
711 Third Avenue, New York, NY 10017

First issued in paperback 2014

Routledge is an imprint of the Taylor and Francis Group, an informa business

© 1956 Rudolf Schlesinger
© 1956 Translation, W. W. Gottlieb

All rights reserved. No part of this book may be reprinted or reproduced or utilized in any form or by any electronic, mechanical, or other means, now known or hereafter invented, including photocopying and recording, or in any information storage or retrieval system, without permission in writing from the publishers.

The publishers have made every effort to contact authors/copyright holders of the works reprinted in *The International Library of Sociology*. This has not been possible in every case, however, and we would welcome correspondence from those individuals/companies we have been unable to trace.

British Library Cataloguing in Publication Data
A CIP catalogue record for this book
is available from the British Library

ISBN 13: 978-0-415-17813-6 (hbk)
ISBN 13: 978-0-415-86873-0 (pbk)

The Nationalities Problem and Soviet Administration
ISBN 0-415-17813-4
The Sociology of the Soviet Union: 8 Volumes
ISBN 0-415-17836-3
The International Library of Sociology: 274 Volumes
ISBN 0-415-17838-X

Publisher's Note
The publisher has gone to great lengths to ensure the quality of this reprint but points out that some imperfections in the original may be apparent

CONTENTS

Introduction *page* 1

PART I: THE FIRST STEPS IN THE ORGANIZATION OF NATIONAL ADMINISTRATION

Document No.

1 The Establishment of the Central Authorities for the Application of the Nationalities Policy 33
(*a*) *Instructions on the Organization of Local Departments for Nationalities:* (*b*) *Decree on the Reorganization of the People's Commissariat for Nationalities:* (*c*) *The Statute of the People's Commissariat for Nationalities:* (*d*) *The Statute of the first Soviet of Nationalities*

2 Reports of some of the Delegations of the National Republics attached to the People's Commissariat 43

PART II: SOVIET NATIONALITIES POLICY UNDER THE NEW ECONOMIC POLICY

3 Stalin's Report and Concluding Remarks at the Fourth Conference of the C.C. with Representatives from the National Republics and Regions on the Application of the Resolution of the XIIth Party Congress on the National Question 61

4 Stalin's Letter to Kaganovich and other Politburo Members on the Ukrainian Question (April 26, 1926) 78

5 Excerpts from F. Khodzhayev's article: On the Revision of the Statutes on the Budget Rights of the Union and the Union Republics 82

6 From the Proceedings of the All-Union Conference on the Re-elections to the Soviets in 1929 86

7 A. Bogdanov: The Koshchi Union in Kazakhstan 90

8 V. Nodel: The Land and Water Reform in the Soviet East 101

Contents

		Page
9	A. Linevski: The Role of the Ethnographer in Soviet Construction in the North	109
10	Excerpts from V. Aliyev's article: The Victory of the Latin Script	123

PART III: THE CRISIS IN THE VILLAGE AND THE STRUGGLE FOR THE COLLECTIVIZATION OF AGRICULTURE

11	I. Sviridov: The Class Struggle in the Azerbaidjan Village	131
12	N. Selimkhanov: Revolutionary Legality protecting the Elections in Azerbaidjan	140
13	K. Kulov: Clan Survivals as a Form of Class Struggle in North Ossetia	144
14	Excerpts from A. Nukhrat's article: Kolkhoz Women of Tataria	152
15	Excerpts from Muhaidzi's and Nazarevski's article: Settling the Nomads in Kirghizia	158
16	P. Rysakov: The Practice of Chauvinism and Local Nationalism	171
17	Excerpts from S.D.'s article: The Struggle against Nationalism and the Lessons of the Ukraine	181

PART IV: THE INDUSTRIAL AND CULTURAL REVOLUTION

18	Excerpts from V. Belitzer's article: The Formation of the National Proletariat in Bashkiria	189
19	Excerpts from K. S. Rykhlevski's article: The Books of the Nationalities of the USSR during Fifteen Years	197
20	M. Nadezhdin and M. Solomonov: How the National School is made Indigenous: Results of an Investigation	204
21	K. Tobolov: On National Cadres	212
22	B.R.: On National Cadres of Specialists	223
23	A. Telikhanov: On National Soviet Cadres	228

Contents

	Page
24 L. Rabinkov: Look after the Fulfilment of the Mandates of the Electors	235
25 T. Kruglov: Complaints from the Working People (Materials from Kalinin's Secretariat)	242

PART V: LATER DEVELOPMENTS IN SOVIET NATIONALITIES POLICIES

26 Excerpts from A. Kurski's article: Administrative Regionalization of the USSR Completed	249
27 P. Tolstoi: Land Nationalization in the New Western Republics and Provinces	262
28 Excerpts from T. A. Zhdanko's article: Everyday Life in a Karakalpak Kolkhoz Aul	280
Index	295

INTRODUCTION

The application of Soviet nationalities policies in the administration of the non-Russian areas may invite the reader's interest for a number of reasons. The subject is one of fairly broad interest in itself; it is directly relevant to important aspects of current history and politics in other parts of the world. While a good deal of fairly frank Soviet documentary evidence is available for the first fifteen years after the Revolution, this evidence is not widely accessible. So far as it has been used in Western publications, such use has been inevitably coloured by the author's standpoint and interests, so that the presentation of a selection of representative original evidence may be helpful to the student who wishes critically to use those publications, and also to the historian or political scientist who works on related subjects without having access to the original Russian documents.

In order to give a selection aiming at a fairly representative illustration (though not at completeness) in a volume of limited length, emphasis on certain stages in the development of Soviet nationalities policies was desirable. Most of the documents from the first period of the Soviet regime deal with the constitutional aspects of nationalities policies; a translation of the most important of these documents is available in W. R. Batsell's *Soviet Rule in Russia* (London, 1929).[1] A presentation of the history of the first five years of Soviet nationalities policies is given in Part III ('Dispersal and Reunion') of Volume I of E. H. Carr's *The Bolshevik Revolution: 1917–1923*, which is likely to remain for many years the standard work on the subject. Anyone who would wish to improve upon it would in any case have to go back to the original sources. In these circumstances, we believed that the treatment of those first five years in the present volume could be reduced to a skeleton of a few documents which may be helpful for the understanding of the developments of the following ten years.

For the opposite reason, the last (fifth) section of our collection was also reduced to a skeleton. While the origins of Soviet national administration are fairly discussed in existing Soviet literature, with

[1] Some documents illustrating the juridical aspects of the struggle for the emancipation of women of the East have been translated in my *Changing Attitudes in Soviet Russia: The Family*, published in 1949 in the International Library of Sociology and Social Reconstruction.

Introduction

the disappearance of overt opposition in the party during the collectivization crisis the direct evidence of political tensions became extremely meagre; the new trends cannot be described by mere reproduction of Soviet documents. We did not aspire, in that section, at giving more than an illustration of the types of documentary Soviet evidence available for the period. The reader should keep in mind that the task of forming his opinion about what has actually happened during that period, with the help of a critical study of the existing books,[1] starts precisely after having seen on what type of Soviet evidence such study is based. It is not the task of a documentation volume to replace interpretation: I felt it necessary, however, to state at the very opening of this volume the limits within which, for different reasons, comprehensiveness at least of illustration has been aimed at for the different periods treated in this book.

It is obviously impossible to eliminate ideological statements in a collection of Soviet documents. By emphasizing the administrative aspects of Soviet nationalities policies I hoped to keep them within certain limits, and to shift the balance towards the practical issues of the daily life of the non-Russian nationalities. Some sidelights on local government in the USSR in general should not be regarded as more than a by-product of our main effort. A collection of the authoritative policy statements is available in Stalin's *Marxism and the National and Colonial Question*.[2] Document 3 of our collection has been chosen from the standpoint of including in this volume such statements of the main architect of Soviet nationalities policy of which only small parts were before available in English, and also of supplying a general survey of the situation of the opening of NEP from a highly practical point of view.

The aim of the nationalities policy of the Russian Bolsheviks, and also of that of the Austrian Social Democrats in polemic against whom many of their arguments originated, was to secure to the working class a leading position in the transformation of a multi-national state. Much confusion about its content has originated from the very different meaning of 'nationality' in Western and Eastern Europe.[3] Only in the Western tradition is nationality

---

[1] An interesting presentation from a standpoint corresponding to that of the 'bourgeois nationalists' in the USSR is available in Walter Kolarz's *Russia and her Colonies* (London, 1952), followed in 1954 by his, even more political, *The Peoples of the Soviet East*.

[2] English edition in the Marxist-Leninist Library, Foreign Language Publication House, Moscow, 1940, to which our quotations refer.

[3] There are exceptions, such as the Irish problem in nineteenth-century Britain, and their study brought the founders of Marxism to solutions not very far from those later attempted in the USSR (cf. my *Marx, his Time and Ours*, International Library of Sociology and Social Reconstruction, 1950, pp. 335 ff.).

Introduction

associated with belonging to a certain national state, in the formation process of which the nation was shaped. In this framework, for example, the recognition of the obvious fact that the Czechs have a history and civilization of their own, different from that of the Austro-Germans, nearly begged the question how to satisfy their legitimate ambitions, and the argument can be extended to far less developed nations. In the eastern half of Europe and the adjacent parts of Asia, however, multi-national states originated in the fifteenth and sixteenth centuries (i.e. slightly after the consolidation of the French and English monarchies in the West). This happened first under the impact of the Tatar invasion upon the Russians and Turks, and after in the struggle of the multi-national empires with each other. Of the four which existed in Europe, the Polish was divided up long before, and the Turkish shortly before, the Austrian and Russian socialists had their opportunity to discuss how the problem could be tackled in the two surviving units (which were enlarged by annexations of parts of the territory of their unlucky competitors).

Stalin, whose first work on the nationalities problem was inspired by a polemic with the Austro-Marxists, when introducing the new USSR constitution in 1936, and again in his election speech of February 1946, noted with pride the very different results achieved by them and his party respectively. Quite apart from the external results (which surely did not depend solely on the nationalities policy pursued by either party), there is, indeed, an impressive contrast between the struggle for the jobs characteristic of the nationalities struggle in the late Austro-Hungarian monarchy and the Soviet communists' efforts to find candidates from the more backward nationalities for the multitude of jobs opened by industrial expansion (cf. Documents 21–23 below). It should, however, not be forgotten that, apart from the Bolsheviks' readiness to combine the solution of the nationalities problem with a straightforward attack on the basic economic structure, the conditions for preserving a multi-national unit of pre-capitalist origins in twentieth-century conditions were, indeed, more favourable in the Russian than in the Austro-Hungarian empire and, perhaps, also more favourable than in any existing colonial empire.

About one-half of the population of the Tsarist empire belonged to the leading nationality, the Great Russians. Amongst the workers, who held the key-position in a socialist revolution, the proportion

This did not, however, prevent them from applying, in general, the West European approach to Eastern nationalities problems, with implications opposed to the development of the small nationalities (*ibid.*, pp. 343 ff.).

Introduction

was considerably stronger.¹ True, the Great Russians had no such clear leadership in the economic and cultural fields as the Austro-Germans had in the Austro-Hungarian monarchy; but the Poles and Finns, who were hardly the Great Russians' inferiors, had a cultural background different from that of nearly all the other nations of the Tsarist empire, and the secession of these two nations, under as friendly a regime as possible, was envisaged by the Bolsheviks from the very start. Lenin fought a prolonged struggle with his Polish friends because their reluctance to accept this solution might result in a Polish regime much less friendly than it otherwise might have been; Stalin's first act as People's Commissar for Nationalities was to sign the decree which recognized the Finns' secession.² In the West, the three Baltic republics were lost in the course of civil war and foreign intervention, nothwithstanding the strong support given at least by the workers of Latvia and Estonia to the Bolsheviks before and after the 1917 Revolution (for their return in 1940 see Document 27). With the sole exceptions of the Buryat-Mongols (who were Lamaist Buddhists) in the Far East, and a number of very backward tribes (comparable to the Eskimos in the extreme north of the New World) who inhabited the immense territories from the White Sea to the Pacific, all the peoples to whom Soviet nationalities policies were applied after the end of the civil war had a cultural background which was Byzantine-Orthodox or Islamic. Within this group of peoples the hegemony of the Great Russians was a long-established fact: the Revolution needed only to abolish its obsolete forms in order to enable its restoration on sounder foundations, fitting an industrial and democratic age.

With the exception of Finland, which seceded immediately after the Revolution, and of the Central Asian khanates of Khiva (Khorezm) and Bokhara, which comprised parts of the Uzbek and Turkmen population and were indirectly ruled by the Tsars through the local

---

¹ Although Stalin could never state this overtly, he always tried to consolidate this advantage by the preservation of the USSR as an intermediate unit between the RSFSR and many of the minor nationalities when the constitutions of 1922 and 1936 were drafted. Cf. my *Federalism in Central and Eastern Europe* (London, International Library of Sociology and Social Reconstruction, 1945, p. 392).

² Soviet Russia's recognition of secession strengthened the Reds in the civil war which, at the time, was going on in Finland and which only by German intervention was decided in favour of the Whites. But even amongst the Reds there was no Bolshevik majority and even in the case of their triumph the chances of Finland's joining a Soviet federation were remote. No special enamourment of Stalin with his early government experience (cf. I. Deutscher, *Stalin*, pp. 481–2) need be supposed in him in order to explain his continuing reluctance to integrate into the USSR—as distinct, of course, from its sphere of influence—alien bodies with a very different type of civilization.

Introduction

feudal regimes,[1] the whole Tsarist empire was administered by a centralized bureaucracy which (with the support of the Orthodox Church) followed a clear policy of Russification. Although some of the non-Russian nationalities had literatures and cultural activities of their own, these were given no official recognition: the empire was simply supposed to be a Russian one. All economic power rested in the hands of the Great Russian bourgeoisie and Russia's foreign creditors, all political power in the hands of the Great Russian aristocracy. There were local exceptions, the most important of which was formed by the Baltic barons (see below, pp. 268–9), who, however, did not affect the territory with which we are concerned. The autonomy granted by the Soviet regime to all, including the most backward, nationalities[2] was bound to appear as a great achievement to all their members, with the obvious exceptions of those who were economic losers from the Revolution and of the 'bourgeois nationalists' who aimed at separation from the Soviet Union and the reconstitution of their national states in a different economic framework. In the further course of its development, the USSR has carried out the industrial and cultural revolution over all its immense territory, creating a modern society upon very narrow foundations so far as the Great Russians were concerned, and upon almost none in the non-Russian territories.

The space available in this volume does not allow for an attempt to illustrate developments even in all the major republics: in order to give those documents which we found most interesting in fair fullness, we had to restrict ourselves to illustrating the most important trends by examples the choice of which was dictated by the quality of the available material at least as much as by the relative importance of the places from which our illustrations were taken. Yet readers may wish to get a general survey of at least the more important of the peoples with which Soviet nationalities policy is concerned.[3]

[1] After the Revolution, they were transformed into 'People's Republics', whose governments were dominated by the local national intelligentsia. The arrangement, not very satisfactory from the communist point of view (see below, pp. 71ff.), was eventually abolished by the redistribution of the Soviet territory according to strictly national lines. See also below, p. 255.
[2] On the dates of its development (see below, Document 26, pp. 251–2). I have given a summary of the constitutional developments in Part III of my *Federalism in Central and Eastern Europe*.
[3] Lists of the peoples important from the standpoint of certain cultural activities will be found below, pp. 126 (with the obvious omission of the Slavic and Transcaucasian peoples), 201–2 and 226–7. The lists differ according to the connection in which they were established: obviously not every people which is given literacy in the mother tongue, and gets elementary schoolbooks and propaganda literature, qualifies as a possible candidate for a higher educational system of its own.

Introduction

The Great Russians, the leading nationality of the Russian empire, inhabited as a compact body the central part of the East European plain and a broad strip reaching across the Urals to the Pacific (along which eventually the Trans-Siberian Railway was built), conquered during the prolonged colonization movement between the end of the sixteenth and that of the twentieth century; apart from this they formed considerable minorities in nearly all the parts of the empire north of the Caucasus. To the west of them live two kindred East Slavonic nations: the Ukrainians, the second largest nationality of the Union, numerically and economically not inferior to the Spaniards or Italians, and, further north, the much less numerous and more backward Belorussians. By the Riga Peace Treaty of 1920, only three-quarters of the Ukrainians and less than half of the Belorussians were left within Soviet territory.[1] The Ukraine contained industrial centres (true, with a mainly Great Russian working class) of great importance already in Tsarist times; the modern civilization of Belorussia is of purely Soviet origin.

South of the Caucasus range lived two peoples with very ancient but non-industrial civilizations: the Armenians and the Georgians, with one and one and a half millions respectively at the time of the end of the civil war. Separated from Russia by foreign intervention, the Armenians, to whom Russian hegemony had always been an alternative preferable to the fate of their brethren under Turkish rule, had returned as soon as the course of the civil war allowed it; in Georgia, however, the predominant Mensheviks attempted to uphold separation from Bolshevik Russia until it was broken by an internal insurrection combined with the intervention of the Red Army. Further to the east lies Azerbaidjan, with the cosmopolitan centre Baku, which already in Tsarist time was a main centre of industry as well as a stronghold of Bolshevism, but also with mountain districts the backwardness of which even in later times is illustrated in Documents 10 and 11; as distinct from the two other Transcaucasian republics it has a Mohammedan majority. Beyond the Caspian Sea follow, from west to east, the Turkmens, Uzbeks and Kirghiz, north

The complexity of the nationalities problems of the USSR is greatly enhanced by the original tendency to develop separate national cultures even amongst very small tribes, who would thus be separated from kindred neighbours. This policy, grown from an exaggeration of the communists' natural tendency to favour the awakening of the 'non-historical' nationalities (see below, p. 10), is now regarded as mistaken (cf. M. N. Kalinin, 'The Might of the Soviet State', in *Bolshevik*, 1944, No. 7–8); in no case could dwarf nationalities be preserved in an era of industralization and mass-migrations.

[1] On the first stages of the reunification process (which was repeated after the defeat of the German invasion and eventually completed by the cession of the Carpatho-Ukraine by Czechoslovakia) see Document 27 below.

Introduction

of them the Kazakhs and southwards the Tadjiks. With the exception of the Kazakhs and the Uzbeks, who numbered over three million each, all of them were numerically weak, and—with the exception of the Uzbeks, whose cities contained major centres of traditional Islamic civilization—extremely backward, to a large extent even nomadic. Even in Uzbekistan nearly all the work of creating a modern civilization had to be performed under the Soviet regime.

All the nations mentioned had Autonomous Republics which by the time of the adoption of the 1936 constitution had become Union Republics, i.e. direct members of the Union.[1] Further within the Great-Russian–Ukrainian bloc we find a number of other nationalities which were granted only Autonomous Republic status. Such an autonomy was enjoyed by the Crimean Tatars (whose ancestors had dominated Southern Russia), though they formed only a minority of the Crimean population, and by the tribes north of the Caucasus, from the Cherkess, Kabardians and Balkars (in the western part of the Central Range) over North Ossetia to the Chechens and Ingushs, and the peoples of the Daghestan republic on the shores of the Caspian. The internecine struggles of these tribes, notorious already under the Tsarist regime, helped the Bolsheviks in that during the civil war some of the tribes sided with them against the Whites. But the experience was repeated during the German invasion, when the Balkars, Chechens and Ingushs, sided with the invaders; so also did the Crimean Tatars and the Kalmyks to the west of the lower Volga, whose settlement from the nomadic status had provided a continuous source of friction. In consequence, all these nationalities were removed from their seats to Siberia and Central Asia and their Autonomous Republics abolished[2]; the same fate had already befallen the Volga Germans (in the Saratov region) in 1941, as a preventive measure against a repetition of Sudeten-German experiences.

Further north, on the middle Volga, we find the Tatars, in Tsarist times the most developed of the Islamic peoples of the empire, and to the east their kindred but more backward neighbours the Bashkirs, the integration of which into a Greater Tataria was frequently

[1] In 1940, Union Republic status was also conferred upon the three Baltic republics (Lithuania, Latvia, Estonia) and upon the Karelo-Finnish and Moldavian republics, created by enlargement of formerly existing Autonomous Republics in consequence of the cession of the Viborg territory by Finland and of Bessarabia by Roumania. In consequence, the number of Union Republics, eleven at the time of the Stalin constitution (see below, p. 258), rose to the present sixteen.

[2] From the title of the Kabardino-Balkarian Autonomous Republic the mention of the Balkars was removed: this indicated that, under the test of the invasion, the ways of the two neighbouring tribes had divided, as so often in their earlier history.

Introduction

sought by Tatar nationalists.[1] Further to the north, between the upper Volga and the Urals, we find the Finnish tribes of the Mordwins, Chuvashs, Mari, Udmurts, and Komi, who owe their cultural and economic development from extreme primitivity to the Soviet regime; they are followed by the already mentioned tribes of the Far North, whose problems are illustrated in our Document 9. To the east of them, in a territory larger than Europe, live the Yakuts —a Turkic tribe whose Autonomous Republic is the only one in Northern Siberia. On Siberia's southern fringe we find that of the already mentioned Buryat-Mongols.

This short survey may indicate the manifoldness of the problems to be met by the Bolsheviks' nationalities policies. On the one hand— in the Ukraine, Tataria and Transcaucasia—they had to tackle problems of self-conscious nationalities, analogous to those which brought about the downfall of the Hapsburg monarchy; on the other hand, on the upper Volga, in the Far North and in other places they had the opportunity to show that under a socialist regime modern civilization can be brought to primitive peoples without destroying their subsistence and identity. Yet the most characteristic type of Soviet nationalities problems lay in between these extremes. The XIth Party Congress, in 1922, drew attention to the fact that amongst the 140 million people living in Soviet territory there were about thirty million, mainly Turkish peoples, 'who, in the majority of cases, preserve the pastoral and tribal form of life (Kirghizia, Bashkiria, the Northern Caucasus) or who have not yet progressed completely beyond the semi-patriarchal, semi-feudal form of life (Azerbaidjan, the Crimea, etc.).'[2]

The existence of nationalities problems of this type on a large

[1] Some manifestations of this tendency, such as a tendency to exclude Bashkirs in favour of Tatars from the benefits of *korenizatsiya* (see below, p. 208) and from skilled jobs (see also below, p. 196), are enumerated in A. Kavalev's article, 'Some Peculiarities of the Struggle on Two Fronts in Bashkiria', in *Revolutsiya i Natsionalnosti*, 1933, No. 12. Kovalev mentions also, apart from local Bashkir 'bourgeois nationalism', a tendency of 'Great Russian chauvinists and bourgeois nationalists . . . to abolish the Bashkir republic on the grounds that the Bashkirs do not represent the predominant nationality of the republic.'

In view of the strong intermixture of nationalities, many of the Autonomous Republics, shaped in order to give some backward nationality opportunities of development, must have been exposed to similar criticism. If the title-giving but still underdeveloped 'leading' nationality of such a republic made good progress and behaved loyally, as did the Bashkirs, such criticism would be rejected as 'Great Russian' (or Tatar) chauvinism'; if it behaved disloyally, as did the Crimean Tatars, its forming a mere minority in 'its' republic provided an additional argument in favour of its abolition. (The Crimea was at first included in Russia but eventually, in 1954, on the occasion of the 300th anniversary of the union of the Ukraine with Russia, transferred to the Ukraine, which had always provided a considerable number of settlers and is geographically adjacent.)

[2] Stalin, *op. cit.*, Appendix, pp. 246–7.

Introduction

scale provided a lot of additional difficulties, but the possibility of quick and impressive achievements in fields such as elementary education, emancipation of women, at a later date land reform, provided the Soviet regime with a reserve of internal strength which far outweighed such resistance as bey and mullah could offer. Moreover, the close connection of these problems with those found in the colonies of other Great Powers and the fact that, because of the similarity of the pre-revolutionary regime in 'motherland' and 'colonies', the emancipation of colonial peoples could be carried out by constitutional reform without severing the links between them and the 'motherland', did strengthen the Soviet Union's appeal to the 'under-dog' nations all over the world.

This is not the place to decide the highly controversial question whether—apart from the propagandist advantage just mentioned—the Bolshevik solution of the nationalities problem has profited from the fact that the 'colonies' of Tsarist Russia were separated from the 'motherland' by mountains and deserts instead of by the high seas. The practical problems of reconstruction were made more difficult by this type of connection, and we shall see (below, pp. 45 and 48) how modest results were regarded as worth mentioning in times of disruption of the railway system. (In times of predominant air transport, the USSR may enjoy the political benefits of its past without being handicapped by transport problems of the present: such a prospect, however, lies outside the scope of the period treated in this book.) The 'moving frontier', as it has frequently been called, made for a type of settlement which differed from that of the British in East India or Africa, who occupied only leading positions in economics and administration, as well as from that in America or Australia, where the aborigines were practically eliminated (this happened, by the way, also in parts of Siberia). Though the Russian official or entrepreneur was conspicuous in Tsarist times, the majority of the Great Russians living in the Ukraine or in Central Asia were workers and peasants. Though they enjoyed a standard of life undoubtedly superior to that of the local nationalities, and the Soviet Government had ample opportunity to gain local sympathies by the abolition of the privileges granted to the Russian settlers (see below, pp. 102 and 212), it remains a fact that both in 1905 and in October of 1917 the (Russian) workers of Tashkent played a conspicuous part in the vanguard of the all-Russian revolution. The fact that they were led by the Bolshevik Party, which taught them to regard themselves as workers first and as Great Russians second, enabled such moves as the temporary suggestion that, in order better to be able to lead their fellows, they should submit to 'Ukrainization'

Introduction

(see below, p. 79). In the long run it had the result that both the cause for which they stood and the national civilization which had reared them became stronger than before.

The evaluation of this result clearly depends on the critic's standpoint. From the standpoint of what the communists describe as 'bourgeois nationalism' it is an unmitigated evil, as both the new social structure and the impossibility of establishing a purely (local) national society are resented; from the standpoint of the standards with which the Bolsheviks approached the great transformation the social and educational achievements are obvious, and the change in national structure (greatly promoted by migrations such as happened during World War II) is nothing deplorable, as long as the civilization of the local nationalities (of course, in the desired social setting) develops at least as quickly as that of the Russian minorities.

An even more controversial aspect of Soviet nationalities policies concerns the hierarchy amongst the non-ruling nations which was in existence at the time of the Revolution. The problem is common not only to the Russian and Austro-Hungarian multi-national empires, but also to colonial territories such as India and large parts of Africa. For convenience's sake, it may be described in terms of the political jargon of the controversies in the Austro-Hungarian monarchy (from which much of the existing literature on the subject originated) as an issue of 'historical versus non-historical nations'. A 'non-historical nation' is not a nation without a long and rich national history—surely the Czechs and Serbs in Austria, the Ukrainians, Armenians or even Tadjiks in the USSR were not inferior in this respect to Poles, Croats, Georgians or Uzbeks who enjoyed a more favourable position in the multi-national empire. The term denotes a nation which lost its national leading class in consequence of conquest by the empire, or by one of the earlier states by absorption of which the multi-national empire was formed. As the multi-national empires of the East were formed before the start of capitalist development, the leading class destroyed was the national aristocracy. The 'non-historical nations' continued as nationalities of peasants and domestic servants, supplying unskilled workers when, eventually, capitalist industrialization started. If conditions were comparatively favourable, as with the Czechs in the Hapsburg monarchy and the Armenians in Russia, the 'non-historical' nation might eventually develop a bourgeoisie of its own, with a grievance against the subjection of the industries of the periphery to big business and the banks, dominated by the leading nationality, if not even by foreign investors, and against a political regime which favoured nations with a big share in the ruling nobility.

Introduction

In unfavourable conditions the nation of serfs would be eventually transformed into one of smallholders and labourers, supplying unskilled labour for industry and with no national bourgeoisie proper. In the worst cases, such as the Carpatho-Ukrainians in Hungary and many of the smaller nationalities of the Tsarist empire, the formation of any kind of national intelligentsia other than village priests would be prevented.

An 'historical' nation, on the other hand, was in many cases an instrument of indirect rule of the multi-national empire (for example, the Austrian Poles in relation to the Ukrainians, or the Uzbek aristocracy in Central Asia). In any case it enjoyed a privileged position because of the integration of its ruling class in the existing state machine. It might strongly resent its junior status in the multinational empire: nations such as the Magyars and Italians in the Hapsburg monarchy, or the Poles in Russia, were conspicuous claimants for full political independence, as distinct from 'non-historical' nations subject to them, some of which might regard the continuation of the multi-national empire as at least a partial protection against their masters.[1] When a revolution not of their making offered the 'historical nations' the opportunity of independence, they would try to carry as much as possible of their former subjects into the new 'national' state (in post-1919 Poland the Poles formed only a narrow majority of the population); when they remained in the framework of a reconstructed multi-national state (as happened in the USSR) they would demand such an organization of that state as secured them regional hegemony. When making policy decisions, the CPSU had to face many issues of this kind. However diverse the institutional forms,[2] the gist of the decision was always in favour of the smaller, 'non-historical' nations as against the claims of the larger ones to establish their regional hegemony, not to speak of larger units inspired by Pan-Turkism, Pan-Islamism and similar anti-communist ideologies, possibly with help from outside.

The communists' tendency to favour the small and undeveloped nations naturally invited an explanation, on the part of the 'historical nations' and their well-wishers abroad, in terms of 'divide and rule'. Surely, the communists were not unhappy if the application of their nationalities policy weakened the position of potential separatists.

[1] For this reason, they were highly unpopular with Western progressive opinion, including the founders of Marxism; cf. my *Marx*, etc., pp. 303 ff. and 333–4.
[2] In Transcaucasia these included the establishment of a sub-federation under the USSR in order to prevent the Georgians from playing a predominant part as against the local minorities (see also below, p. 179); in Central Asia, on the other hand, each nationality got a completely delimitated unit so as to prevent a general hegemony of the Uzbek intelligentsia.

Introduction

But there were consistent inherent reasons for that policy. If the main task of communist nationalities policies was to bring the tasks of socialist construction as near as possible to the understanding of the peasant masses and to facilitate the recruitment of industrial workers and future specialists from their ranks (see below, pp. 65 and 227), surely the 'backward' nationality of peasants was more important than the aspirations of the intelligentsia of the nation which dreamed of a great past and of the possibilities of reviving it under its own leadership over a number of 'kindred' peoples. The communists did not refrain from implications of the emancipation of the backward nationalities, such as land reforms carried out against the interests of Russian settlers or discrimination in the public services in favour of national as distinct from Russian candidates for well-paid jobs.[1] Soviet communism came into being as a means of carrying out certain social purposes, and not as a means for realizing Russian, Ukrainian, Georgian, Tatar or any other nation's 'historical aspirations'.

The intellectual tools needed for the solution of these tasks had been shaped in the internal disputes of pre-1914 Social Democracy. There has never been, nor could be, disagreement amongst Marxists about the desirability of large political units as the framework for economic reconstruction, but there were quite opposite views about the way in which this need could be reconciled with the national divisions in Central and Eastern Europe. Most German Marxists tended to define internationalism as denying the smaller nationalities' claim to development.[2] The tendency predominant amongst the Austrian Marxists did not discourage those nations' claim for cultural development, but restricted demands for constitutional reform to the offer of national self-government in cultural matters, thus by-passing the most important economic issues of the nationalities struggle and supporting the *status quo*—i.e. the control of Czech industry by Viennese high finance, and refusal of land reform as involving national discrimination in regions where landlords and peasants were of different nationality.[3] This programme appeared to combine broad-mindedness in cultural issues with preservation of the existing economic units and won great popularity amongst the Russian Mensheviks. The Bolsheviks, however, opposed it because

[1] See below, pp. 77, 212 and 220.
[2] Cf. Kautsky's criticism of Bauer's book on the nationalities problem (*Nationalitaet and Internationalitaet*, Supplement to *Neue Zeit*, No. 1, 1908, pp. 4 ff.) and my *Marx*, etc., note 37 on p. 338.
[3] See my *Federalism*, etc., pp. 213 ff., and E. Marz's paper: 'Some Economic Aspects of the Nationality Conflict in the Hapsburg Empire', in the *Journal of European Affairs* (USA), Vol. XIII (1953), No. 2.

Introduction

it implied both a waiving of the use of the national revolutionary movements as allies against the existing regime, and a concentration of the demands of the workers of the 'underdog' nations precisely in the cultural field which they shared with the national bourgeoisie. Stalin (*op. cit.*, pp. 26 ff.) reproached the Austro-Marxists with organizing national communities instead of the class-struggle between Czech workers and Czech bourgeois, as would be possible if the Czechs had a territory of their own. Precisely such organization of national communities was the main reason for the acceptance of the Austro-Marxist platform by the Jewish *Bund*, which desired to organize the Jewish workers (who only in very few parts of Russia formed a majority of the working class) in separate organizations as distinct from the Russian (Bolshevik and Menshevik) Social Democrats. When Stalin attacked this position[1] he defended the unity of the Russian labour movement, both the fractions of which recruited quite a few of their activists from among the Jews. Apart from such direct effects of organization on a national-cultural basis, the question arose whether once the ghetto walls were broken and free access to all occupations was granted to all citizens, any contents other than religious would be left to the national culture of a people such as the Jews. This issue gained in topicality when the right-wing Social Democrats in Stalin's Caucasus suggested the introduction of personal-cultural autonomy for the minor tribes, whose present culture was clearly dominated by the mullahs.[2]

The Bolsheviks' answer to the complicated entanglement of national issues, as formulated in 1913 in Stalin's *Marxism and the National Question*, is dominated by the desire both to account for

[1] *Op. cit.*, pp. 31 ff. Even Otto Bauer, the shaper of the Austro-Marxist theory of national autonomy, had refused its application to the Jews, as he saw their future in assimilation. Zionism, i.e. recognition of a Jewish nation on a racial basis, with a 'national home' (based upon nationalist *mystique* before the impact of the Hitlerite invasion both upon surviving Jews and Gentiles collaborating with the Nazis was felt), was rejected by any variety of Russian Social Democracy, including even the *Bund*. The latter aimed at cultivating a Yiddish, not a Hebrew civilization: in cultural matters, it differed from the communists in that it ascribed to this civilization a permanent value, independently of whether the Jews would eventually acquire a territory where they might grow to nationhood (in the sense of Stalin's theory of nation). To the Marxists of both the Social Democrat fractions, the *Bund* represented the resistance of the persecuted Jewry of the Tsarist settlement belt to fusion with the general Russian revolutionary movement. This issue was quite different from that of the cultural policies most conducive to a painless assimilation of the Yiddish-speaking population, and from that of the socialists' attitude to the creation of a Jewish nation on a territory of its own, which might very much depend upon the economic and international framework within which such an attempt would be made. For this reason the communists have opposed Jewish settlement in Palestine but made an effort of their own in Birobidjan.

[2] *Ibid.*, pp. 35-6, and 43.

Introduction

the realities of the national struggles in Russia, which were seen as part of the impending bourgeois-democratic revolution, and to preserve unity amongst the workers of different nationalities who lived within certain regions. 'The Social Democratic Party', Stalin says, 'can reckon only with real nations, which act and move, and therefore insist on being reckoned upon' (*op. cit.*, p. 11). A real nation is not only an ideological but also at least as much an economic entity; as the Bolsheviks expected the Russian revolution to be largely a peasants' revolution, possession of a definite territory tilled by members of the nation was one of the essential characteristics of nationhood. From this followed as well an answer to the entanglement of 'historical' and 'unhistorical' nations (the Ukrainian and Bashkir peasants were just as right against Polish nobles and Tatar merchants as the Poles and Tatars within their national confines were right against Tsarist Russia), as also the denial of the nationhood of the Jews who had no national territory and only an insignificant minority of whom tilled the soil (p. 31).

The Bolsheviks demanded regional autonomy for territories such as Poland, Lithuania, the Ukraine, the Caucasus and so forth: this implied control of the economic life of the region by the local majority nation (if any), with guarantees for full equality in matters such as schools and language for the local minority nations (such as the Jews in Poland, the Poles in the Ukraine, the Russians in the Caucasus). If some backward nationalities of the Caucasus would thereby be drawn into the common stream of a higher civilization, so much the better (p. 43). No other nation could order any nationality how to organize its national life, but Social Democracy as a party was free, while fighting for the right of nations to self-determination, to agitate in favour of solutions which it deemed proper and against solutions which it deemed pernicious. Thus it would agitate against secession of the Tatars, or against cultural autonomy (on a personal basis) for the Caucasian nationalities (p. 46). The use of its right to self-determination by any nation depended on the contingencies of the class-struggle: in cases such as that of the Poles and Finns the Bolsheviks would eventually support,[1] in others they would oppose its application. There was nothing contradictory in the combination, in one decree of the Soviet Government,[2] of recognition of the Ukraine's independence with an ultimatum to her bourgeois-nationalist government, based upon the latter's support of the Russian Whites, nor in the outcome of that ultimatum, i.e. support of the Ukrainian Soviets by the Russian Soviets. As early as 1913

[1] See above, p. 4.
[2] Of December 6, 1917, No. 90/1917 in the Collection of Laws and Decrees.

Introduction

Stalin had stated that the recognition of every nation's right to self-determination

'does not mean that Social Democrats will support every demand of a nation. A nation has the right even to return to the old order of things; but this does not mean that Social Democrats will subscribe to such a decision if taken by any institution of the said nation. The obligations of Social Democrats, who defend the interests of the proletariat, and the rights of a nation, which consists of various classes, are two different things.

'In fighting for the right of nations to self-determination, the aim of the Social Democrats is to put an end to the policy of national oppression, to render it impossible, and thereby to remove the grounds of hostility between nations, to take the edge off that hostility and reduce it to a minimum.' (*Op. cit.*, p. 17.)

Amongst the diverse possible solutions of the nationalities problem that which was eventually applied by the Bolsheviks, i.e. federation, was rather unpopular with them in times of the struggle against the Tsarist regime, mainly because of its likely implications upon the party's fighting unity. The Austrian example demonstrated that disintegration of the Socialist Party along national lines would occur long before the party had any opportunity to reshape the constitution, and might deprive it of such opportunity. Nor were the possibilities of managing a federal constitution with the help of a homogeneous state party in those days realized. Stalin (*op. cit.*, p. 16) mentioned federation just as one of the diverse possible uses of the right of self-determination, immediately before the above-quoted passage. Lenin opposed it as tending to weaken the economic links and unsuitable for a united state. 'We are', he continued, 'in favour of the *right* to secede (but not of [actual] *secession* of all). Autonomy is *our* plan for the construction of a democratic state.'[1] During the heydays of post-revolutionary 'self-determination' the term 'autonomy'—more modest, but more realistic as it was—receded into the background of propaganda, but Stalin used it as early as 1920, including in the concept diverse degrees from a narrow administrative autonomy (as enjoyed, at the time, by Volga Germans, Chuvashs, and Karelians) to the status of autonomous and even of independent republics entering into mere contractual relations with Soviet Russia.[2] As regards 'self-determination', Stalin remarked at the Xth Party Congress in 1921, that this slogan had been discarded

---

[1] Letter to Shaumann of December 6, 1913, *Sochinenya*, Vol. 19, p. 453.
[2] *Op. cit.*, p. 70. For a more recent application of the concept of 'Soviet autonomy' as embracing the diverse federal institutions, cf. Trainin in *Sovetskoye Gosudarstvo i Pravo*, 1938, No. 2, p. 95.

Introduction

already two years before, with the adaptation of the party programme: there remained only the 'right to secession', which was important for imperialist colonies but would not be applied by the peoples of the RSFSR.[1]

The Third Soviet Congress, in its declaration of January 27, 1918, established 'the fundamental principles of a Federation of Soviet Republics in Russia', 'in order to create a really free and voluntary, and therefore a more complete and lasting union of the toiling classes of all the nations of Russia.' In the deliberations of the Committee which drafted the new Constitution, Reissner's suggestion to apply federalist principles to the union of the different economic regions was rejected by Stalin and the majority of the Bolshevik members of the Committee: thus federalism was clearly restricted to the solution of the nationalities problem.[2] With complete separation as the alternative, federalism supplemented centralization. During the civil war, it was applied only to the peoples of inner Russia: the border regions, when under Soviet rule, were linked up with the Russian federation by mere alliances, strengthened by the unity of the party caucus.[3] The replacement, in 1922, of that system of alliances by a federal union between the RSFSR and its former allies implied progress in centralization, but also in the opportunities of the former allies to participate in the central institutions of party and state. In the circumstances of civil war and reconstruction, and even more with the transition to centralized planning, the centralist character of the Soviet state was a given fact. Notwithstanding some scuffling about the distribution of administrative competences and financial resources, as characteristic of more orthodox federations,[4] the real issue for the constituent national units was their capacity to participate in the formation of decisions arrived at at the centre. Documents 1 and 2 illustrate the process in which what later became the Second Chamber in the federal constitution arose from an administrative arrangement intended to safeguard the liaison of the People's Commissariat for Nationalities with the periphery which it had to serve.

The definition of the units of regional autonomy changed after

---

[1] *Op. cit.*, p. 93. Such a realistic approach, however, did not prevent Stalin from using that theoretical right in 1936 to avoid straightforward statements of his opinion that the preservation of a Great-Russian-dominated nucleus federation was essential for the unity of the USSR.

[2] Cf. Batsell, *op. cit.*, pp. 60–1.

[3] The degree of its centralization was characterized by the removal, in 1920, of the Ukrainian C.C. (which was dominated by the 'Democratic Centralist' opposition group) by a decision of the All-Russian C.C. (in which, of course, the Ukraine too was represented). Cf. Popov, *Outline History of the CPSU* (Engl. ed.), Vol. II, pp. 87–8.

[4] See Document 5.

Introduction

the Bolshevik conquest of power. The only practical application of 'regional autonomy' for large 'crystallized units' selected was the temporary establishment of the Turkestan Soviet Republic[1]; this Republic was dissolved as soon as the progress of the social revolution in the former khanates of Khiva and Bokhara allowed for a redivision of the Central Asiatic territory according to nationality. There was no longer any reason to desire the absorption even of the most backward nationalities by more advanced ones once the mullahs need no longer be in control of the development of those national civilizations. The new state, bound to pursue a policy of emancipation of all the hitherto oppressed, had to support the backward nationalities and to help them in building an economic and cultural life of their own. Since May 1918 in Russia and later in the outlying regions (in Central Asia as late as 1924), the Bolsheviks' alliance with the whole of the peasantry and with the bourgeoisie of the nationalities oppressed by Tsarism (in the periphery by the White generals) broke down and had to be replaced by an alliance with the poorest strata of the peasantry, directed against the kulak as well as against the local bourgeoisie. In many places this implied a policy of supporting the most backward nationalities against the leading strata of the 'historical nationalities'. Finally, the needs of reconstruction, which culminated in the Five-Year Plans, demanded maximum recourse to the forces slumbering in the backward nationalities; helping those nationalities in building an economic and cultural life of their own, spreading education in the native tongue, emancipating their womenfolk were the best means to bring these forces to the fore.

In 1923, at the culmination of NEP, Stalin described the establishment of proper relations between the Great Russian working class and the peasantry of the formerly oppressed nationalities as the class essence of the national question (*op. cit.*, pp. 133–5). Two years later, after having elaborated the concept of 'socialism in one country', he came to the conclusion that the socialist content of the future civilization would be poured into diverse national moulds, that some national cultures might disappear in the transition process by assimilation but that others would rise; the partial process of assimilation was a by-product of the general process of development of nationalities (*ibid.*, pp. 183 ff.). This process included radical land reforms in all the parts of the former empire and the systematic creation of a national working class and a national intelligentsia even amongst the most backward nationalities[2]; it did in no way exclude systematic struggle against nationalism with the undesirable

[1] See below, pp. 70–1.   [2] See Documents Nos. 21–23.

Introduction

social content, culminating in the resettlement and enforced assimilation of those nationalities who behaved disloyally during World War II. There have been shifts in the type of national tradition cultivated, from the original praise of all anti-Tsarist movements to the present disapproval of all anti-Russian traditions amongst the non-Russian nationalities. These shifts were obviously conditioned by the development of the internal and external position of the USSR. More recently, the encouragement of the development even of dwarf nationalities has been recognized as an error,[1] but there has been no change in the desire to encourage the development of a large number of national civilizations so as to bring the socialist content as near as possible to the broadest masses of the people, nor in the principle that the content of every national civilization, including the Great Russian, has to be appreciated according to the accepted social standard. The concept of uninterrupted continuity (*neprerivny potok*) of the development of some civilizations or even of the progressive elements within it, is rejected wherever it occurs.[2]

The development of Soviet nationalities policy can be understood only in the framework of the general development of Soviet society. The establishment of the administrative machinery of Soviet federalism roughly coincides with the end of the civil war and the introduction of NEP.[3] By way of introduction we illustrate, in Document 1 of our collection, the growth of the People's Commissariat for Nationalities into a broad institution with an advisory board which eventually became the Second Chamber of the multi-national state.

[1] See note above, p. 6.
[2] See below, p. 28, and my article in *Soviet Studies*, Vol. II, p. 147.
[3] The People's Commissariat for Nationalities, under Stalin, was established immediately after the October Revolution; during the first year of its existence, however, its activities were restricted to advising the Government on arrangements concerning individual nationalities. Document 1*a* of our collection represents the first attempt to create a centralized administration for nationalities problems in general.
About the same time, in the particular field of education, provision was made to secure the rights of all the nationalities and national minorities to education in their mother tongue (this included, of course, also the Great Russians where they formed the local minority and such national minorities as the (Yiddish-speaking) Jews who had no compact settlements and therefore no national administrative unit of their own). By a decree of the P.C. of Education (*Izvestiya VTsIK*, October 31, 1918) such rights were granted to every nationality which had, in a given locality, at least 25 schoolchildren in each age group (form); the study of the language of the majority in a given region was made compulsory also in the national minority schools (this implied, in contrast to later attitudes, that non-Russian minorities in non-Russian territories had no compulsory Russian). By decree of February 14, 1919, Sub-Departments for National Minorities Education were established in the localities; it is worth mentioning that the elimination of 'manifestation of harmful tendencies (such as nationalistic ones) from the cultural and educational work of the local national minorities' was mentioned amongst their tasks (point 7 of the Instruction).

Introduction

Document 2 illustrates the elementary problems with which the representatives of the nationalities were concerned at the time, and the modest character of the achievements possible in conditions of war and later of famine.

The second section of our collection deals with the period of NEP, during which the unified political and administrative approach to the nationalities problem was elaborated. The party, after having made all kinds of compromises even with obviously reactionary varieties of 'bourgeois nationalism' such as Pan-Turkism and Pan-Islamism[1] when this was opportune in the emergencies of the civil war, aimed at developing in the national regions a policy of its own directed against all the bourgeois tendencies flourishing in the conditions of NEP: first of all against an arrogant attitude of Russian Soviet officials towards the needs and requirements of the non-Russian nationalities, but also against excessive claims of the bourgeois upper stratum of those nationalities, directed against the Russians, and even more, against weaker neighbour-nations. The description of these two deviations as 'Great Power nationalism' and (local) 'bourgeois nationalism' was elaborated by Stalin at the XIIth Party Congress.[2] During the following decade, policy decisions on nationalities administration were made in terms of assessment of the comparative danger involved in either of these deviations, as illustrated in Documents 8, 16 and 17. After Hitler's accession to power in Germany, however, emphasis shifts to struggle against the potentially separatist tendencies, though the old terminology is preserved for some time longer (see below, pp. 185–6).

The XIIth Party Congress was followed by a conference (the fourth) of the C.C. with the leaders of the national party organizations, in June 1923: we translate, as Document 3, Stalin's report and reply to the discussion on the practical measures to carry out the Resolution of the Party Congress.[3] The convocation of the

[1] Even after the explosion of the conspiracy of Sultan Galiyev, Stalin, in 1923, stated (*op. cit.*, p. 155) that the mere *propaganda* of Pan-Turkist and Pan-Islamist views within the ranks of the party, might be tolerated, and theoretically criticized within the party's ranks: only the practice of this theory by collaboration with the Basmach anti-Soviet insurgents had to be repressed. Still Stalin paid compliments to the Tatar leaders ('splendid practical workers in spite of their lack of ideological stamina') who had expressed their solidarity with Sultan Galiyev.
[2] *Op. cit.*, pp. 123 ff., 136 ff. and 149 ff.
[3] Stalin's *Marxism and the National and Colonial Question* contains, apart from his speech on the Sultan Galiyev case (see note 1 above), only a short passage from the report (pp. 159 ff.). From our following document, the letter to Kaganovich, only a part is included (*ibid.*, pp. 201 ff.). The decisions of the XIIth Party Congress were in the minds of all the participants of the Nationalities Conference and needed only occasionally to be hinted at by Stalin; for an understanding of the Conference the Congress documents (*ibid.*, pp. 121 ff., 130 ff. and 249 ff.) are essential.

Introduction

Conference appears to have been caused by the exposure of the unreliability of some of the nationalist supporters of the party in the Sultan Galiyev case in Bashkiria, but the main emphasis of the criticism was directed against Great Russian chauvinism, which might be strengthened by the reconciliation of many of the pre-revolutionary officials and intellectuals with the Soviet regime under NEP.[1] Stalin supported Grinko's suggestion to discriminate in promotion in favour of Ukrainian officials, and described the industry inherited by the Ukraine from Tsarist times in terms which might favour 'Ukrainization'. A few years later, however, he warned against excesses in both directions, as Ukrainian nationalism was assuming an anti-Russian character (Document 4). Problems familiar to politicians working in other federations with great diversity in economic structure are dealt with in Document 5, which expresses the typical demands of a local leader for less dependence on federal subsidies. A particular note is introduced by the Soviet use of differentiated taxation as a means to encourage certain branches of production. Khodzhayev pleads for a share even of the local budget in turnover tax on raw cotton, to remove the disincentive for local authorities to promote its cultivation created by the incentive given to the farmers. It is a different question whether, at that time, such demands could be satisfied without destroying the whole foundations of the federal budget which, up to the most recent times, was mainly based upon revenue from turnover tax.

From these arguments on the highest level we proceed, in Document 6, to the conflicts proceeding in village administration at the end of the NEP period. Documents 6, 7 and 8 should be read together: indeed, some readers may criticize their arrangement in that order, which is based upon the chronology of their origin. From the political point of view, they proceed from the description of social tensions as developed in the framework of NEP (in Document 6) to the overt denunciation of the right-wing opposition at the end of Document 8. As for their content, Document 8 describes economic processes in Central Asia since the October Revolution, Document

---

[1] In Stalin's writings on the problem, as in all the party documents of the time (cf. the Resolution of the XIIth Party Conference, Aug. 1922, *VKP(b) v Resolutsiakh*, Vol. I, 1935 ed., p. 475), this trend was described as *Smenovekhovtsi* ('Change the Signals' people)—from a self-styled bourgeois group (in the USSR and also in the emigration) which favoured reconciliation with the Soviet regime, as it was supposed to be bound to develop NEP in a bourgeois sense, and in any case was restoring the ancient greatness of Russia. Cf. Lenin, *Sel. Works*, Vol. IX, pp. 346 ff. For the counterpart of the *Smenovekhovtsi* amongst the non-Russian nationalities (i.e. local nationalists who hoped that the Revolution would not go beyond the abolition of national oppression) see below, Document 21, p. 212.

Introduction

7 describes the part played by a particular organization of the village poor in these processes (in a republic which appears to have been particularly backward at the time, see below, p. 91), and Document 6 indicates the general political setting in the village of the time.

While in the European territories of the USSR individual peasant enterprise as created by the anti-landlord and anti-kulak upheaval of 1917–18 was consolidated under NEP, in Soviet Central Asia the Revolution, being national in character, had been supported by part of the local aristocracy (beys) and even by the most wealthy of the non-Russian peasants. As soon as Soviet power was consolidated, land reform proceeded on the lines established in Russia already during the civil war period, adapted to the local conditions where control of water for irrigation had provided at least as important an opportunity for the smallholders' exploitation as unequal distribution of land. Documents 7 and 8 illustrate this process and its consequences. The first is written from the standpoint of an organizer who complains of the shortcomings of the local organizations of the village poor; the second sees the issues in the general framework of party politics.

Document 9 carries us to civilizations which, faced with the impact of modern industrial civilization, would be bound to disappear, as the North American Indians have done, unless reasonable guidance were offered for the adaptation to modern conditions. Notwithstanding the difference in underlying principles of social and economic reorganization, students of corresponding problems in other backward regions will find in this document familiar features—including the ethnographer's emphasis on the central importance of his job,[1] but also the problem involved in both preserving the primitive nationality and causing its members to make a positive contribution to economic reconstruction.

Document 10 illustrates an important aspect of the cultural revolution carried out amongst those nationalities of the former Tsarist empire which had no written language of their own, or only one which by force of its character and difficulty of access was restricted to a small upper stratum. The former held true of most of the peoples of the North, the latter of the Islamic peoples, bound by tradition to the Arabic script and a system of religious schools which served only a small minority of the indigenous population. The Russian school system mainly served the settlers: in the Turkestan of

---

[1] Occasionally (cf. p. 113) carried to the point of making him the guardian of elementary attention to local conditions even of well-known and civilized peoples.

Introduction

1906, with a total population of 6·7 millions, there were 30,326 children at school, some 20 per cent of whom were indigenous.[1] A larger number of children learned in the religious schools to recite from the Koran; still, total literacy at the beginning of the century amounted to 0·5 per cent amongst the Kirghiz and 2 per cent amongst the Kazakhs. Conditions were more favourable amongst the Volga Tatars, Azerbaidjanis and Uzbeks, yet even amongst those peoples the large majority was illiterate: in 1911 the 20 million Moslem population had 320,000 children in Moslem religious and 46,000 in Russian elementary schools.

Replacement of the Arabic script by the Latin one was suggested already before the Revolution by progressive Moslems in Azerbaidjan (where, as our document shows, also the post-revolutionary movement for script reform originated). It met, however, with sharp resistance by the Moslem clergy and traditionalists as well as by the Tsarist government. Efforts made by some Russian missionaries to introduce the Russian script for writing the native tongues found more favour with the government but were regarded by the indigenous population as a refined method of Russification. In a prolonged struggle the Soviet Government achieved the introduction of a latinized script, against the opposition not only of the Moslem clergy (which was met also by the parallel reforms in Kemalist Turkey) but also of the Pan-Turkist elements, who rightly feared that the introduction of written languages adapted to the national tongues would bring the differences between the diverse 'Turkic' peoples into the open and thereby destroy the foundations of their Utopia. The Soviet Government did not dare to suggest the use of the Cyrillic script, which was associated with the Tsarist policy of Russification[2]; at that time, it was more interested in extending the influence of Soviet Turkic literature to related peoples who were undergoing similar reforms beyond the border. Some Westernizing intellectuals such as Lunacharsky suggested even Latinization of the Russian script. Already in those days such suggestions were regarded by most people as Utopian in the case of a great nation with an ancient and well-developed literary tongue (to-day they would be condemned as an extreme expression of 'cosmopolitanism'). For those nationalities,

[1] Official materials, quoted by M. Holdsworth in *Soviet Studies*, Vol. III, p. 260.
[2] Characteristic is the incident reported by Winner (as quoted in the next note, p. 137) from the Second Conference of Uzbek Educational Workers in 1922: the principle of Latinization received theoretical approval, but the mere suggestion to supplement the Latin alphabet with a few Cyrillic symbols for Uzbek sounds unexpressible in the Latin script met 'the fiercest possible opposition on the part of all delegates'. See also below, p. 207, for the eagerness with which the Cyrillic script in a typewriter was exchanged for a Latin one.

Introduction

however, who lacked a national secular literature, if not any written language of their own, Latinization appeared as the correct solution and was carried on long after the acceptance of the principle of 'socialism in one country'.

On March 13, 1938, Russian was introduced as the compulsory secondary language in all schools of the Union, as the means of communication in the multi-national state. Already before, teachers had frequently enough resorted to the Russian language in teaching general educational subjects, though the practice was disapproved of[1]; when good successes in Russian were regarded as an important element of scholastic achievement, the teaching of two alphabets in the schools of the non-Slavic nationalities was bound to be regarded as a superfluous complication, threatening not only teaching in school but, more important, the pupils' access, in later life, to Russian literature. Thus Latinization was followed at a short interval (for some nationalities before it had been accomplished for others) by the introduction of the Cyrillic alphabet for writing the national languages—of course, with the exception of the Georgians and Armenians, who had long-standing alphabets of their own adapted to their national tongues.[2] Though the change implied some shift from an international to an inter-Soviet appeal, and followed a definite change in the USSR's relations with Kemalist Turkey and the corresponding trends in the Islamic world, it is sufficiently explained by the above-discussed educational considerations. Notwithstanding the success story told in Document 10, the elimination of illiteracy amongst the backward peoples was a slow process: as late as 1930 promotion of people whose economic interests coincided with the Government's policies might involve acceptance of large proportions of illiterates amongst members of the local Soviets (see below, pp. 139 and 229). No wonder that, after the 'Second Revolution', with the implied demands upon the general educational level, efficiency was regarded as the most important consideration in the educational as well as in other fields.

Soviet nationalities policy, like most aspects of Soviet life, received its definite shape in that 'Second Revolution', the struggle for the collectivization of agriculture and planned industrialization of the country: the third and fourth sections of our collection are designed to illustrate these developments. Their importance justifies a fairly

[1] See Document 20 below, p. 209.
[2] Surveys of these developments have been published by E. Koutaissoff ('Literacy and the Place of Russian in the non-Slav Republics of the USSR', in *Soviet Studies*, Vol. III, 1951, pp. 113 ff.) and by Th. G. Winner ('Problems of Alphabetic Reform amongst the Turkic Peoples of Soviet Central Asia, 1920–21') in *The Slavonic and East European Review*, December 1952.

Introduction

large share in the space available and only very few remarks by way of introduction are needed. The collectivization of agriculture on a larger than experimental scale arose from the failure of the individual-peasant system to supply the increasing industrial population. The 'suppliers' strike' in early 1928 brought the tensions between Stalin's majority group and the right-wingers in the Politburo into the open. At the Plenary Meeting of the C.C. in November of that year the victory of those who would answer the crisis by increasing speed of industrialization, and a reorganization of agriculture which would make supplies independent of speculative considerations, was decided.

The first steps on the new road, entered already in January 1928,[1] implied, as before in the crisis of summer 1918, mobilization of the poor peasants against the rich on the basis of the existing mode of production; only gradually did collectivization become the prime task of the poor peasants' organization. Because of the backwardness of Central Asia the developments illustrated in Documents 6 to 8 of the second section coincided in time with the first steps of collectivization in Russia and the Ukraine; they immediately led to the developments reflected in the first two documents (Nos. 11 and 12) of the third section. Like some other documents in our collection (Nos. 6 and 24), these two are coloured by a definite campaign, namely Soviet elections under the 1918 Constitution[2]; they illustrate, however, the development of the class-struggle in the village and the way in which all major issues of social and cultural life were involved in the great dispute.

The following three documents illustrate the specific aspects of the struggle for the collectivization of agriculture amongst the peoples of the East, including one so backward as the nomad Kirghiz (Document 15, a report by an investigation commission). These are followed by two documents (Nos. 16 and 17) of a directly political

[1] Cf. the documents first published in 1949 in Stalin's *Sochineniya*, Vol. XI, pp. 4 ff.

[2] Elections were indirect and open, yet because of the very dispersal of the actual elections into thousands of localities in few of which the party had organizations there was an actual struggle concerning the political physiognomy of the non-party peasants who would form the large majority of those elected. The campaign might also serve as a check on the local party organizations' activities—for example, when an increased percentage of medium peasants amongst the elected (as against the local communists' natural preference for the village poor) was insisted upon (see below, p. 39); in backward mountain districts of Azerbaidjan the check might also involve the medium peasants' willingness to serve on institutions described by the mullah as devilish, or the Mohammedan women's readiness to face prejudice by standing for election (the party, properly instructed, would presumably see to it that suitable women candidates, if prepared to stand, would also be elected).

Introduction

nature: these illustrate the struggle against Great Russian as well as local chauvinism which had opened during NEP (Documents 3 and 4), but assumed additional importance at a time when collectivization might appear as an initiative of the Russian proletariat directed against the national peasantry. Development of the national civilizations on the desired lines formed an important condition of successful recruitment of industrial workers from the non-Russian nationalities. The last of these documents expresses, overtly enough, the change of political emphasis brought about by Hitler's accession to power in Germany and the involved danger of political separatism (see, especially, pp. 185-6).

The fourth section of our collection is devoted to industrial, cultural and administrative developments. Document 18 deals with the formation of a national working class and industrial development in a particularly backward region; we have already noted[1] the special difficulties arising from the Bashkirs' traditional association with unskilled and seasonal jobs and the Tatars' unwillingness to recognize that 'making Bashkir industry indigenous' implied training those very Bashkirs for skilled jobs. There is plenty of literature on industrial development in the non-Russian territories available[2]; for evaluation of its impact upon the solution of the nationalities problem discussions of the contribution made by the diverse nationalities to the skilled labour force needed for these industries, such as that given in Document 18, are all-important.

The industrial was necessarily accompanied by a cultural revolution: the industrialization of the new territories required an educated national working class. Documents 19 and 20 illustrate this process, the first with pride of achievement, the second in a more critical vein. As the number of printed textbooks given in Document 19 need not be questioned, it evidently still lagged far behind the demands of a country in quick industrialization, general obligatory education just being introduced. In Document 21 we find a discussion of the difficulties caused by the lack of qualified new cadres, in view of the political tensions with the old national intelligentsia as illustrated already in Documents 16 and 17: the solution of the problems is still sought in a prolonged combination of old and new cadres. Document 22, however, which originated two years later, puts all the emphasis on the training of a new generation of specialists; Document 23 illustrates the discrepancy between such training as there is and the needs of the administration. The last two documents

---

[1] Note 1 above, p. 8.
[2] A statistical survey, to the critical assessment of which I tried to make my contribution in a note, is given in the table in Document 26, p. 260.

Introduction

of this part illustrate some of the checks on local administration: the one—with a strong propagandist vein—that by the electorate, the other that by the supreme state organ.

The documents of the collectivization period (as were, in their field, those originating in earlier periods) are quite frank about the resistance met by government policies. Documents 12 and 13 give a picture of the resistance against collectivization, just as documents such as Nos. 14 and 21[1] show the strength of 'bourgeois nationalism'. There was no point in hiding such facts, as Soviet policy was explained as one of continuing class-struggle, and the hard measures applied in the course of that struggle were justified by the exposition of enemy action, such as given, e.g., in Documents 12 and 16. But however frankly the resistance still met, and the insufficient preparedness of the forces supporting the government policies, were illustrated, it was taken for granted that, within *every* nationality, these forces were potentially by far the stronger ones, i.e. that, eventually, however long and hard the way, there would be a flourishing civilization, 'socialist in content, national in form', for every one of the nationalities inhabiting the USSR. What shortcomings there were, were regarded as administrative shortcomings in the application of a policy the eventual full success of which everywhere would be brought about by the frankest criticism and self-criticism. No one expected in those days that the insufficient participation of the Tatars in reconstruction in the Crimea or the difficulties met in finding indigenous officials of political reliability in Kabardino-Balkaria (Document 23, p. 230) heralded what eventually happened under the stern test of the war. Even if anyone had foreseen such things, he could have drawn no consequences from such foresight: no nationality could be written off as a supporter of the Soviet regime before all possible efforts to strengthen the regime's support amongst its members had been made.

With the completion of the collectivization of agriculture frank speaking about the difficulties met with in the non-Russian regions came to an end, at least for the time being. It is yet too early even to attempt a comprehensive picture of the subsequent changes. The external difficulties, which culminated in World War II, were bound to put 'bourgeois nationalism' in a light different from that current at the time when it was more or less a specific colouring for the widespread resistance against collectivization. With the enormous population moves during the war any idea of avoiding major minority problems (including those of a large Russian minority) in

[1] See also document 10, p. 125, on the length of self-sacrifice to which the clerical opponents of Latinization were prepared to go.

Introduction

the national republics was absurd. Nothwithstanding, or perhaps just because of, the development of a large national intelligentsia, friction appears to have continued. The emphasis on ideological homogeneity current in the post-war USSR was bound to result in discoveries of 'bourgeois-national deviation' where there was perhaps no more than a competition in national pride. Document 17 (p. 186) just shows the shift in emphasis from the description of Great Russian chauvinism as the greater political danger, as was current before and during collectivization, to the setting of the period of the purges and of later times, when the 'bourgeois-nationalist' trend was regarded as a threat of treason. Important shifts also in this field of nationalities policies have undoubtedly been proceeding during the period before and following Stalin's death: it is not the task of this volume to essay in speculation.

In these circumstances, the fifth part of our collection does not attempt anything beyond an illustration of the type of documentation available for the post-collectivization period. Its first document illustrates the degree of economic reconstruction achieved at the end of the Second Five-Year Plan and gives some impression of the degree of industrialization with which the national territories entered World War II. The following document (No. 27) illustrates the problems involved in the annexation of the territories where not collectivization but land reform of the type carried out in Russia immediately after the October Revolution was regarded as the immediate task: it may thus be regarded as a summary of the lessons which the Soviet leaders drew from their earlier experience. The last document (No. 28) gives an example, selected by the Soviet publication because of its ethnographical interest, of the fusion between tribal tradition and modern kolkhoz organization which may be characteristic of much of Soviet Asia. The example would hardly have been published had it not been regarded as good, in spite of the fact that the position of women, though greatly improved, surely remains behind what was aimed at in earlier years,[1] and that (as evident from the parts of the article not translated here) only a minority of the women kolkhoz members worked the statutory

---

[1] It is evident from recent Soviet publications that, apart from extreme cases of buying wives, bigamy, etc., the application of the articles of the Penal Code which deal with 'Offences Rooted in the Traditional Way of Life' (*bytovye*, see below, pp. 117 and 145, and my *Changing Attitudes: The Family*, pp. 188 ff.) is avoided. M. P. Kareva (*Law and Morals in Socialist Society*—in Russian—pp. 157–8) still quotes a decision of the Supreme Court of the USSR, of April 10, 1941, which is directed against this lenient approach, as representative of the Soviet view; she emphasizes herself, however, that in the present stage of development propagandist methods of fighting backward traditions are by far the most important ones.

Introduction

minimum of labour days (the distributions per labour day keep within the range of what may be regarded as typical of a cotton-growing district). To some extent, Document 28 may be regarded as a following-up to Documents 9 and 15.

Like every documentation based on administrative regulations and experience, the present collection will leave its readers with open questions of the first order of magnitude. Soviet administration, in the national perhaps more than in any other field, is characterized by a combination of maximum centralization in the interests of planning and defence, the main instrument of which is the control of all important institutions by the strongly centralized Communist Party, with a system of devolution intended to attract the participation of a maximum number of citizens in the execution of public policies: these policies are brought nearer to their understanding and interest by the transfer of manifold functions to the local organs and the systematic promotion of 'national cadres' in all fields of Soviet administration. The respective strengths of the centralising and the decentralising elements cannot be assessed on the basis of ideological, or even of political statements, the predominant bias of which might be caused by the very predominance of the trend criticized at the time when those documents originated: there is no need to suppose that the non-Russian nationalities were weaker at a time when preference in promotion to minor posts was granted even to the illiterate amongst their members than to-day when universities and scientific academies of theirs have to be warned off excesses of national self-assertion. We need much more documentation on everyday life and everyday administration in the USSR before we can conclude from the available documentation more than, at best, a formulation of relevant questions.

Some of these questions lie outside the field of administrative documentation. We can only guess, but not even estimate, the importance of the shifts in population and intermingling of nationalities caused by the last war; we have no post-collectivization statistics of the share of the diverse nationalities in the diverse occupations, and not even of the share of industrial and agricultural population in the diverse regions (though estimates on that account may be possible on the basis of documents such as the confidential Plan for 1941). We can hardly say what people, when arguing about the assessment of some Kirghiz or even Azerbaidjan national tradition, are actually fighting about—beyond the ideological surface value, in which we are not interested, as our present study is devoted neither to ideology, nor to local history, nor even to the effects of 'political warfare'.

Introduction

Other issues belong to the realm of political philosophy and moral evaluation rather than to that of scientific analysis. Clearly a very gifted Kazakh or Tadjik girl, at a certain point of an academic career, will have to make up her mind whether to make full use of all the opportunities of a giant country and a literature of world importance, implying the possibility that if not she herself, then her children will become Russians, or to devote all her energies to the development of her local civilization, possibly including the overcoming of prejudices against women scholars which she would not notice if moving to some Research Institute of the Moscow Academy of Science. Another girl, of average gifts, may enjoy the local opportunities of promotion implied in the party's policy of demonstrating its interest in the emancipation of women. A thousand decisions of this kind will obviously affect the respective future of Kazakh, Tadjik and Russian civilization: but we cannot count and even less measure them. Least of all should we, *qua* scholars, say whether they are good or bad. Nor can we say that there will be no proper Kirghiz civilization when children will have grown up who have been acquainted with the national *epos* only in an appropriate selection. It is not the task of our study to answer questions of this kind.

A selection of documents like the present one, even within its defined terms of reference, is exposed to manifold criticism. In a constitutional history or in a presentation of party dogma certain well-definable items have to be included; the application of policies to administration, however, is expressed in hundreds of documents the choice amongst which—quite apart from accidents of accessibility—cannot avoid including subjective assessments. The best I can hope for is that my critics, while disagreeing with me (and, presumably, also amongst themselves) about issues of priority, will agree that all the issues touched in the documentation are relevant. In order to restrict the subjective element involved in every selection, I omitted from the materials selected for translation only obvious technicalities and repetitions, and most of the phraseological introductions and conclusions which are so tedious in Soviet publications. To omit them completely appeared to me inadvisable, not only because it would distort the reader's impression of the original material, and involuntarily may shift the balance of his judgment, but also because at least some of the conventional formulae carry important overtones for those familiar with the subject (see, for example, above, p. 19, and below, p. 222). On the whole, I tried rather to err on the side of excessive fidelity to my original material than to risk some future student's reproach that I deprived him of

Introduction

interesting detail. In some clearly indicated cases, only the most interesting parts of lengthy articles, which otherwise would have occupied a disproportionate share of the space available, have been translated: in these cases the student interested in detail will presumably resort to the originals. Our approach to the problems of translation has been guided primarily by the desire to present, to the student who has no access to the original, the material as it actually emerged from its peculiar historical setting. Hence the deliberate preservation of the style and form of the documents, and their occasional clumsiness of expression, even when this implied a sacrifice of English style for the sake of greater accuracy.

As my attempt to supply a picture of the general framework has been made in this introduction, footnotes are restricted to the unavoidable minimum of explanation: unless they have been marked by Dr. Gottlieb as 'translator's note', or initialled by me, notes have originated from the Soviet author of the document translated.

The production of this volume has been made possible by the active support of the Department for the Study of the Social and Economic Institutions of the USSR in the University of Glasgow; I use this opportunity to thank all its members for their help.

Invereoch, Kilmun, Argyll,　　　　　　　　RUDOLF SCHLESINGER
March 1955

PART I

The First Steps in the Organization of National Administration

DOCUMENT NO. 1

THE ESTABLISHMENT OF THE CENTRAL AUTHORITIES FOR THE APPLICATION OF THE NATIONALITIES POLICY

(a) *Instructions on the Organization of Local Departments for Nationalities*[1]

1 In the localities of the RSFSR populated by mixed nationalities, departments for nationalities are organized at the soviets [*sovdeps*], in accordance with requirements, on an equal footing with the other departments.
2 In the local departments for nationalities, national sections are established corresponding to the nationalities residing in the territory.
3 Each department for nationalities must be established with the knowledge of the competent Provincial Executive Committee and confirmed by the People's Commissariat for Nationalities.
4 The national sections are confirmed by the People's Commissariat for Nationalities on the recommendation of the appropriate national central departments (commissariats).
5 The departments for nationalities attached to the local soviets:
   (*a*) see to it that the principles of the Soviet regime are applied in every nationality in its native tongue;
   (*b*) carry out all the decrees of the People's Commissariat for Nationalities;
   (*c*) adopt all measures aimed at raising the cultural level and the class consciousness of the working masses of the nationalities residing in the territory;
   (*d*) fight counter-revolution in its national manifestations (the struggle against the 'national'-bourgeois 'governments' and so forth).
6 The heads of the local departments for nationalities are elected by the executive committees and confirmed by the People's Commissariat for Nationalities.
7 The heads of the national sections of the department are elected by the executive committees and confirmed by the corresponding

[1] From: *The Nationalities Policy of the Soviet Government for the Three Years 1917—XI—1920*, (Russian) State Publishing House, 1920, pp. 144–5.

The Organization of National Administration

national central department (commissariat) attached to the People's Commissariat for Nationalities.

8 A board consisting of the heads of the national sections of the department is attached to the head of the department, and placed under his chairmanship.

9 The local departments for nationalities, while subordinated in the ordinary way to the local executive committees, are, at the same time, executive organs of the People's Commissariat for Nationalities. If differences on questions of principle arise between the department and the executive committee, these must be brought to the notice of the People's Commissariat, which takes the appropriate measures to elucidate and resolve them in accordance with the general principles of the Constitution of the RSFSR.

10 The estimates [of expenditure] are drawn up by the department and its national sections and submitted for confirmation to the board of the department and thereafter to the executive committee. After confirmation by the executive committee, the estimates are submitted for confirmation to the People's Commissariat for Nationalities, which includes them in its general estimates.

11 The local departments for nationalities, as a whole, are accountable not only to the executive committee but also to the People's Commissariat for Nationalities.[1] The national sections are accountable both to the local department for nationalities and the executive committee, as well as to the central department (commissariat) attached to the People's Commissariat for Nationalities.

(*Zhizn Natsionalnostei*, December 15, 1918, No. 6.)

People's Commissar for Nationalities: STALIN
Secretary of the Board: IVAN TOVSTUKHA

(*b*) *Decree on the Reorganization of the People's Commissariat for Nationalities*[2]

The All-Russian Central Executive Committee decrees:

In order to ensure fraternal co-operation among the nationalities and tribes of the RSFSR, the People's Commissariat for Nationalities shall be reorganized on the following basis:

1 Every nationality within the RSFSR appoints, directly from the local soviets and their congresses or through its autonomous government, where such exists, a special Delegation to the People's

---

[1] This is one of the first applications of the principle of 'double subordination' which became an established principle of Soviet administration after the VIIth Soviet Congress in the following year.—R.S.

[2] From: *ibid.*, p. 147, published in *Izv. VTsIK*, May 22, 1920, No. 109. *Sobr. Uzak.* May 27, No. 45, p. 202. *Zhizn Natsionalnostei*, May 23, 1920, No. 15.

Establishment of the Central Authorities for the Nationalities Policy

Commissariat for Nationalities, consisting of a chairman and two members.

2 The Delegations of the nationalities are in charge of the corresponding departments of the People's Commissariat for Nationalities, and may reorganize them in accordance with the needs and requirements of the working masses of their nationalities.

3 The People's Commissariat for Nationalities is subordinated to the Soviet of Nationalities composed of representatives of the above-mentioned national Delegations.

4 The Soviet of Nationalities is presided over by the People's Commissar for Nationalities assisted by a board of five members.

5 The People's Commissariat for Nationalities is given the following immediate tasks:

(*a*) to work out and apply all the measures required to ensure fraternal co-operation among the nationalities and tribes of the RSFSR;

(*b*) to work out and apply all the measures required to guarantee the interests of the national minorities residing in the territory of other nationalities within the RSFSR;

(*c*) to solve all disputes arising from the overlapping of national settlements.

6 The People's Commissariat for Nationalities is instructed to issue appropriate instructions to this effect.

May 19, 1920.

Chairman of VTsIK: M. KALININ
People's Commissar for Nationalities: J. STALIN
Secretary of VTsIK: A. YENUKIDZE

(*c*) *The Statute of the People's Commissariat for Nationalities*[1]
[*Tasks*]

Para. 1: It is the task of the People's Commissariat for Nationalities (*Narkomnats*):

(*a*) to secure the peaceful co-existence and fraternal co-operation of all the nationalities and tribes of the RSFSR, and of the friendly Soviet Republics which are linked with it by treaty;

(*b*) to promote their material and spiritual development, in conformity with the peculiarities of their conditions of life (*byt*), state of culture and economic position;

(*c*) to supervise the application of the national policy of the Soviet regime.

[1] From: *The Reference Book* [*Spravochnik*] *of the People's Commissariat for Nationalities*, Moscow, 1921, pp. 5 ff.

The Organization of National Administration

Para. 2: To carry out these tasks, the People's Commissariat for Nationalities:

(*a*) draws up the appropriate draft measures in the sphere of the nationalities policy and submits these, according to competence, either to the All-Russian Central Executive Committee or the Council of People's Commissars;

(*b*) unifies and directs the work of the national Delegations of the various Autonomous Republics, provinces and communes within the borders of the RSFSR;

(*c*) takes into account the experience of Soviet construction in the national territories, and outlines the ways of satisfying their needs and desires in conformity with the peculiarities of the economy, culture and conditions of life of each nationality;

(*d*) protects the rights of the national minorities on the entire territory of the RSFSR;

(*e*) assists the Autonomous Republics, provinces and communes and the separate national groups in their relations with the central institutions of the RSFSR;

(*f*) presents its conclusions on all draft measures of the People's Commissariats of the RSFSR affecting the Autonomous Republics and the Soviet Republics linked by treaty to the RSFSR;

(*g*) supervises the fulfilment, by the institutions as well as by the Delegations of the RSFSR and the Autonomous Republics, provinces and communes, of the relevant articles of the Constitution, decrees, treaties and resolutions affecting the various nationalities;

(*h*) establishes its Representatives at the Central Executive Committees and the Councils of People's Commissars of the Autonomous Republics and the corresponding Executive Committees of the autonomous provinces, as well as at the Delegations of the Soviet Treaty Republics not included in the Federation;

(*i*) conducts negotiations with the representatives of the nationalities within the RSFSR, and makes suggestions for the formation of new autonomous units to the All-Russian Central Executive Committee and the Council of People's Commissars;

(*j*) presents its conclusions on the estimates, both financial and material, submitted by the Autonomous Republics, provinces and communes;

(*k*) collects and studies material on the life of the nationalities within the RSFSR and beyond its borders, and publishes relevant information reports;

(*l*) sets up special learned societies and educational institutions to

Establishment of the Central Authorities for the Nationalities Policy

study the life of the nationalities and to train cadres of political workers of non-Russian nationality;

(*m*) issues a periodical and special publications on the national question, and directs the national publishing house of the Delegations and the departments for nationalities at the People's Commissariat for Nationalities.

[*The Structure of the People's Commissariat for Nationalities*]

Para. 3: The People's Commissariat for Nationalities, by virtue of its functions, is subdivided into:

(*a*) Delegations accredited to the centre by the Autonomous Republics, provinces and communes;

(*b*) Representatives of the People's Commissariat for Nationalities accredited to the governments of the Autonomous Republics, the executive committees of the autonomous provinces and communes, and to the governments of the Soviet Republics linked to the RSFSR by treaty;

(*c*) departments for the separate nationalities;

(*d*) departments for information, editing and publishing; for educational institutions and learned societies; and the internal administration.

Note: A Soviet of Nationalities is attached to the People's Commissariat for Nationalities.

[*The Soviet of Nationalities*] Para. 4:

(*a*) The Soviet of Nationalities is a consultative representative organ attached to the People's Commissariat for Nationalities which establishes, by means of the Delegations and departments for nationalities, a living and indissoluble link among the nationalities, systematizes the practical experience gained in applying the national policy of the Soviet regime, and outlines ways of satisfying the needs and requirements of the working masses of the nationalities to promote their economic, cultural and political development;

(*b*) the Soviet of Nationalities includes the People's Commissar (chairman), the members of the Board, the chairmen of the Delegations of the Autonomous Republics, provinces and communes, and the heads of the departments for nationalities.

[*The National Delegations at the People's Commissariat for Nationalities*] Para. 5:

(*a*) Each autonomous national-territorial state unit on the territory of the RSFSR maintains, at the People's Commissariat

The Organization of National Administration

for Nationalities, its own Delegation which has deparmental status and forms an organic part of the Commissariat;

(b) the Delegations, consisting of a chairman and two members, are appointed by the Council of People's Commissars or the executive committee of the autonomous units, and confirmed by the All-Russian Central Executive Committee;

(c) the tasks of each Delegation are: to establish a link between the Autonomous Republics and provinces with the centre and *vice versa*, to take part, through the Soviet of Nationalities, in working out the measures affecting the nationalities of the RSFSR, to pilot through the appropriate central institutions the financial as well as material estimates of the Republics and provinces which they represent, and to promote their cultural and economic development;

(d) in accordance with its tasks, each Delegation may maintain a general section, an information section and an economic section.

[*The Departments for Nationalities*] Para. 6:

(a) Nationalities residing within the RSFSR as national minorities but having corresponding territorial units which are not part of the RSFSR and are neither allied nor Soviet Republics (Poles, Latvians, Estonians, Lithuanians, Finns and others), as well as Jews, have appropriate departments for nationalities at the People's Commissariat for Nationalities;

(b) the departments for nationalities are set up by the People's Commissariat for Nationalities with the direct collaboration of the workers' organizations of the corresponding national groups on the territory of the RSFSR;

(c) the departments for nationalities may be divided into sub-departments: for general affairs, for editing and publishing, and for information and instruction.

Para. 7:

(a) The Department for National Minorities unifies and directs the work of the provincial and district [*uyezd*] departments for nationalities serving those national groups (minorities) on the territory of the RSFSR which have no departments for nationalities of their own at the People's Commissariat for Nationalities, and do not form part of corresponding national-territorial units;

(b) the Department for National Minorities contains a sub-department for organization and instruction and sub-departments for the corresponding national groups.

Establishment of the Central Authorities for the Nationalities Policy

Para. 8:
(*a*) The internal administration is in charge of questions of an administrative, financial and technical nature, and directs the corresponding departments of the People's Commissariat for Nationalities which are an organic part of the administration;
(*b*) the following are organic parts of the administration:
  1 the general office,
  2 the secretariat of the board,
  3 the financial sub-department,
  4 the economic sub-department.

Para. 9:
(*a*) The information department collects, systematizes and works out the data on the economy, politics, culture and conditions of life of all the nationalities and national groups connected, in one form or other, with the RSFSR; it publishes weekly information reports, drawn from these data, for the People s Commissariats of the RSFSR on the state of affairs in the provinces and Autonomous and Treaty Republics, and supplies the Soviet press with corresponding information;
(*b*) the information department is divided into two sub-departments:
  1 for statistics, libraries and archives, and
  2 for general information,
both of which contain corresponding national sections.

Para. 10:
(*a*) The tasks of the department for educational establishments and learned societies are to centralize the study of the East, to relate oriental studies closely to the practical requirements of life of the respective peoples, and to train cadres of political workers for the Eastern Republics and provinces;
(*b*) the department is in charge of the Society for Oriental Studies, the Communist University for the Working Peoples of the East, the Instructors' School of the People's Commissariat for Nationalities, and so forth;
(*c*) all institutions and organizations mentioned in point (*b*) function on the basis of special decrees and of the explanations added to them.

Para. 11: The editorial and publishing department unifies the work of editing and issuing the publications of the People's Commissariat for Nationalities and its departments for nationalities; it also renders technical and literary assistance in this field to the autonomous units and national minorities.

[*On the Departments for Nationalities attached to the Provincial Executive Committees*]

Para. 12: The provincial and district departments for nationalities unify the work among the national minorities residing on the territory of a given province or district, and take part in the work of the other Soviet institutions in questions affecting the national minorities.

Para. 13: The tasks of the departments for nationalities are:
(*a*) to consolidate the principles of Soviet construction, and to apply the measures of the Soviet regime among the national minorities on the territory of a given province or district;
(*b*) to raise the political, economic and cultural level of the national minorities of a given locality;
(*c*) to publish periodical and non-periodical literature for the national minorities.

Para. 14: The Department for Nationalities is divided into national sub-departments corresponding to the national groups of the territory. Apart from the national sub-departments, the Provincial Department for Nationalities has the following sub-departments:
  1 the sub-department for general affairs,
  2 the information and instructional sub-department,
  3 the literary and publishing sub-department.

[*The Representatives of the People's Commissariat for Nationalities*]
Para. 15:
(*a*) For the purpose of systematizing the practical experience gained by applying the policy of the Soviet regime in the autonomous provinces and Republics, as well as in the Treaty Republics, and for the purpose of supervising the fulfilment of the decrees issued by the Central Federal Authority of the RSFSR on the basis of article 22 of the Constitution of the RSFSR protecting the rights and interests of the national minorities, the People's Commissariat for Nationalities sends its Representatives to the governments of the Autonomous and Treaty Republics, and to the executive committees of the Autonomous Regions.

Establishment of the Central Authorities for the Nationalities Policy

(*b*) the Representatives of the People's Commissariat for Nationalities function on the basis of special statutes issued in relation to them.

Moscow, Kremlin, May 26, 1921.

Chairman of VTsIK: M. KALININ
Chairman of the Council of People's Commissars:
V. ULYANOV (Lenin)
Secretary: A. YENUKIDZE

(*d*) *Statute on the Soviet of Nationalities attached to the People's Commissariat for Nationalities, confirmed by the Praesidium of the All-Russian Central Executive Committee on April 21, 1921.*[1]

In pursuance of the resolution of VTsIK of May 22, 1920 (on the reorganization of the People's Commissariat for Nationalities), and the People's Commissariat for Nationalities of June 9, 1920, the Soviet of Nationalities decrees:

1 The Soviet of Nationalities is the representative organ, attached to the People's Commissariat for Nationalities, reflecting the peculiarities of the economy, culture and conditions of life of the Autonomous Republics, provinces, communes and national minorities of the RSFSR, and serving as a living and indissoluble link between the nationalities.

2 The tasks of the Soviet of Nationalities are:
(*a*) to satisfy the needs and desires of the Autonomous Republics, provinces, communes and national minorities of the RSFSR;
(*b*) to outline the means of satisfying the needs and desires of the above-mentioned units in conformity with the peculiarities of the economy, culture and conditions of life of each nationality;
(*c*) to consolidate the peaceful co-existence and fraternal co-operation of the working masses of the nationalities and national groups of the RSFSR;
(*d*) to systematize the practical experience gained by applying the national policy of the Soviet regime in the peripheries.

3 In order to carry out these tasks, the Soviet of Nationalities:
(*a*) maintains a close link, through the national Delegations and the Departments for Nationalities, with the Autonomous Republics, provinces, communes and national minorities; it keeps the local authorities regularly informed, receives reports from the localities and, on the basis of the material received, draws up the measures and draft laws designed to satisfy the needs and desires of a given nationality;

[1] From: *ibid.*, pp. 9–10.

The Organization of National Administration

(b) formulates its opinions and makes suggestions to the All-Russian Executive Committee and the Council of People's Commissars on all questions of state life, which are subject to the decision of these institutions, and which have a bearing on the national policy of the RSFSR;

(c) discusses, by way of preliminary examination, draft bills and projects of the All-Russian Executive Committee and the Council of People's Commissars which have an exclusive bearing on some nationality and require changes in, or amendments to, the existing decrees and resolutions or the promulgation of new ones;

(d) discusses, and arrives at conclusions, on all questions and measures of People's Commmissariats which affect in matters of principle the Autonomous Republics, provinces and communes, as well as the separate national minorities;

(e) makes suggestions to People's Commissariats for changes in amendments to instructions or the promulgation of new instructions by them on questions affecting the work of these People's Commissariats, so that the latter should be able to fulfil in the best possible way their tasks among the particular nationalities and give complete satisfaction to the needs and requirements of the latter;

(f) co-ordinates the activity of the various People's Commissariats and organs in relation to the Autonomous Republics, provinces, communes and national minorities.

4 The following are permanent members of the Soviet of Nationalities: The People's Commissar, the members of the board of the People's Commissariat for Nationalities, the chairmen of the National Delegations of the Bashkir, Buryat, Votsk, Gorsk, Mari, Karelian, [Volga] German, Daghestan, Zyryan, Kalmyk, Kirghiz, Turkestan, Tatar, Crimean, Chuvash and Yakut Autonomous Republics and provinces, and the heads of the Jewish, Latvian, Lithuanian, Polish, Finnish and Estonian Departments for Nationalities.

Note: The chairman of the Soviet of Nationalities is the People's Commissar for Nationalities.

5 The Soviet of Nationalities nominates the candidates to the board of the People's Commissariat for Nationalities.

People's Commissar for Nationalities: STALIN
Secretary: AINSHTEIN

DOCUMENT NO. 2

REPORTS OF SOME OF THE DELEGATIONS OF THE NATIONAL REPUBLICS ATTACHED TO THE PEOPLE'S COMMISSARIAT FOR NATIONALITIES[1]

DELEGATION OF THE DAGHESTAN SSR

The Delegation began its existence in February 1921. At that time it consisted of a chairman and a secretary. Gradually the staff was enlarged, and the work of the General Section was steadily improved.

The General Section carried out the following important directives from the Revolutionary Committee of the Republic:

1 Providing the Republic with Soviet officials and specialists. In accordance with this directive, 550 people were assigned to the People's Commissariat for Labour; but the Delegation was only able to select and despatch 133. This list did not include those sent directly from the People's Commissariats of the RSFSR. It was mainly the People's Commissariats for Health, Agriculture, and the Interior which were supplied with personnel. The very difficult transport conditions and the unstable food position on the spot presented the greatest obstacles.

2 The People's Commissariat for Education of the RSFSR has complied with the decision to despatch an expedition of instructors to Daghestan. The expedition was assembled and despatched by the Delegation at the expense of the RSFSR People's Commissariat for Education and returned with a great deal of material, particularly for the Museum of the Revolution.

3 A scientific expedition was organized, equipped and despatched to investigate the mining resources of Daghestan. This expedition has already returned, and a map of the mining resources of Daghestan is being prepared on the basis of its data.

4 A special commission was equipped by *Glavsteklo* [the Central Administration of the Glass Industry] to inspect the glass factory *Dagestanskiye Ogni*, and an estimate for its restoration was drawn up and adopted. At present, the Economic Department is engaged in transferring workers to this factory.

[1] Excerpts from: *Report of the People's Commissariat for Nationalities for 1921* (in Russian), Moscow, December 1921.

The Organization of National Administration

5 The question of organizing and equipping a separate Daghestan brigade has been raised and tackled.

6 The question of transferring a wool-weaving factory to Daghestan has been raised and approved. The Economic Section is at present engaged with the technical aspects of this project.

7 The question of setting up in Daghestan the First State Museum for Painting and Sculpture, the accomplishment of which in 1921 was impeded by the lack of estimate provisions and was therefore transferred to 1922, has been raised and worked out.

The Information Section of the Daghestan Delegation started full-scale work only in June. Until then, absolutely no current information material was available from the Republic. Nevertheless great efforts were made, by drawing on the accumulated material, to prepare placards and diagrams for the various People's Commissariats, and a history of the revolutionary movement for the Comintern exhibition. The same material was used for the album *Soviet Daghestan*.

On the whole, from August onwards, the work began to function properly.

Liaison was established with the People's Commissariats of the RSFSR and the various political bodies, from whom material was received in the form of instructions, placards and statutes concerning all the departments of the People's Commissariats, and these were sent regularly to the corresponding People's Commissariats of the Republic of Daghestan. The largest amount of the material accumulated and sent was for the People's Commissariats for Education, Health and Agriculture.

In the second half of the year a great deal of work was also done in enrolling in the higher educational establishments the students sent (*komandirovannykh*) from Daghestan. The Daghestan Delegation has placed altogether 62 students in the Sverdlov University, the General Staff and technical and special higher educational institutions.

The business of making economic estimates and placing orders for the Daghestan Soviet Socialist Republic which was entrusted to Comrade Takho-Godi, secretary of the Extraordinary Delegation, member of the VTsIK and chairman of the VTsIK Commission for the supply of Daghestan, and the transport side of which was entrusted to Comrade Korova, was completed by May 1.

The Delegation, not yet fully organized at the time, gave only technical assistance in this work. The provisioning of the Republic for the first half of 1921, therefore, proceeded without the participation of the Delegation. After the departure of Comrade Takho-Godi the Delegation got through only a few applications which had been

Reports of the Delegations of the National Republics

left uncompleted by him. It was difficult to make further applications because information from the People's Commissariats of the Daghestan Socialist Republic was not received in time.

Altogether, during the first half of 1921, 39 wagons of freight were sent from Moscow to Daghestan, including eight wagons of drugs for the People's Commissariat of Health, six of machines for the People's Commissariat of Agriculture, two of uniforms for the Commissariat of War, 18 of cloth for the People's Commissariat of Education, and three of mixed freight for various People's Commissariats.

At the end of July, the Delegation was joined by the member of the Board of the Representation and manager of the Economic Department, the former chairman of the Daghestan Soviet of National Economy, Comrade Ulusski, who had been appointed by the Daghestan Revolutionary Committee and by the representative of the Daghestan Revolutionary Committee at the Supreme Council for National Economy, Comrade Korobov; he was accompanied by other members of the Daghestan Soviet of National Economy, who brought with them a considerable amount of information and estimates. The Economic Section is in the process of reorganization and will now be able to do a great deal of important work in supplying industry.

For the second half of the year the following freights were despatched to Daghestan: two wagons of flour-milling machines, two of drugs and medical instruments, two of sawing and timber-processing machines, one of chloride of lime, three of instructions[1] and other materials for the Soviet of National Economy, two wagons of various materials for the People's Commissariat of Education, one wagon of seeds for the People's Commissariat of Agriculture, 10 wagons of industrial sugar, five wagons of sugar for the People's Commissariat of Food, one wagon of turners' lathes and one wagon of various materials for Sovnarkhoz, three wagons of sugar and honey for the People's Commissariat of Food, a motorized hospital (13 wagons) for the People's Commissariat of Health, another wagon of sugar for the People's Commissariat of Food, three of cast iron for the Soviet of National Economy and one of arsenic for the People's Commissariat of Agriculture. A total of 51 wagons by December 1.

In addition, the Economic Section organized the transfer of a 300-h.p. steam engine from Rybinsk, of a wool-weaving factory, and of workers for the glass factory *Daghestanskiye Ogni*.

For the whole period the Delegation received 164,148,385 rubles for expenses.

---

[1] The text says 'instructors'—which may be a printer's error.

The Organization of National Administration

Owing to the fact that the sums or money allocations from the various People's Commissariats for defraying the cost of their commissions were not received in time, there were faults in the expenditure of the sums and even in the accounts which were recorded by the Workers' and Peasants' Inspectorate at the last inspection. The main defect lies in bad liaison with the People's Commissariats of the Daghestan SSR and weaknesses in the organization of the work in these Commissariats. Thus, the Delegation is still unable to prevail upon the People's Commissariats that it should be informed of the safe arrival of goods despatched, or that it should be sent clearance for advances made and so forth. Lately, in connection with the universal change-over to payment for supplies,[1] the Economic Section, being without credits and failing to receive them from the Republic, was put in a hopeless position. The attachment of the Daghestan Republic, in the economic field, to the south-eastern district is responsible for a radical change in its work and organization. At the present moment the Economic Section is engaged in working out the project for its reorganization into a trading agency, and negotiations are in progress with the Moscow Centre of Consumers' Co-operatives about commercial links with Daghestan, since Moscow was (Daghestan's) basic market for the sale of agricultural, wine-making and market-gardening produce, as well as for the output of domestic crafts. Negotiations are also being held with Rostov about the organization of an economic delegation of the Daghestan SSR, which is to be attached to the (permanent) Economic Conference of the South East.

THE DELEGATION OF THE TATAR SSR

It is not possible to give an account of the activity of the Delegation for the whole of 1921, since prior to the appointment, in August of the current year, of its new chairman, Ganeyev, no trace of its work was preserved.

Until then, the apparatus of the Delegation did not function properly and the 30 warrants,[2] which had accumulated for the People's Commissariat of Education, the Central Veterinary Administration and others could not be fully carried out, so that

---

[1] As distinct from the distribution in kind (*payok*) which had been current under War Communism.—R.S.

[2] Warrants (*naryady*) were issued by the supreme planning bodies and the Government on recognition of the priority of some claim: as can be seen from this document, considerable efforts on the part of the Department which had obtained a warrant were still needed to secure actual supply by the factories, stores, etc., to which the warrant was addressed.—R.S.

Reports of the Delegations of the National Republics

some of them were cancelled. The liaison with the People's Commissariats of the Tatar SSR was weak, and the Delegation was not informed of all the needs of, and requests from, the institutions of the Republic. Moreover, the Delegation, having no estimates for its own maintenance, was in extreme need of funds.

This state of affairs shaped the immediate course of the Delegation's work. The first urgent task was to carry out the warrants it had received—and the second to establish a close and living link with the People's Commissariats of the Tatar SSR, and to put an end to their separate relations with the People's Commissariats of the RSFSR.

The General Section, during that time, did mainly office work and kept a register of people sent from the Tatar Republic to Moscow, and of those returning from these missions.

In connection with allocations for higher education, the General Section was instructed to distribute and direct students who were natives of the Tatar Republic to higher educational establishments. Altogether 80 students were involved.

Moreover the General Section supplied all the required information in answer to enquiries, and issued explanations and instructions to all those making direct approaches to the Delegation.

The activity of the Information and Statistical Department during that time was as follows:

The statistical material received from the Tatar Statistical Administration was systematized and transmitted to the Information Department of the People's Commissariat for Nationalities; data on the exact frontiers of the Tatar Republic and their changes—copies of the minutes of the conference of the mixed commission for frontier delimitation—have been collected. The entire material was sent to the Tatar People's Commissariat for Internal Affairs. Informational liaison was established with the People's Commissariats for Food, Agriculture, Education, Social Security, the Chief Administration for Political Education and other departments of the RSFSR, and the same kind of link was organized with the institutions and commissions of the Tatar Republic. The Information Department of the People's Commissariat for Nationalities was kept informed of all developments, and reports were given to the newspaper *Zhizn Natsionalnostei*.

In addition to this, literature received from the People's Commissariats of the RSFSR was sent to Kazan; and literature in the Tatar language was sent by request to the Culture and Education Section of the Moscow-Kazan, Kazanburg Railway and the Vyatka Provincial Section for National Minorities.

The activity of the Delegation was more successful in provisioning

The Organization of National Administration

the Tatar Republic, and from March to December of this year the following warrants were received and carried out:

1 For building materials: 20,717 poods of alabaster, lime, whiting and so forth; 939,190 poods of brick; 2,500 pieces and 37 cases of glass; 154 poods and 35 pounds of metals (steels, iron, zinc and others).

2 Materials of chemical production: 1,126 poods 22 pounds (sulphur, drying oil, vitriol and so forth).

3 Approximately $62\frac{1}{2}$ kilogrammes of drugs and medical instruments, 1,000 ampules of caffeine and 1,000 ampules of camphor, 2,788 bottles of wine and 5,174 items such as forceps, lancets, clamps, douches and so forth.

4 34,454 arshins of textiles.

5 Carpenter's, locksmith's and blacksmith's tools—1,545 pieces; blacksmith's, carpenter's and locksmith's materials: 541 gross of screws, 200 poods of bolts, 2,000 sheets of emery paper, 5 poods 25 pounds of emery, 512 arshins of leather and driving belts, 152 metres of copper tubing.

6 2,875 poods of paper.

7 Agricultural implements and objects of agricultural use: 4 ploughs, 18 rakes, 1 locomobile, 60,765 saws, choppers, locks and so forth, $181\frac{1}{2}$ dozens of files, 365 poods of nails, 540 poods of string, 15 poods of leather, 120 poods of pitch.

8 Goods of mass consumption: 107 gross of thread, $415\frac{1}{2}$ dozen skeins of thread, $40\frac{1}{2}$ poods of coarse thread, 350 arshins of braid, 50 lamps, 600 glass lamp funnels, and so on.

9 Office appliances: 1,035 pencils, 30 reams of paper, 1,045 notebooks and 197 other small items.

10 Motor-vehicle materials: 25 covers, 25 tyre tubes, 1,105 autoparts (ball-bearings and so forth).

11 Electrical appliances: 4,595 electrical bulbs, 195 switches, plugs and so forth, 18 poods 38 pounds of bolts, 75 sazhens of electrical flex.

Apart from these materials, the following items were received: 139 pieces of clothing, 47 pieces of underwear, 273 pieces of linen, 198 pairs of boots, 1,000 pairs of socks, 235 pairs of children's shoes and so on. On behalf of the Tatar People's Commissariat of Education, the Delegation obtained the following items: 164,588 arshins of cloth, 1,000 pairs of American footwear, 1,977 pairs of stockings, 1,047 knitted and cotton shawls, 730 pairs of socks, 67 children's fur collars, 24 cut-out furs, 7 poods of rubber soles, 46 school appliances, 30 bottles of sulphuric acid, and office equipment.

By presenting additional estimates the norm of supply was

increased from 3 per cent to 5·9 per cent. Warrants have been issued for 1,500 poods of vegetables from Penza and Samara, 500 pairs of shoes from Kazan, 10½ poods of leather scraps, 19 poods of soap, 49 poods of washing powder and about 10,000 pieces of crockery from Kazan.[1]

Of the 13 warrants for the People's Commissariat for Local Security, for reasons beyond the Delegation's control only two have so far been carried out, i.e. for 80,000 arshins of woollen cloth and for office equipment.

For the period from September 20 to October 30, 203 wagons of grain were consigned by warrant to the Tatar People's Commissariat of Food.

THE DELEGATION OF THE BASHKIR SSR

Owing to last year's food shortage and this year's famine, the activity of the Delegation centred almost entirely on supplying the Republic with all necessary products and materials. Under these conditions, most of the work had obviously to be done by the Economic Section.

The provisioning of the Bashkir Republic proceeded along two parallel lines: by plan and by extraordinary unplanned procedure, as well as by private purchases and some goods exchange in conformity with the New Economic Policy.

In order to establish work according to plan, the Economic Section tried to see that all the orders from the Bashkir Republic be concentrated in the Delegation. It was only due to the weak liaison with the government of the Bashkir SSR that strict observance of this procedure was occasionally impeded.

As soon as the Bashkir Republic was put in the category of famine districts (September 5), the Economic Section took an active part in relief work. It obtained warrants for approximately 100 wagons of various freight for Bashkiria, and some 30,000 poods of grain have already been despatched.

By request of the Delegation, two fully equipped hospital trains were sent to Orenburg and Rayevka in October to evacuate children from the Bashkir Republic into Turkestan. Authorization was also received for 10 equipped railway wagons to evacuate 50 families to Siberia. The Delegation took also an active part in providing the various Commissariats of the Bashkir SSR with money and diverse commodities of which 2,937 items (35 wagons) were despatched between February 25 and November 1.

In addition to the Economic Section, the General Section has

[1] Evidently of the needs as estimated by the local authorities.—R.S.

been active. In addition to correspondence, it has assumed the legal and social protection of the Bashkirs' interests.

The Information Section, too, has done much work in sifting and analysing all the information received from the Republic, and on tasks received from the Information Department of the People's Commissariat for Nationalities.

As regards the other fields of the Delegation's work, it was due to its insistence that a certain number of vacancies in various higher educational establishments in the capital and the other big cities of the RSFSR were reserved for the Bashkir Administration of Professional Education. The Delegation keeps in touch with the students of whom, according to its information, the following are in Moscow: 42 in the University of the Toilers of the East, 8 in the Institute of the Living Languages of the East, 5 in the Workers' Faculties, 25 in the Sverdlov Communist University, and 27 in other educational establishments.

Omitting various other activities connected with Bashkiria's frontier problems and a great many other questions of a political nature, the Delegation emphasizes that, owing to the particularly critical position of Bashkiria, its main attention in the current year has been devoted to problems of supply.

THE DELEGATION OF THE KIRGHIZ [KAZAKH] SSR

Prior to the confirmation by the Praesidium of VTsIK of the Statute on the Organization of the Delegations of the Autonomous Soviet Republics, the Delegation of the Kirghiz SSR in Moscow functioned on the basis of the Statute on the Delegation of the Kirghiz territory confirmed by the Kirghiz Military Revolutionary Committee on July 9, 1920.

The duties of the Delegation included: (1) participation in the discussion of all questions affecting the Kirghiz territory, and (2) directing the supply of all the required materials, funds and workers from the central institutions of the Republic to the Revolutionary Committee and its departments.

The work of the Delegation during that period failed to take definite shape mainly because the state organization of the Kirghiz territory itself was fluid, and the entire work of the Delegation was reduced to the political, state aspect, to working out the Statute of the Kirghiz Republic, and partly also to getting the supply business under way.

With the promulgation of the decree of VTsIK and the Council of People's Commissars on recognition of the Kirghiz Republic on August 26, 1920, the activity of the Kirghiz Delegation assumed more

Reports of the Delegations of the National Republics

definite form; and in addition to the political work, much attention is now paid also to economic work, i.e. the work of supply.

A clear picture of the conditions under which the Kirghiz Revolutionary Committee had to work emerged from the first Congress of Soviets of the Kirghiz SSR in October 1920: the Semipalatinsk and Akmolinsk provinces were subordinated to the Siberian Revolutionary Committee; the Uralsk to the Revolutionary Military Committee of the IVth Army; the Bukeyevsk Orda was completely severed from the Kirghiz Revolutionary Committee; the Kustanai district was attached to Chelyabinsk province, and only [its] remaining portion was left under the jurisdiction of the Kirghiz Revolutionary Committee.

Owing to this territorial muddle, the work of the Delegation met with incredible difficulties. To this must be added the fact that the relations of the Kirghiz People's Commissariats with the Delegation had not been regularized so that the latter found itself ignored and indirectly counteracted. The Delegation was given neither personnel nor funds, nor even the required information (claims, estimates and so forth). It was neither financed, nor were its members of staff provided with anything. This state of affairs continued for some time. It was only in May of this year that the territorial delimitation of the Kirghiz SSR (the incorporation of Semipalatinsk and Akmolinsk provinces) was concluded and a decree promulgated by the Central Executive Committee of the Kirghiz SSR, giving the Delegation an appropriate status and inviting all People's Commissariats to pay serious attention to the Delegation and to satisfy its requests for the resources required.

Unfortunately, even this authoritative decree is carried out with great difficulty.

When examining the conditions of work of the Delegation regarding its relations with the People's Commissariats of the RSFSR, we find that until quite recently the People's Commissariats of the RSFSR took little notice of the Delegation.

Until recently there had been no response to the continuous demand that the People's Commissariats and Administrations (*Glavki*) should not despatch goods and materials without a certificate (*visa*) from the Delegation, a demand aimed at achieving supply according to plan and supervision of the work of the agents sent from the Republic.

This is how the business of supplying the Kirghiz SSR escaped the attention of the Delegation, with the result that the principle of planning was violated in the field of supply.

In view of the above, it is impossible to give a well-balanced and

The Organization of National Administration

graphic picture of the work of the Delegation for the whole time of its existence. It was only this year that the Delegations started more or less systematic work. But even then the work suffered from interruptions.

First of all, the Information Section saw to it that all newspapers published in the RSFSR were received, and that all decrees and resolutions of the Delegations were recorded. It also conducts a register of all the people arriving from the Kirghiz Republic, with notes on the purpose of their assignment, and supplies them with information relating to their work in Moscow. All available publications concerning every People's Commissariat (decrees, circulars, instructions, statistical information and so forth) were collected. All institutions of the Kirghiz SSR were requested to furnish the statistical information at their disposal, and all Congresses, Conferences, educational establishments, competitions (competitive examinations) and so forth, are registered and reported to Kirghizia. With the assistance of the People's Commissariat of Nationalities, the Kirghiz Delegation in Moscow has equipped 40 institutions (People's Commissariats and Departments) in the Orenburg, Bukeyev, Uralsk, Akmolinsk and Semipalatinsk provinces. A large proportion of the expenditure (approximately 15 million) falls on the Bukeyev Soviet of National Economy. The expenditure on the other People's Commissariats and departments comes to approximately 1 to 3 million each.

From September 1, 1920, until May 1, 1921, i.e. during the first eight months of the Delegation's existence, a total of 19 wagons of goods and materials were despatched from the depot of the Delegation, and 49 wagons from elsewhere.

For the period from May 1 to September 1921, 24 wagons were despatched from the depot of the Delegation and eight wagons from elsewhere.

The goods sent included metallurgical, electrical, chemical, leather, rubber and textile materials as well as drugs, and school and office appliances.

The work for some People's Commissariats was difficult to organize and suffered great interruptions. This was due above all to a shortage of staff in general and of specialists in particular.

Systematic work for the People's Commissariat of Education on a territorial scale, which was on the point of getting under way in the autumn of 1920, was interrupted in winter owing to several unfavourable circumstances such as the loss of liaison with the Kirghiz People's Commissariat of Education, and a lack of specialists. That work was not resumed until the spring of 1921. Owing to the persistence shown by the Delegation and the support given to it by the Kirghiz People's Commissariat of Education which sent personnel and funds, it was possible to get permission from the Chief Clothing Administration to carry out warrants for cloth which had hitherto received no attention. A warrant obtained for 750,000 arshins of cloth for the Kirghiz SSR and 250,000 arshins for Uralsk has been carried out. A warrant for 500,000 arshins of cloth for children was received through the Commission for Improving the Conditions of Life for Children, and this cloth is being supplied in the form of ready-made clothing: of this order, [only] 36,000 pieces (produced from 250–300,000 arshins) have been supplied. The delay is due to a shortage of sewing shops. An application has been made for cloth in bales. 7,060 caps have been received. The delivery of school and other books was delayed by accident: the depots were sealed up owing to a change of management. Orders for office equipment have been fulfilled.

The Delegation took a direct part in the organization of the Archaeological Institute and the nuclei of the future Kirghiz State University: the Agricultural Technicum, the Institute for Scientific Education, the Technical School and, at the present time, the Workers' Faculty. A campaign was held recently for allocating students of the Kirghiz SSR to higher educational establishments.

Despite the outstanding importance of supplying the Kirghiz People's Commissariat of Food, the Delegation was compelled by the lack of means to neglect that Commissariat and to throw it back on its own organization and resources. The Delegation must, however, state that the needs of the Kirghiz SSR were not always sufficiently catered for by the People's Commissariat of Food, so that fulfilment of the warrants was extremely slow, and at times did not take place at all. The Delegation has reported this in good time to VTsIK. It was not until quite recently that an Inspectorate for the People's Commissariat of Food was organized.

The following tasks have been fulfilled:

(a) Removal of the restrictions on fisheries. The Delegation took a direct part in the conferences dealing with this question and upheld in various commissions the need for such action. The result of the work of those commissions was embodied in the decree of the Council of People's Commissars of May 31, on the fishing industry.

(b) A campaign against the tax in kind.[1] The Delegation strongly

---

[1] By decree of March 1921, the compulsory delivery of all the agricultural products which exceeded the producer's personal needs was replaced by a tax in kind, after the payment of which peasants were left free to market the excess product.—R.S.

supported the idea that the decree on the tax in kind was inapplicable in the conditions of life of the nomadic and semi-nomadic population of the Kirghiz, and that it should be replaced by commodity exchange. As a result, the tax in kind was cancelled for the Kirghiz SSR and it was recognized that the state must obtain the raw materials required solely by means of commodity exchange.

(c) A campaign to mobilize Kirghiz workers for the spring fishing season.

(d) The solution of some problems concerning the provisioning of the workers.

(e) The fulfilment of a warrant obtained for 600,000 arshins of cloth for Bukeyev province over and above the plan.

Already in the summer it became clear that, according to information from the Kirghiz Central Executive Committee, the Kirghiz Republic was overtaken by an immense catastrophe—famine. Urgent measures had to be taken to render maximum assistance to the starving.

As a result of the steps taken a resolution of the Praesidium of VTsIK of August 13 included the Orenburg, Uralsk, Aktubinsk, Bukeyevsk, Kustanai (without the Kustanai *uyezd*) provinces and the Adayevsk district among the provinces envisaged for famine relief. The Delegation took part in the conferences of various commissions on famine problems and adopted urgent measures to obtain and fulfil warrants by sending agents to the localities to see to the movement of freight on the spot.

Apart from the work in the Central Commission for Famine Relief attached to VTsIK, the Delegation has been, and continues to be called upon to join the VTsIK Commission for Improving the Conditions of Life for Children for the purpose of ascertaining the actual requirements and conditions of children's institutions in the famine-stricken areas of the Kirghiz SSR.

The Delegation has worked hard in drawing up, instead of a budget, a preliminary statement on the required quantity of grain, amounting to 15 million poods, for the famine-stricken provinces of the Kirghiz Republic. Simultaneously a statement was drafted on the amount of potatoes required. It was very difficult to do so, since there was no precise information from the localities even on the population total, let alone other essential information. Only partial data were available, so that obviously not all the budget figures are exact.

Only after continuous and urgent queries to the localities and requests for immediate information on famine problems, did the

Reports of the Delegations of the National Republics

Kirghiz Delegation begin to receive more or less detailed and precise information.

The Delegation has taken appropriate measures to increase the number of provincial and subsidiary feeding and medical centres in the Kirghiz SSR, on the plea that, whereas more than 10 feeding centres are projected in Samara, Saratov and other provinces, only four feeding centres (consisting of two main and two subsidiary ones) are contemplated for five famine-stricken provinces of the Kirghiz SSR. Such an arrangement would have only given each famine-stricken province of the Kirghiz SSR two-thirds of a feeding centre. In view of the particular conditions of the Kirghiz SSR and the insufficiency of the railway network, the Delegation urged that it is necessary to organize two types of feeding centres: those on the railway lines and those elsewhere.

The Delegation took up the fact that the People's Commissariat of Food had completely excluded Aktubinsk and Kustanai provinces from the allocation of food and grain for the five famine provinces of the Kirghiz SSR.

Compared to the famous provinces of the Volga region, the Kirghiz Republic has received too little food for its famine areas. The Delegation has requested the People's Commissariat for Nationalities to see to it that such abnormalities should be avoided.

In the field of famine relief, the Delegation has achieved the following results:

Altogether 464,000 poods of seed grain were designated for the Kirghiz Republic of which, according to the information of the Central Transport Agency, 197,000 poods went to Orenburg, and 193,000 poods to Uralsk. In addition, according to a telegram from the People's Commissariat of Food, 90,000 poods from the Samara food base are to go to Orenburg.

The items designated include: 98,000 poods of grain, 25,000 poods of fish, 200 cases of glass, 100 units of crockery (for two provinces only), 140 pails, 230 pieces of cast-iron dishes, 350 pieces of iron and tinware, 50 dozen knives and forks, six wagons of rice, 110 poods of cocoa, 9,800 poods of groats, 3,116 poods of sugar, 1,705 poods of salt, 843 poods of confectionery, 10,047 poods of coffee, 1,178 poods of ordinary soap, 789 poods of washing powder, 308 poods of green soap, and eight poods of soap powder; 5,500 poods of drugs against epidemics were sent to the Kirghiz People's Commissariat of Health. Of these, 1,500 poods went to the Semipalatinsk Provincial Health Section, and 2,000 poods to the Akmolinsk Provincial Health Section. Three hundred and sixty arshin of woollen fabrics were despatched to children's institutions.

It was also decided to release, for the Section for the Protection of Mothers and Infants, ten complete outfits for crèches, children's homes and so forth, with drugs and textiles, for 30 people each. Of these, two outfits were for the Uralsk province and 8 for the remaining provinces.

Finally, on September 23, the Delegation received from the pharmacy of the Centre for the Protection of Mothers and Infants a warrant for drugs and instruments for two more establishments out of the 40 designated for the famine provinces. A warrant for inventory and linen for these two establishments was also obtained. The Delegation made also great efforts to secure the despatch of drugs against cholera and other plagues.

The Delegation consists at present of the board of representatives and of the general, economic, information, business and finance sections (temporarily).

THE DELEGATION OF THE TURKESTAN SSR

The Delegation started its work in Moscow on April 1, and was preoccupied with:
1 the internal work of organizing its sections in conformity with the instructions from the People's Commissariat for Nationalities;
2 drawing in experienced specialists;
3 establishing business liaison with the central institutions;
4 establishing a continuous liaison and timely exchange of information between the Delegation and Turkestan, and vice versa;
5 defending and protecting, in the central institutions, the economic needs of Turkestan;
6 supervising the fulfilment of the plans for supplying Turkestan with required goods, and carrying out the warrants obtained from the head Administrations and People's Commissariats by receiving the freights and despatching them to Turkestan by non-stop trains, and finally,
7 working out, applying and regularizing the measures, arising from the New Economic Policy, for commodity exchange between the centre and Turkestan.

To provide Turkestan with experienced and qualified officials, the Delegation invited specialists for the various branches of political, economic, cultural and educational life of the Turkestan territory. It organized and despatched to Turkestan (*a*) an expedition for the fight against plant pests; (*b*) an expedition of the Institute for Land-Surveying; (*c*) an expedition of the Commission for the Preservation of Artistic and Ancient Monuments; (*d*) an expedition for the

Reports of the Delegations of the National Republics

exploration of Lake Balkhash; (*e*) an expedition for irrigation and other technical work; (*f*) an expedition of the geological committee; (*g*) an expedition to fight malaria; (*h*) an expedition for purchases (*zagatovka*) of castor-oil plants.

The labour force of 1,500 people released after the construction of the Algai-Embsk railway was transferred to Turkestan for the construction of the Semirechensk railway line.

An expedition is being organized for the investigation and study of stock-raising and horse-breeding in Turkestan.

By taking an active part in the work of the central institutions in matters affecting Turkestan, the Delegation (1) helped to obtain an increase of funds for Turkestan up to 15 thousand million rubles per month, beginning from July 1 this year; moreover, there was a single allocation of $2\frac{1}{2}$ thousand million rubles for wine-making, 1 thousand million for *Turkgukom*, 75 thousand million for the cotton committee, 35,000 [rubles] in gold valuta for the purchase abroad of materials for the Kaushchinsk sugar works; (2) established relations with the VTsIK commission for the transfer of cattle from the famine provinces to Turkestan; (3) adopted measures for regularizing the provision of Turkestan with required goods by commodity exchange to be handled in Turkestan by the central workers' co-operative; (4) by request from the Turkestan Delegation, the RSFSR Commission for Utilizing Resources allotted to Turkestan, above the planned allocation, 0·1 per cent of its entire reserve fund of goods, and the Delegation has already received, and partly fulfilled, the warrants for these goods.

The goods transport to Turkestan is impeded chiefly by the overloading of the Samara-Zlatoust and of the Tashkent railways, which caused the People's Commissariat for Communications and Transport to impose restrictions from March 1921 that are still in force. This is why since May the following items have not been despatched: 57,000 poods of cement, 8,000 poods of iron, 25,000 poods of plywood, 250 poods of asphalt, 50 poods of tar, 30,000 poods of boiler-plate scraps and one wagon of pharmaceutical crockery.

In spite of these difficulties, the Turkestan Delegation in the period of April 1 to October 31, 1921, has despatched to Tashkent c/o the Turkestan Central Executive Committee seven through goods trains with the following items: 1,100 poods of iron, 500 poods of various technical appliances, 1,400 poods of petrol, 31,500 poods of textiles, 900 poods of wire, 400 poods of lime, 400 poods of shoe polish, 1,000 poods of footwear, 400 poods of knitted wear, 6,500 poods of various goods, 500 poods of paper, 400 poods of metal for casting

The Organization of National Administration

typographical letters, 700 poods of automobile stock, 300 poods of university equipment, 400 poods of lignine cotton wool, 300 poods of turner's lathes, 7,500 poods of fire-proof bricks, 6,000 poods of hoes, 800 poods of uniforms, 200 poods of printed material, 200 poods of cement, 200 poods of sulphuric acid, 20,000 poods of cast iron, 12,500 poods of agricultural implements, 2,000 poods of empty barrels, 3,100 poods of tobacco.

In addition, 5,000 poods of various goods have been sent through the Turkestan Representation by Central Co-operative Union. A total of 103,700 poods [of various commodities] has been despatched.[1]

[1] One pood=16·38 kilogrammes; one arshin=28 inches.—Tr. N.

PART II

Soviet Nationalities Policy under the New Economic Policy

DOCUMENT NO. 3

REPORT AT THE FOURTH CONFERENCE OF THE CC WITH NATIONALITIES OFFICIALS, JUNE 10, 1923, ON THE PRACTICAL MEASURES FOR APPLYING THE RESOLUTION ON THE NATIONAL QUESTION OF THE TWELFTH PARTY CONGRESS[1]

by J. V. STALIN

Comrades, you must have received by now the Politburo's draft programme on the national question.... The proposals of the Politburo may be divided into three groups.

The first group of problems deals with the consolidation of communist cadres of local people in the Republics and provinces.

The second group of problems deals with the practical application of the concrete resolutions on the national question of the XIIth Congress, namely: the questions of how to draw the working elements of the local population into the process of building up of the party and the soviets, the questions of what measures are required to raise the cultural level of the local population, the questions of improving the economic position of the Republics and provinces with regard to the specific peculiarities of their daily life; and finally the questions of the co-operative movement in the provinces and Republics, of the transfer of factories, the establishment of industrial centres and so forth. This group of problems affects the economic, cultural and governmental tasks of the provinces and Republics in conformity with local conditions.

The third group of questions deals with the Constitution of the Union of Republics in general and, in particular, with the question of amending the Constitution so as to establish a second chamber of the Central Executive Committee of the Union of Republics. ...

I now pass to the first group of problems—the methods of training and consolidating Marxist cadres of local people, cadres capable of serving as the most important and, in the long run, decisive stronghold of the Soviet regime in the peripheries. If we examine the development of our party (I take its Russian section, which is the

[1] *Sochineniya*, Vol. V, pp. 313–39—slightly abridged.

basic section) and follow the main stages of its development, and if in the same way we draw up an outline of the development in the immediate future of our communist organizations in the provinces and Republics, then I think we shall be able to find the key to the specific features which, in those countries, mark the development of our party in the peripheries.

The basic task in the first period of the development of our party, of its Russian section, was to create cadres. These Marxist cadres were made and forged in our fight with Menshevism. The task of these cadres at that period—I take the period from the foundation of the Bolshevik Party to the expulsion from the party of the liquidators, the most complete embodiments of Menshevism—their basic task was to win over to the side of the Bolsheviks the most alert, honest and outstanding members of the working class, to create cadres, to forge a vanguard. In this respect the struggle was waged primarily against tendencies of a bourgeois nature—especially against Menshevism—which impeded the consolidation of cadres and their fusion into a single unit, into the basic core of the party. At that time the party was not yet faced with the task of establishing, as a matter of immediate and vital urgency, extensive links with the millions of the working class masses and the toiling peasantry, nor with the task of gaining control over these masses, and in winning a majority in the country. The party had not reached that stage yet.

Only in the following stage in the development of our party, only in its second phase, when these cadres had matured, when they had become the basic core of our party, when the sympathies of the best elements of the working class had already been won or almost won—only then did it become the task of the party, as a matter of immediate urgency, to gain control of the millions of working masses, to transform the party cadres into a real workers' mass party. During this period the core of our party had to struggle not so much against Menshevism as against the 'left' elements within our party, the *Otzovists*[1] of all kinds, who were attempting to substitute revolutionary verbiage for a serious study of the distinctive features of the new conditions after 1905, impeding by their over-simplified 'revolutionary' tactics the conversion of the cadres of our party into a genuine mass party and threatening, by their activities, to divorce the party from the broad working masses. There is hardly any need

---

[1] The fraction expelled in 1909 from the Bolshevik ranks, so called because of its demand to recall *otozvatj* the Social Democratic M.P.'s from the Duma. Stalin speaks of 'all kinds' because there were diverse nuances of radical anti-parliamentarians.—R.S.

to prove that had the party not resolutely struggled against, and overcome, this 'left' danger it could not have gained control over the millions of the working masses.

Such, roughly, is the picture of the struggle on two fronts, against the 'right-wingers', i.e. the Mensheviks, and the 'left-wingers,' the picture of the development of the basic, the Russian, section of our party.

Comrade Lenin has outlined convincingly enough this essential and inevitable development of Communist Parties in his pamphlet *'Left Wing' Communism, an Infantile Disorder*. In it Lenin showed that the Communist Parties in the West must pass, and are already passing, through approximately the same stages of development. We will add for our own part that this applies also to the development of our communist organizations and Communist Parties in the peripheries.

It should, however, be noted that, despite the analogy between the experiences of our party in the past and the present experiences of our party organizations in the peripheries, there are none the less some essential peculiarities in the development of our party in the National Republics and Regions, which we must under all circumstances allow for. For, if we fail to take them thoroughly into account, we run the risk of committing the grossest errors when defining the tasks of training Marxist cadres from the local people in the peripheries.

Let us now examine these peculiarities.

The fight against the right-wing and 'left'-wing elements in our organizations in the peripheries is necessary and obligatory, for otherwise we shall not succeed in training Marxist cadres which are closely connected with the masses. That is obvious. But the peculiarity of the situation in the peripheries and its difference from the past development of our party lies in the fact that the forging of cadres and their conversion into a mass party in the peripheries is taking place not under a bourgeois system, as was the case in our party's past, but under a Soviet system, under the dictatorship of the proletariat. At that time, under the bourgeois system, it was possible and necessary, in accordance with the previous circumstances, to struggle *first* against the Mensheviks (in order to forge Marxist cadres) and *then* against the Otzovists (in order to turn these cadres into a mass party); and the struggle against these two deviations made up two entire periods in the history of our party. Now, under the present conditions, we cannot do this at all, for now the party is in power; and, being in power, the party needs in the peripheries dependable Marxist cadres of local people who are, at the same time, connected with the broad masses of the population. Now we can no longer struggle *first* against the right-wing menace with the help of the 'left'-wingers, as we did in the past history of our party, and *then* against the 'left' danger with the help of the right-wingers. Now we must struggle on both fronts and overcome both dangers *simultaneously* in order to obtain in the peripheries cadres of local people schooled in Marxism and linked with the masses. In the past we could speak of cadres not yet linked with the broad masses, but to be linked with the latter in the next stage of development. Now it would be ridiculous even to discuss such a thing, because it is impossible, under the Soviet regime, to imagine Marxist cadres not connected in one way or other with the broad masses. Such cadres would have nothing in common either with Marxism or with a mass party. All this complicates matters considerably and makes it imperative for our party organizations in the peripheries to struggle simultaneously against both the right-wingers and the 'leftists'. That is why our party has taken the position of fighting on two fronts, against both deviations simultaneously.

Furthermore, the fact should be noted that the development of our communist organizations in the peripheries does not proceed in isolation, as was the case in the past history of our party, as regards its Russian section, but under the direct influence of the basic core of our party which is experienced not only in forming Marxist cadres but also in linking them with the broad masses of the population, and in revolutionary manœuvring in the struggle for Soviet power. The peculiarity of the situation in the peripheries in this respect lies in the fact that our party organizations in those countries, in accordance with the conditions under which the Soviet regime is developing there, can and must, in their manœuvres designed to strengthen their links with the broad masses of the population, draw for this purpose on the rich store of experience accumulated by our party in the preceding period. Until recently the Central Committee of the Russian Communist Party used to make these manœuvres in the peripheries by itself, over the heads of the communist organizations there, sometimes even by-passing these organizations, and drawing into the general work of Soviet construction all and sundry more or less loyal national elements. But this work must be performed by the party organizations in the peripheries themselves. They can do it, and must do it, bearing in mind that this is the best way of converting the Marxist cadres of local people into a genuine mass party capable of rallying the majority of the population in the country.

Such are the two peculiarities which must strictly be taken into account when defining our party line in the peripheries regarding the training of Marxist cadres and their gaining control of the broad masses of the population.

I now pass to the second group of problems. . . .

In the first place: 'measures for attracting the proletarian and semi-proletarian elements into the process of building up the party and the soviets.' What is the purpose of this? It is to bring the apparatus of the party, and especially of the soviets, close to the people. These apparatuses must function in languages understood by the broad masses of the population, or else there can be no closeness between them. If it is the task of our party to convince the masses that the soviet system is their own system, then this can only be done when that system is understood by them. The people directing state institutions, and the institutions themselves, must conduct their work in a language intelligible to the population. The chauvinist elements which are destroying the feelings of friendship and solidarity among the peoples of the Union of Republics must be expelled from our institutions both in Moscow and in the Republics. Local people who are familiar with the language and customs of the population must be appointed to the management of state institutions in the Republics.

I remember that, two years ago, the chairman of the Council of People's Commissars in the Kirghiz Republic was Pestkovski, a man who did not know the Kirghiz language. This circumstance made it very difficult, at that time, to strengthen the links of the government of the Kirghiz Republic with the Kirghiz peasant masses. That is precisely why the party has seen to it that the chairman of the Council of People's Commissars of the Kirghiz Republic should be a Kirghiz.

I remember, too, that a group of comrades from Bashkiria last year proposed to nominate a Russian comrade as chairman of the Council of People's Commissars of Bashkiria. The party resolutely rejected this proposal and secured the nomination of a Bashkir for that post.

It is our task to apply this line and, in general, the line of gradually nationalizing the governmental institutions in all the National Republics and provinces and, above all, in such an important Republic as the Ukraine.

Secondly: 'the selection and inclusion of the more or less loyal elements of the local intelligentsia, coupled with simultaneous efforts to form soviet cadres from members of the party.' This clause requires no special explanation. Now that the working class is in power and has rallied the majority of the population, there is no reason to be afraid of drawing into the building up of the soviets the more or less loyal elements, including even former *Octobrists*.[1] It is, on the contrary, absolutely necessary to draw all these elements into the work in the national provinces and Republics in order to assimilate and sovietise them in the course of that work.

Thirdly: 'convocation of non-party conferences of workers and peasants, for members of the government to report on the measures taken by the Soviet regime.' I know that many People's Commissars in the Republics, for example in the Kirghiz Republic, have no desire to visit the localities, to attend peasants' gatherings, to speak at meetings, to acquaint the broad masses with the work of the party and the Soviet Government in matters which are of particular importance to the peasants. This state of affairs must be ended. It is absolutely necessary to hold non-party conferences of workers and peasants to acquaint them with what the Soviet Government is doing. Without this, the contact between the state apparatus and the people is unthinkable.

Furthermore: 'measures to raise the cultural level of the local population.' Several measures, which cannot of course be considered exhaustive, have been proposed, namely: (*a*) 'to organize (non-party) clubs and other educational institutions for popular enlightenment in the local languages'; (*b*) 'to extend the network of educational establishments of all grades in the local languages'; (*c*) 'to draw in the more or less loyal national teachers'; (*d*) 'to establish a network of societies spreading literacy in the local languages'; (*e*) 'to organize the publishing business.' All these measures are obvious and intelligible. They require no special explanation.

Further: 'economic development in the National Republics and provinces in line with the peculiarities of national character and day-to-day life.' In this respect the Politburo proposes the following measures: (*a*) 'to regulate and where required, to stop migration'; (*b*) 'to provide the local *working* population with land out of the state land fund'; (*c*) to grant the local population agricultural credit on easy terms'; (*d*) 'to intensify irrigation work'; (*e*) 'to move factories and plants to Republics which are rich in raw materials'; (*f*) 'to set up trade and technical schools'; (*g*) 'to arrange courses on agriculture', and finally, (*h*) 'to assist in every way the co-operative movement and, in particular, the producers' co-operatives (in order to attract the handicraftsmen) (*kustari*).'

I have to dwell on this last point because of its particular importance. Whereas formerly under the Tsar the development proceeded

---

[1] The more conservative of the bourgeois parties existing under the Tsarist regime, so called because it accepted as its platform the constitutional monarchy promised in the Manifesto of October 17, 1905.—R.S.

in such a way that the kulak grew [in wealth], agricultural capital expanded, the situation of the mass of medium farmers was unstable, while the broad peasant masses, the broad mass of petty farmer proprietors were compelled to flounder in the grip of ruin and impoverishment, now, under the dictatorship of the proletariat, when credit, land and [political] power are in the hands of the working class, the development cannot take the old course—despite NEP and the revival of private capital. It is quite incorrect to allege, as some comrades do, that owing to the development of NEP, we are compelled to re-enact the old story of nurturing the kulaks by bringing about the mass ruin of the peasant majority. This is not our way. Under the new conditions with the proletariat in power and holding all the basic threads of the economy, the development is bound to take a different course—that of drawing together the petty village proprietors in all kinds of co-operatives, and giving them state support in their struggle against private capital, gradually drawing the millions of petty farmers through the co-operatives into socialist construction, gradually improving (instead of worsening) their economic position. In this sense, 'assistance of every kind to the co-operative movement' in the peripheries, in those predominantly peasant countries, is of paramount importance for the future economic development of the Union of Republics.

Further: 'on the practical measures of setting up national army units.' I think that we are rather late in the matter of working out measures for this purpose. We must set up national army units. Obviously this cannot be done in a day, but it is possible and necessary at once to proceed with establishing military schools in the Republics and provinces so as to train, within a certain time, a staff of commanders from local people, capable of serving later as a core for organizing national army units. It is absolutely essential to make a start in this matter and to push it ahead. If we had reliable national army units with a reliable commanding staff in Republics such as Turkestan, the Ukraine, Belorussia, Georgia, Armenia, Azerbaidjan, then our Republic would be far better provided than is now the case both in respect of defence and of offensive operations if such should be forced upon us. We must make an immediate start. Owing to this, of course we shall have to increase the number of our troops by 20–25 thousand,[1] but this cannot be considered an unsurmountable obstacle.

I shall not enlarge on the remaining points (see the draft programme) since they are self-evident and require no explanation.

[1] At the time of Stalin's speech, the army's strength in peace-time was being reduced to slightly over half a million men.—R.S.

The third group of problems is connected with the establishment of the Second Chamber of the Central Executive Committee of the Union and the organization of People's Commissariats of the Union of Republics. In this respect the most striking questions have been selected, but they do not, of course, cover everything.

The Politburo envisages the Second Chamber as an organic part of the Central Executive Committee of the USSR. It had been proposed to set up, side by side with the existing Central Executive Committee, a Supreme Soviet of Nationalities which would not form part of the Central Executive Committee. This draft was rejected, and the Politburo arrived at the conclusion that it is more expedient to divide the Central Executive Committee itself into two chambers. Of these, the First Chamber may be called the Soviet of the Union, which is to be elected at a Congress of the Soviets of the Union of Republics, while the Second Chamber, which ought to be called the Soviet of Nationalities, is elected by the Central Executive Committees of the Republics and the Provincial Soviet Congresses of the National Regions at the ratio of five representatives from each Republic and one from each province. The elected representatives are to be confirmed by the Congress of Soviets of the Union of Republics.

As regards the powers of the Second Chamber in relation to the First Chamber, we have arrived at the principle of equal powers for both. The two chambers have each a Praesidium without legislative functions. Both chambers elect in joint session the common Praesidium which holds supreme power in the interval between the sessions of the Central Executive Committee. No bill tabled in one of the chambers acquires the force of law without having been passed by both chambers, so that a complete balance between the two chambers is established.

Now to the Praesidium of the Central Executive Committee, which I mentioned in passing. The Politburo considers that the existence of two legislative Praesidiums is inadmissible. The Praesidium as the holder of supreme power cannot be divided into two or more parts; the supreme power must be undivided. With this in view, it is considered expedient to form a joint Praesidium of the Central Executive Committee of the USSR, from the Praesidiums of the two chambers with the addition of some individuals elected in a joint session of both chambers, i.e. in a plenary session of the Central Executive Committee.

Now, the question of the number of All-Union Commissariats. You know that under the old constitution, as confirmed last year at the Congress of Soviets of the Union of Republics, the Commissariats of War, Foreign Affairs, Foreign Trade, Posts and Telegraphs, and Railways are concentrated in the hands of the Council of People's Commissars of the Union of Republics, that five other Commissariats, i.e. those of Food, Finance, Labour, the Supreme Council for National Economy and the Workers' and Peasants' Inspectorate are subordinated to the respective Republican governments and at the same time to the All-Union Government, while the remaining six Commissariats are independent Republican Commissariats. This draft was criticized by several Ukrainians, Rakovski, Skrypnik and others, but the Politburo has rejected the proposal of the Ukrainians to transfer the People's Commissariats for Foreign Affairs and Foreign Trade from the category of All-Union Commissariats to the second category and has adopted basically the main clauses of the Constitution in the sense of last year's decisions.

. . . .

I take it that, as regards the Constitution of the Union of Republics and the Second Chamber, the conference will have to confine itself to a short exchange of views, especially since this question is being dealt with in the commission of the plenary session of the Central Committee.[1] The question of what practical measures must be taken in pursuance of the resolution of the XIIth Congress will, in my opinion, have to be discussed in greater detail. A great part of the debate will have to be devoted to the question of how to consolidate Marxist cadres from local people.

I think that, before opening the debate, it would be expedient to hear the reports of the comrades from the Republics and provinces on the material from the local authorities.

Stalin's Concluding Remarks, June 12, 1923

First of all, I should like to say a few words on the reports made by the comrades, and in general on the nature of the conference in the light of these reports. Although this conference is the fourth since the establishment of the Soviet regime, it is nevertheless the only one which has been complete, with more or less complete and well-based reports from the Republics and provinces. It can be seen from the reports that the communist cadres in the provinces and

[1] According to a footnote added in Stalin's *Sochineniga* this commission, under his chairmanship, was composed of representatives of the party organizations of all the Union Republics (at that time the RSFSR, the Ukraine, Belorussia and the Transcaucasian Federation).—R.S.

Republics have matured, and that they are learning to work independently. I assume that the rich material put before us by the comrades at the conference, and the practical working experience revealed by them at the conference must without fail be made accessible to our entire party in the form of minutes of this conference. The people have matured and are going ahead. They are acquiring the art of administration—such is the first conclusion, the first impression derived from these reports.

As for the content of the reports, the materials presented can be divided into two groups: reports from socialist Republics, and reports from non-socialist People's Republics (Bokhara, Khorezm [*Khiva*]).

Let us examine the first group of reports. The reports show that, in the sense of closeness of the party and, particularly, the state apparatus to the language and daily life of the people, Georgia is the most highly developed and advanced Republic. Georgia is followed by Armenia, and after them come the other Republics and provinces. This conclusion, in my opinion, is incontestable. This fact is due to the higher degree of culture achieved by Georgia and Armenia. In Georgia, the percentage of literacy is fairly high—it reaches 80 and in Armenia not less than 40. This is the secret why these two countries are ahead of the other Republics: the higher the degree of culture and literacy of a country, Republic or province, the closer the party and soviet apparatus is to its people, its language and daily life—all other conditions being equal, of course. This is clear, and there is nothing new in that conclusion; but precisely because it contains nothing new, that conclusion is often forgotten; and not infrequently the attempt is made to blame cultural backwardness and the consequent backwardness in state organization on 'errors' in party policy, on conflicts and so forth, whereas, in fact, it is a matter of inadequate literacy and cultural standards. If you want your country to advance to a higher form of state organization, then raise the level of literacy among the population, raise the standard of culture of your country—the rest will follow.

If we appraise from this angle the position in the individual Republics in the light of the reports at hand, we have to admit that the present position in Turkestan is the most unfavourable and alarming one. The picture is one of cultural backwardness, a devastatingly low percentage of literacy, isolation of the state apparatus from the language and life of the peoples of Turkestan, a devastatingly slow rate of development. Yet it is clear that, of all the Soviet Republics, Turkestan is the most important from the point of view of revolutionizing the East, not only because Turkestan is a combination of nationalities which have more links with the East than any others, but also because, geographically, it cuts into the heart of that [part of] the East which is the most exploited and most explosive in the struggle against imperialism. That is why Turkestan as it is now is the weakest point of the Soviet regime. The task is to transform Turkestan into a model Republic, into the outpost of revolution in the East. That is precisely why it is necessary to concentrate attention on Turkestan for the purpose of raising the cultural level of the masses, nationalizing the state apparatus and so forth. We have to solve this task, cost what it may, without sparing our strength or shirking sacrifices.

As the second weak point of the Soviet regime we have to consider the Ukraine. The state of affairs here, in respect of culture, literacy and so forth, is the same, or almost the same, as in Turkestan. The state apparatus in the Ukraine is as far removed from the language and life of the people as in Turkestan. Yet the Ukraine has the same importance for the peoples of the West as Turkestan has for the peoples of the East. The position in the Ukraine is further complicated by some peculiarities in the industrial development of the country. The point is that, in the Ukraine, the basic branches of industry—coal and metallurgy—have not arisen in the Ukraine from below, through a natural development of national economy, but have been introduced from above, by artificial implantations from outside. Owing to this, the workers in these branches of industry are not of local origin, not Ukrainian in language. And this brings about a situation in which the cultural influence of the town on the village and the fusion of the proletariat and peasantry are very much impeded by these differences in the national composition of the proletariat and the peasantry. All these circumstances must be taken into account in our efforts to transform the Ukraine into a model Republic, but transform her into a model Republic, in view of her immense importance for the peoples of the West, we must.

I pass now to the reports on Khorezm and Bokhara. I shall say nothing on Khorezm because of the absence of the representative from it. It is awkward to criticize the work of the Khorezm Communist Party and the Khorezm government only on the basis of the materials at the disposal of the Central Committee. What Broido has said here on Khorezm refers to the past and has little relevance to its present position. As regards the party, he said that 50 per cent of its members are merchants and so forth. Perhaps this was so in the past, but at present there is a purge on there; not one of the unified party tickets has yet been issued to Khorezm; strictly speaking the party does not exist there; there will be a question of the party

Soviet Nationalities Policy under the NEP

there only after the purge.[1] There are said to be several thousand party members in Khorezm. I think that no more than a few hundred will be left after the purge. It was exactly the same thing in Bokhara last year, when they had 16,000 party members, of whom, after the purge, not more than a thousand were left.

I come to the report on Bokhara. Speaking of Bokhara, I have first to say a few words on the general tenor and nature of the reports made. I consider that the reports on the Republics and provinces have on the whole been truthful, and that on the whole they did not diverge from reality. Only one report did radically diverge from reality—the report on Bokhara. This was not even so much a report as a wholesale display of diplomacy, for everything negative in Bokhara was concealed and glossed over, while everything superficially bright and striking was boosted for show. The conclusion is that all is well in Bokhara. I think that we have not come to this meeting to play diplomats, nor to make sheep's eyes to one another and, at the same time, diddle one another when backs are turned. I think that we have come here to tell the whole truth, to reveal, in a communist way, all the sores, to open them up, and to work out the remedies. Only under this condition can we advance. From this point of view, the report on Bokhara distinguishes itself from all the others by its untruthfulness. It was not by accident that I have

---

[1] The 'revision of the personal composition of the Party', more shortly described as *chistka* (purge), was started at the end of 1921, with the intention to secure the party's ideological homogeneity as well as to eliminate the type of members who might not be safe against the temptations of holding public office under the conditions of NEP; Stalin's observations indicate that, under the particular conditions of Soviet Central Asia, he expected most of the expulsions to fall under the second heading. In order to secure homogeneity of standards of this scrutiny, this purge, like others up to the last in 1934–5, was accompanied by the issue of new party tickets (the 'unified party tickets' mentioned by Stalin) to all those who had gone through the scrutiny; a person who had not yet got this ticket (in the Central Asian cases because the purge commissions had not yet finished their work) could not join another party organization without special scrutiny. At the XIIth Party Congress, when—apart from the two People's Republics mentioned by Stalin—the purge was in substance completed, it was reported that 20 per cent of the party members existing before the purge had been expelled, another 2·7 per cent had left voluntarily; Stalin's above-translated observations indicate very different standards for the scrutiny in Central Asia.

In the West, the term 'purge', which indicated the periodical revisions of party membership envisaged by the Rules of the CPSU and applied up to 1934, has become the current description for the elimination of actual or supposed oppositionists during the crisis of 1936–8, and expectations of the repetition of similar events. In fact, the purge proper was an organizational device of the party caucus resulting, as a rule, in the 'purged' members continuing to work in a non-party capacity: criminal or political police procedures, which were characteristic of the 1936–8 'purge', originated from the purges proper only occasionally, if the scrutiny revealed, say, instances of bribery or other misuse of official power, as distinct from a general background, or attitude, too accommodating to NEP men which would result in the unsafe member's expulsion from the Party.—R.S.

questioned here the speaker on the composition of the Council of Nazirs in Bokhara. The Council of Nazirs is the Council of People's Commissars. Does it include any dekhans, i.e. ordinary peasants? The speaker did not reply. But I have information on this, and, you see, it appears that there is not a single peasant in the Bokhara government. Out of 9 or 11 members of the government, one is the son of a rich merchant, another a trader, yet another an intellectual, then a mullah, one more trader, an intellectual, and again a trader, but there is not a single dekhan. And yet Bokhara, as is well known, is exclusively a peasant country.

This question has a direct bearing on the question of the policy of the Bokhara government. What is the policy of that government, which is headed by communists? Does it consider the interests of the peasantry, of its own peasantry? I should like to mention only two facts which illustrate the policy of the Bokhara government at the head of which are communists. A document signed by the most responsible comrades and old members of the party shows, for example, that, during the time of its existence, the Bokhara State Bank has advanced 75 per cent of its credits to private merchants, but only 2 per cent to peasant co-operatives. In absolute figures: 7 million gold rubles to the merchants, and 220,000 gold rubles to the peasants. Furthermore, no land has been confiscated in Bokhara. They did confiscate the emirs' cattle—for the benefit of the peasantry. And what was the result? From the same document it appears that, while some 2,000 head of cattle have been confiscated for the peasants, only some 200 head of cattle have passed into their hands—the rest has been sold—of course to the well-to-do.

And this government calls itself a soviet—a people's government! It is hardly necessary to say that there is nothing soviet, nothing popular in these actions of the Bokhara government.

The speaker has dealt in very rosy hues with the question of the relations of the people of Bokhara to the RSFSR and the Union of Republics. According to him, in this respect too, all is well. The Bokhara Republic, it appears, wishes to become part of the Union. The speaker seems to think that it is sufficient to wish to enter the Union of Republics for its gates to burst wide open. No, comrades, it is not as easy as all that. You must also enquire whether the Union of Republics will admit you. Before being able to become a part of the Union, you must, in the eyes of the Soviet people of the Union, deserve the right of entry, you must become worthy of that right. I have to remind the comrades from Bokhara that the Soviet Union cannot be regarded as a dumping place.

Finally, in finishing the first part of my concluding remarks on the reports, I should like to mention one characteristic feature of these reports. No one, not a single speaker, has answered the question on the agenda of the conference as to what unused reserves of local officials are available. No answer was given to that question, nor has anyone touched on it, except Grinko who, however, was not making a report. And yet this is a question of paramount importance. Are there, in the Republics and provinces, officials from local people available but not being made use of? If there are—why have they not been made use of? But if there are no such reserves, while the shortage of such officials still prevails—with which national elements will the vacant party and soviet posts be staffed? All these questions are of the utmost importance for the party. I know that in the Republics and provinces a proportion of leading officials, mainly Russian, sometimes stand in the way of officials from the local people, impede their promotion to certain posts, and refuse to give them a chance. Such things have happened, which is one of the causes of discontent in the Republics and provinces. But the main and basic reason of discontent lies in the appalling shortage, or rather the total absence, of reserves of local people capable of work. This is a crucial point. If there is a shortage of local officials then, obviously, it is necessary to employ non-local officials, people of other nationalities, for time does not stand still, you must build and run the administration, while cadres of local people are maturing slowly. I think that, at the conference, the officials from the provinces and Republics have somewhat cunningly passed over this circumstance. Yet it is clear that nine-tenths of the misunderstandings are due to the shortage of officials recruited from local people. Hence there can be only one conclusion: the party must be given the urgent task of accelerating the formation of cadres of soviet and party officials from local people.

From the reports I pass over to the speeches. Comrades, I have to note that no one, not one speaker, has criticized the statement of principles in the draft programme proposed by the Politburo. (A voice from the floor: 'It is beyond criticism.') I take this to imply the consent of the conference, as an expression of the solidarity of the conference with the theses set forth in the statement of principles in the programme. (Voices from the floor: 'Correct.')

Trotsky's amendment, which he had spoken about, or the amendment (which relates to principles) should be adopted, for it makes absolutely no change in the character of the statement of principles in the resolutions: it follows naturally from it. This all the more, since Trotsky's amendment is essentially a reiteration of the well-known clause of the resolution of the Xth Congress on the national question, according to which it is inadmissible mechanically to transplant Petrograd and Moscow standards into the provinces and Republics. This would of course be a repetition, but I consider that to repeat certain things does no harm sometimes. In view of this I do not intend to dwell on the statement of principles in the resolution. Skrypnik's speech gives some grounds for concluding that he is interpreting this statement of principles in his own way. While facing up to the basic task—the struggle against Great-Russian chauvinism, which is the main danger—he is trying to gloss over the other danger, that of local nationalism. But such an interpretation is profoundly erroneous.

The second part of the Politburo programme deals with the questions of the nature of the Union of Republics, and some amendments to the Constitution of the Union of Republics with a view to establishing a so-called Second Chamber. I must say that, in this respect, the Politburo has some difference of opinion with the Ukrainian comrades. The draft programme of the Politburo has been adopted unanimously by it. But some points are contested by Rakovski. This was expressed, *inter alia*, in the commission of the plenary session of the Central Committee. Perhaps I ought not to speak about it, because this question is not being decided here. I have already reported on this part of the programme, when I said that this question is being worked out in the commission of the plenary session of the Central Committee and in the commission of the Praesidium of the Central Executive Committee of the Union. But once we have touched on this question I cannot evade it.

It is incorrect to say that the question of whether it is to be a confederation or federation is a trivial one. Was it by accident that the Ukrainian comrades, when examining the well-known draft constitution adopted by the congress of the Union of Republics, have crossed out the phrase that the Republics 'are uniting in a single Union state'? Was this an accident, or have they not done so? Why have they crossed out that phrase? Was it by accident that the Ukrainian comrades proposed in their counter draft, that the People's Commissariat of Foreign Trade and the Peoples Commissariat of Foreign Affairs should not be merged, but transferred to the category of Republican Commissariats subject to mere directives from Union Commissariats? What sort of a Union is this, if every Republic keeps its own People's Commissariat of Foreign Affairs and People's Commissariat of Foreign Trade? Was it by accident that, in their counter draft, the Ukrainians have reduced to zero the power of the Praesidium of the Central Executive Committee, by dividing it between two praesidiums of two chambers?

All these amendments by Rakovski have been recorded, examined by the commission of the plenary session of the Central Committee, and rejected. Then why repeat them again here? I perceive in this persistence of some Ukrainian comrades the desire to obtain, in the definition of the nature of the Union, something between a confederation and federation, with the odds in favour of a confederation. Yet it is clear that we are not establishing a confederation, but a federation of Republics, a single Union, unifying the Departments of War, Foreign Affairs, Foreign Trade and others, a state which does not diminish the sovereignty of the individual Republics.

If we should have in the Union a People's Commissariat of Foreign Affairs, a People's Commissariat of Foreign Trade, and others, and if, at the same time, such People's Commissariats should also operate in the Republics forming part of the Union, then—as far as the outside world is concerned—the Union as a whole, as a single state, would obviously cease to exist; for there can be only one of two alternatives: either we merge these apparatuses and act, in face of the external enemy, as a single Union, or we do not merge them and do not establish a Union, but a conglomerate of Republics —in which case each Republic must have its own apparatus parallel to that of the others. In my opinion Comrade Manuilski is right here and not Rakovski and Skrypnik.

. . . .

I cannot pass over in silence one of Grinko's proposals that certain preferential conditions should be introduced to facilitate the entry into the party and the promotion to its leading organs of local people of the less cultured and, perhaps, less proletarian nationalities. This is a correct proposal, and should, in my opinion, be adopted.

. . . .

I have not dwelt on the question of establishing, under the Central Committee, a commission on the national question. Comrades, I have some doubts about the expediency of establishing such an organization, in the first place because the Republics and provinces will certainly not give us leading officials for this business. I am convinced of that. In the second place, I think that the provincial committees and the national Central Committees will not consent to yield to the commission attached to the Central Committee a fraction of their rights in the matter of allocating officials. At present, when distributing our forces, we generally consult the provincial committees and the national Central Committees. If there is a commission, the centre of gravity will naturally shift to it. There is no analogy between a commission on the national question and the commissions on the co-operative movement or on work among the peasants. The commission on work in the village and the commission on the co-operative movement usually work out general instructions. But in the national question we require not general instructions but specific measures for the individual Republics and provinces, a thing which the general commission would not be in a position to do. A commission of this kind would hardly be able to work out and adopt decisions of any sort, say for the Ukrainian Republic: two or three people from the Ukraine cannot act as substitutes for the Central Committee of the Ukrainian *CP(B)*. That is why I think that such a commission will give us nothing substantial. The step which is contemplated here—the introduction of national elements into the basic departments of the Central Committee—is, in my opinion, quite sufficient for the time being. If we have no particular successes in half a year, then it will be possible to raise the question of establishing a special commission.

DOCUMENT NO. 4

A LETTER TO COMRADE KAGANOVICH AND OTHER MEMBERS OF THE POLITBURO[1]

by J. V. STALIN

I had a talk with Shumski. . . . You know that he is dissatisfied with the state of affairs in the Ukraine. The reasons for his discontent can be reduced to two basic points.

1 He considers that the progress of Ukrainization is slow and that it is regarded as a duty fulfilled reluctantly, with great delay. He considers that the development of Ukrainian culture and the Ukrainian intelligentsia is proceeding quickly, and that it may by-pass us, if we do not assume control of this movement. He considers that this movement must be led by people who believe in the cause of Ukrainian culture, who are familiar, and want to be familiar, with that culture, who support and are able to support the growing movement for a Ukrainian culture. He is particularly dissatisfied with the conduct of the party and trade union leadership in the Ukraine which, in his opinion, is impeding Ukrainization. He thinks that one of the basic sins of the party and trade union leadership lies in its failure to draw into the leadership of party and trade union work those communists who have direct links with Ukrainian culture. He thinks that Ukrainization must be carried through, in the first place, in the ranks of the party and among the proletariat.

2 He thinks that, in order to correct these defects, it is necessary, above all, to make changes in the party and soviet leadership so as to make it more Ukrainian, and that only if this is done will it be possible to bring about a radical change in the cadres of our officials in the direction of Ukrainization. He suggests that Grinko be appointed Chairman of the Council of People's Commissars, and Chubar political secretary of the Central Committee of the Ukrainian *CP(B)*, that the staff of the secretariat in the Politburo should be improved and so forth. He thinks that, unless these or similar changes are made, it will be impossible for him to work in the Ukraine. He says that, if the Central Committee insists, he will be prepared to return to the Ukraine, even with present conditions of work remaining unaltered, but he is convinced that [in such a case]

[1] *Sochineniya*, Vol. VIII, pp. 149–57.

Stalin's Letter to Kaganovich on the Ukraine

the result will be nil. He is particularly dissatisfied with the work of Kaganovich. He considers that Kaganovich has succeeded in setting up the organizational work of the party, but, in his opinion, the predominance of the organizational approach in the work of Comrade Kaganovich makes normal work impossible. He asserts that the consequences of organizational pressure in Comrade Kaganovich's work, the consequences of the method of pushing aside the highest Soviet [Ukrainian] institutions and their directors, will tell in the near future. And he is not sure that these consequences will not result in a serious conflict.

My opinion in this respect is:

1 Shumski's assertions on the first point are to some extent correct. It is true that a widespread movement for a Ukrainian culture and Ukrainian public life has begun and is developing in the Ukraine. It is true that this movement must in no circumstances be allowed to fall into the hands of elements alien to us. It is true that many communists in the Ukraine fail to understand the meaning and significance of this movement and are therefore taking no measures to gain control of it. It is true that a radical change must be brought about among the cadres of our party and soviet officials who are still ironical and sceptical about Ukrainian culture and Ukrainian public life. It is true that we must carefully select and create cadres of people capable of gaining control of the new movement in the Ukraine. All this is true. Nevertheless, Shumski commits at least two serious errors.

In the first place, he confuses the Ukrainization of our party and of the apparatuses with the Ukrainization of the proletariat. We can and must gradually ukrainize our party, state and other apparatuses serving the population. But we cannot ukrainize the proletariat from above. The Russian working masses cannot be *compelled* to renounce the Russian language and Russian culture and to adopt the Ukrainian culture and language as their own. This would be contrary to the principle of the free development of nationalities. This would not be national freedom, but a peculiar form of national oppression. There can be no doubt that the composition of the Ukrainian proletariat will change with the industrial development of the Ukraine, in proportion to the influx into industry of Ukrainian workers from the surrounding villages. There can be no doubt that the Ukrainian proletariat will be ukrainized in the same way as the proletariat of, say, Latvia and Hungary which, at one time German in character, subsequently became latvianized and magyarized. But this is a lengthy, spontaneous and natural process. To attempt to replace this spontaneous process by a forcible Ukrainization of the proletariat from above would be a utopian and harmful policy capable of arousing anti-Ukrainian chauvinism among the non-Ukrainian strata of the proletariat in the Ukraine. It seems to me that Shumski has an incorrect understanding of Ukrainization, and that he overlooks this latter danger.

In the second place, while Shumski is perfectly correct in emphasizing the positive nature of the new movement in the Ukraine for a Ukrainian culture and public life, he does not, however, see the darker sides of that movement. Shumski fails to realize that, in view of the weakness of the indigenous communist cadres in the Ukraine, this movement, which is very often led by the non-communist intelligentsia, may in some places assume the character of a fight for alienating Ukrainian culture and Ukrainian society from Soviet culture and society as a whole. He fails to realize that it may turn into a struggle against 'Moscow' in general, against the Russians in general, against Russian culture and its supreme achievement—Leninism. I shall not attempt to prove that this danger is becoming increasingly real in the Ukraine. I should only like to say that even some Ukrainian communists are not free from such taints. I have in mind such a well-known fact as the article by the communist Khvilevoi which appeared in the Ukrainian press. Khvilevoi's demand for an '*immediate* de-Russification of the proletariat' in the Ukraine, his view that 'Ukrainian poetry must get away as quickly as possible from Russian literature and its style', his assertion that 'we are familiar with the ideas of the proletariat without the help of Moscow art', his enthusiasm for some sort of Messianic role to be played by the 'young' Ukrainian intelligentsia, and his ludicrous non-Marxist attempt to divorce culture from politics—all this and a lot of similar stuff now sounds (and cannot but sound) more than strange from the lips of a Ukrainian communist. At a time when the workers of Western Europe and their Communist Parties are full of sympathy for 'Moscow', the citadel of the international revolutionary movement and of Leninism; at a time when the workers of Western Europe look with admiration at the banner waving over Moscow, the Ukrainian communist Khvilevoi has nothing better to say for 'Moscow' than to appeal to Ukrainian public men 'as quickly as possible to run away from "Moscow".' And this is called internationalism! What is one to say of other Ukrainian intellectuals of the non-communist camp, if communists begin to talk, and not only talk, but also write in our Soviet press in the language of Khvilevoi? Shumski does not understand that control over the new movement for a Ukrainian culture in the Ukraine can only be gained by combating extremes such as those of Khvilevoi in the communist ranks. Shumski does not understand that it is only in the struggle against such extremes that the developing Ukrainian culture and Ukrainian public life can be *sovietized*.

2 Shumski is right in asserting that the higher ranks of the party and other leadership in the Ukraine must be ukrainized. But he errs in regard to the rate at which this is to be done. And this question of the rate is at present the main thing. He forgets that there are still not enough purely Ukrainian Marxist cadres for the task of Ukrainization. He forgets that such cadres cannot be produced artificially. He forgets that such cadres can only arise in the course of the work, and that this requires time.... What would be the meaning of now appointing Grinko Chairman of the Council of People's Commissars? What would the party as a whole and the party cadres in particular make of it? Would they not interpret it in the sense that we have embarked on reducing the standing of the Council of People's Commissars? For, after all, it is impossible to conceal from the party that Grinko's party and revolutionary record is much below that of Chubar. Can we take such a step at present when we are reviving the soviets and raising the standing of the soviet organs? Would it not be better, for the time being, to drop such plans in the interest of the cause and in the interests of Grinko? I am for strengthening the Secretariat and the Politburo of the Central Committee of the Ukrainian *CP(C)* as well as the higher Soviet leadership with Ukrainian elements. But it is impossible to say there are no Ukrainians in the leading party and soviet organs. What about Skrypnik and Zatonski, Chubar and Petrovski, Grinko and Shumski—are they not Ukrainians? Shumski's error in this respect is that, although he has the correct prospect, he does not consider the rate of development, and the rate of development is at present the main thing.

April 26, 1926.   With communist greetings,
                                                                    J. STALIN

DOCUMENT NO. 5

Excerpts from: ON THE REVISION OF THE STATUTES ON THE BUDGET RIGHTS OF THE UNION AND THE UNION REPUBLICS[1]

by F. KHODZHAYEV (1929)

The most vital problem of the mutual relations between the Union and the Union Republics in the field of the budget has been removed from the agenda of the fourth session of the Central Executive Committee of the USSR which has just been concluded. This was done because this question had not been studied enough and requires a preliminary and most thorough discussion in the Union Republics.

Our task is rendered more difficult by the considerable differences in the economic structure of the various Republics, and yet it is essential to find common norms reconciling the diverse interests and satisfying to an equal extent the requirements of the Union Republics and the Union as a whole. . . .

The prospect that the new law will solve completely all these difficult problems is not very bright. No doubt it will be necessary later on to introduce various changes and amendments based on practical experience provided by the rapid economic growth of the Union as a whole, and in its component parts. But it is decidedly necessary for the projected law to anticipate and tackle the aspects revealed by the experiences gained in budget work. . . .

This problem is much facilitated by the fact that, in the USSR, the interests of the Union and the interests of the individual Republics do not contradict each other, as they do in bourgeois federations. Planning, the fixed principle of our work will enhance the success of our task.

Let us note the most important problems which must be solved by the new budget legislation.

The distribution of the various kinds of expenditures between the All-Union and Republican budgets should be regulated from the point of view of their importance for the Union as a whole or the Republics. Even in this respect, there may be certain differences of opinion, but they are more easily resolved. From the practical

[1] *Sovetskoye Stroitelstvo*, 1929, No. 2.

viewpoint it seems necessary in such cases to apply the principle of decentralization. With the consolidation of the Republican apparatus, the volume of its work should be increased by transferring to it various duties from other fields. This will improve the quality of the work and enliven and galvanize its links with the masses. The adoption of this principle for example, in the Uzbek Republic has had precisely such a result. The direction and the volume of the work in the individual Republics must, of course, be kept in the general frame of the plan adopted for the Union as a whole.

Matters are more complicated on the income side. Every ruble, passing from the all-Union to the Republican budget, reduces the former and appears to narrow the scope for handling all-Union resources. On the other hand, under the present state of affairs, some budgets, especially in the weaker Union Republics, show a considerable deficit.

Apart from the question of the economic capacities of these Republics, the deficits are to a large extent due also to defects in the structure of the income side of the Republican budgets. For example, on the income side of the budgets of the Uzbek or Turkmen Republics it is impossible to find any indication of the place occupied in their national economy by the production of cotton, Persian lamb, silk and many other kinds of raw materials. The contribution made by the most important branches of national economy to the income side of the budget is incomparably lower than the place which they actually occupy in national economy. The natural result of this is the budget deficit which is covered by the peculiar device of distributing the income from the stamp duty among the individual Union Republics.

That is why it is necessary for the new law to provide an income structure in the Republican budgets which will reflect fully the economic structure of each individual Republic. In regard to Uzbekistan in particular, we consider that cotton and several key raw materials must occupy an appropriate place in the budget. We shall not, at present, go into detail on the implementation of this principle to be applied in practice. There could, for example, be a special addition to the price of a certain product which is to go to the Republican budget. Since almost all the industries processing basic agricultural raw materials and most of the state purchases of raw materials are handled by state authorities or co-operatives, the technical side of collecting this addition would not be particularly difficult. Yet a relatively small addition, under the conditions prevailing this year, would yield a considerable amount, likely to increase our budget income according to our computations approximately by 20 per cent.

Identical proceedings could be applied to such articles as Persian lamb, silk, dried fruit and so forth.

In our opinion such an addition would introduce no substantial innovation into our legislation. We have already very similar taxes: various kinds of special purpose dues and, in particular, the per-pood due in railway and water transport.

But such a price increase of cotton or other raw materials for light industry must not lead to price increases for finished goods. This will naturally affect the extent of profits of the textile industry and, in the final outcome, the income side of the Union budget. But the reduction in the all-Union income will be deceptive, for the Republican incomes will rise correspondingly and the extent to which the Republican deficit is covered by the all-Union budget will be reduced.

On the other hand, this innovation will considerably increase the active interest and initiative of the local authorities (County and District Executive Committees and Village Soviets). The Republic will seek to expand its economy, for example cotton cultivation in Uzbekistan, not only for the purpose of fulfilling the all-Union task of supplying the raw material to the textile industry, but also to increase the revenue of its local budget.

In this connection it would appear expedient to reduce the extent to which the weak Republican budgets are *adjusted* by the all-Union budget, and correspondingly to increase the Republican sources of revenue.

At the same time, we consider such a general adjustment of Republican budgets by the all-Union budgets as necessary for it will not be possible, without it, to raise the economy and culture of the backward and weaker Republics to the average Union levels; the economic and cultural problems are so great that the Republics lack the capacity to solve them on their own.

It is particularly important that the new law should deal with the position of the local budget.

Many big expenditures have lately been transferred to the local budget, but this process, particularly in some Union Republics, cannot be considered as completeted. It is true that, apart from the transfer of expenditures under the last statute on local finances, the local authorities were also offered a new way of raising additional revenue. . . . But in practice the incomes of the local budget do not suffice to meet, more or less tolerably, the necessary expenditures. There are not enough income items to satisfy the growing requirements of the local authorities.

The revenue side of the local budget has the same defect as that of the state budget. Like the latter, it hardly reflects the basic items of national economy. That is why it is imperative to improve the structure of the income side of the local budget by including in it definite allocations from those sources of revenue which are reserved for the state budget.

But hitherto, for example, cotton which practically did not figure in the Republican budget, was not represented in the local budget either, although, in fact, it is of the greatest importance for the economy of any cotton district.

The local executive committees which have the great and responsible task of fulfilling all kinds of assignments connected with the cotton campaign and the accomplishment of the cotton plan, and whose budgets contain almost no income from cotton cultivation, are naturally raising the question of including this most important branch of economy in the local budget.

As regards cotton, in particular, the expansion of this culture has, strangely enough, the effect of reducing the local revenue owing to the agricultural tax preference which cotton enjoys in comparison to other agricultural crops (half of the tax on grain).

This, of course, must be put right, so that the local budget, too, reflects properly the most important economic items of the district in question.

On the whole, it seems that the relation between the local budgets and the Republican budget should be analogous to that between the Republican budgets and the all-Union budget.

If the deficit in a Republican budget is balanced, when necessary, at the expense of the all-Union budget, then the deficit in a local budget must be covered by the Republican budget. The link between the work of the Republican and local authorities is so close, and the efficiency of the local apparatus has so great a bearing on the way the Republican authorities work and accomplish the plan that the latter must see to it that the relevant measures passed in the local budget are actually financed. . . .

DOCUMENT NO. 6

Excerpts from: THE ALL-UNION CONFERENCE ON
THE RE-ELECTIONS TO THE SOVIETS IN 1929[1]

Comrade Ibrahimov (CC CPSU(B)):
Comrade Kaganovich has said in his speech that, in some regions of Kazakhstan, it is necessary to discuss the forming of soviets. I consider that this applies not only to Kazakhstan, but also some other districts in the National Republics and Provinces. The activity of the local apparatus of soviets in the Republics and Provinces is affected by the same kind of shortcomings. I shall list them.

If we raise the question of the collective work of the village soviet, we find that there is none. In many districts, the whole work is done by the chairman and the secretary of the soviet, so that you can put the entire soviet into the portfolio of its chairman and secretary. Not everywhere have sections been formed, and where they have been, they do not work effectively, so that, essentially, the party directives to organize a local body of activists have been neglected.

Compared to the past, there are considerable improvements in the social composition of the soviets. Nevertheless, the figures presented by some Republics and areas are not quite correct. In the local soviets, kulak and [other] well-to-do elements predominate, whereas few village poor and farm labourers are in charge of the village soviets. That is why, in the forthcoming re-election campaign, all party organizations of the National Republics and Provinces must mainly concentrate on ascertaining how far the local soviets are following the class line of our party and of the soviet regime (*vlast*).

In the higher administrations (the district and, perhaps, the central administrations of the National Republics and Provinces), we come across a great many serious defects and scandals. Think of the decree of the CC of the party and the decree of the soviet organs on the Crimea, and you will see the state of decomposition the soviet apparatus is in, and the extent to which officials who are at the helm of the Republic *are in contact with the kulaks, and are supporting and shielding them.* Yesterday Comrade Kaganovich told us that

[1] Verbatim Report of the Central Executive Committee of the USSR, October 9–11, 1928: Publishing House, *Vlast Sovetov*.

The Re-elections to the Soviets in 1929

peasants in the Votsk province have been whipped and that the apparatus of the land departments is infested with alien elements. In the Northern Caucasus, in Karachai, as can be seen from the note in *Pravda*, former or present beys (landlords) have each been entrenched in the apparatus for some years. That is why, before the re-elections of the soviets, we must raise with greater urgency the problem of the central administration of the Autonomous Republics or Provinces. It is necessary to renew not only the apparatus and the composition of the village and rural district (*volost*) soviets, but also to pay attention to the district (*raionnye*), county (*okruzhnye*) and central apparatuses of the Autonomous Republics and Provinces.

The task of promoting new officials has to be put on the agenda. It must be said frankly that several Republics and Provinces suffer from a kind of stagnation in this respect. For several years no new persons have been promoted to higher posts [*vydvizhentsi*]. Everywhere there are the comrades whom we have known since 1918–20, but there is no activist from among the poor peasants and middle peasants, nor even from the workers. Yet several National Provinces, after the October Revolution, after NEP, and owing to the work of the party and the soviet power in restoring industry, have achieved the emergence of a working class. The Turkmenian Republic which used to have about 200–300 Turkmenian workers, has now approximately 3,000. Uzbekistan, Azerbaidjan, the Tatar and other Republics, too, have now thousands of workers each. By restoring agricultural economy and developing the industry processing local raw materials, we have increased the number of workers in the National Provinces and Republics. This makes it possible to raise in a more acute form the question of promoting new officials to higher posts. Hence in the forthcoming re-election campaign the promotion of new officials should be borne in mind so as to remove the alien kulak elements prevalent in the apparatuses of the National Republics and Provinces.

I am not trying to say that all is well in the other districts of the Union. There are the Smolensk affair and others, but this does not absolve us from centring our attention on the National Republics and Provinces. On the contrary, it goes to show that if there are such districts in the central industrial regions of the Union, then they are all the more likely to be found in the National Republics and Provinces.

I shall now dwell on some aspects of the re-election campaign. Above all—the report-making campaigns. Comrade Kaganovich is quite right in saying that the electoral mandates (*nakazy*)[1] were

---
[1] On *nakazy* see Document 24 below.

drawn up by the Agitation and Propaganda Departments and that very often they have been formulated worse than the reports from the local soviet organs for *Gosplan*, the Council of Labour and Defence or the Council of People's Commissars. Standard mandates have been drawn up, let us say, for the whole Turkmenian Republic, for the whole of Kazakhstan, for the whole of the Smolensk province or others, whereas they should have been adapted to each district. But no one bothered about this business. The mandates were taken as they were and applied, almost without change, to any district or village soviet. Naturally, this was incorrect.

That is why, in the report-making campaign of the re-elections, we must try by a sweeping development of self-criticism, to put before the villages a number of questions on the work of the soviets in the field of culture, economy, expenditure of budget funds, and self-taxation. It is also necessary to check up how *aul* [village] soviets are applying in practice the decrees on the emancipation of women.

Apart from that, greater attention should be paid in the National Republics to checking how the class line of our party was being applied to ascertaining how much assistance has been given by the village soviets to the poor peasants and labourers when collecting agricultural tax and self-tax, granting agricultural credits, and so forth. If such a check should prove that some chairman had failed to protect the interests of the village poor, he will be immediately removed by the people.

It is on the basis of such criticism, by showing up the defects in the work of the village soviets and correcting them, that the mandates applicable to the village concerned must be drawn up. This is the only way in which the question of the mandates can be properly dealt with.

In the National Republics and Provinces (in some of them, at least) the kulaks begin to draw up their lists much earlier than we do. For example, two months before the re-elections in Kirghizia, the kulaks drew up their lists. In these lists you will find names of village poor; the kulaks even earmark poor peasants or farm labourers as chairmen of village soviets, but village poor of their own clan who are in a position of total economic dependence on the kulak. That is why the question of preparing the nominations for the village, district and regional soviets must be raised in good time.

Owing to the conditions in the National Republics and Provinces special attention must be paid to the electoral commissions. For example, in Turkmenia which had strong clan groupings, members of electoral commissions in a great many cases supported the members of their clan endeavouring to get one of them appointed chairman,

The Re-elections to the Soviets in 1929

and so on. It is necessary to form electoral commissions which will apply the correct class line of the party and, in no circumstances, treat this question from the clan angle.

Moreover, there is the question of the election commissioners. Some Republics used to send such commissioners from the centre to the regions, districts and sometimes villages. This system must, evidently, be preserved. The despatch of election commissioners in aid of the local organizations of the soviets is very beneficial.

A few words about preparing our organizations. Very often, the party cells in the *auls*, the komsomol cells, or the unions of *koshchi*[1] and *Dzarly* are entirely unprepared for the re-elections, or else the explanations in the cells begin a few days before the report-making campaign—a day or two before the re-elections. The preparation of the public organizations must start much earlier.

Who, then, is to be drawn into the soviets? The comrades recommend that those exempted from taxation[2] should be drawn into the soviets. That is correct: in the first place those exempted from taxation. Moreover, a cattle-breeding reform is in progress in Kazakhstan. Clearly, those peasants receiving cattle under the reform will have to be elected to the soviets to enable them to defend their rights and, having received cattle, to develop their economy. In Uzbekistan and Turkmenia it will be a question of those who received land and water during the land and water reform. Undoubtedly the peasants who received land and water must be elected to the soviets. This is the main guarantee that the beys and kulaks will not take the land and the water from them. Consequently, it is above all these strata of the village which have to be brought into the soviets.

But to attract into the re-election campaign the broad sections of the village labourers and the village poor in general does not in the least mean that we are going against the middle peasant. Nothing of the kind. We know that in villages, districts and regions of several Autonomous Republics and Provinces the middle peasant at present plays a greater role than the village poor—and that is why, in the present re-election campaign, we must pay greater attention to the village labourer and village poor.

[1] See the following document, pp. 91 ff.
[2] I.e. the poorest peasants and labourers.—R.S.

DOCUMENT NO. 7

THE KOSHCHI UNION IN KAZAKHSTAN[1]

by A. BOGDANOV

The organization of the *koshchi* union has a great past. Its emergence is connected with, and derived from, the national policy of the party and, in particular, the establishment of Soviet power in Central Asia and in Kazakhstan.

Prior to the demarcation of the Central Asiatic Republics, the *koshchi* union was affected by lengthy organizational and political crises, mainly due to the vagueness of its organization and the multitude of duties placed on it; it was also influenced at the time by the general instability of Soviet power in Central Asia. The beginning of the *koshchi* unions in Central Asia goes back to 1920. In Kazakhstan the *koshchi* union was organized in 1926; in southern Kazakhstan (Dzhetysu, the Syr-Daryinsk province and the Kara-Kalpak province) it developed during the fight against the Basmach movement,[2] and in the struggle for the organization of Soviet power in Turkestan. Since then, the union has grown rapidly in strength. Thus, by July 1, 1926, it had 97,461 members in the whole of Kazakhstan; by September 1, 1927, 177,455; and by May 1928, 231,650.

What is the *koshchi* union in organization, composition and class nature, and how does it fulfil the functions of organizing the village labourers and village poor and protecting their economic class interests against exploitation by the kulaks, beys, and semi-feudal elements? To answer these questions, it is necessary to observe the *koshchi* union's participation in several political campaigns. According to its statutes, the union is based on individual membership. Its fundamental aim is to rally the village poor, to liberate them from arbitrary exploitation by the bey and the patriarchal family yoke, to bring out and develop their self-reliance in economic restoration, and to draw the masses of the village poor into the work of Soviet construction.

[1] *Sovetskoye Stroitelstvo*, 1929, No. 4 (slightly abridged).
[2] Bands with a counter-revolutionary (Pan-Turkic) orientation including gangs of ordinary robbers; they operated in Central Asia from 1920 to 1923 as fairly organized groups (Enver Pasha was one of their leaders). Their final dissolution took some more years.—R.S.

The Koshchi Union in Kazakhstan

Let us dwell first on the organizational and practical problems.

The organizational and practical work of the *koshchi* union has great defects. The cells and committees have not taken shape and have not been re-elected for a long time. Almost everywhere the leading bodies of the village district committees of *koshchi* are nominated. Members of the union are mostly recruited without having been consulted. Often some farm labourer who has been enrolled in his absence by the chairman or the secretary of the union cell does not know that he is a member. One had better say nothing about the way the members are living up to their duties, seeing that they do not even fulfil such elementary obligations as paying membership fees or attending general meetings.

The leadership and the instruction of the lower *koshchi* organs by the county and territorial centres are extremely weak. Instructors inspecting the work of the local organs confine themselves to drawing up bureaucratic documents.

The apparatus of the *koshchi* union consumes a great deal of money. . . . The political education of the members is very poor. More than 98 per cent of them are illiterate. The leadership of the district committees and *aul* cells too consists mostly of illiterate people who do not understand their tasks. The People's Commissariat of Education and its organs are doing practically nothing to serve the cultural requirements of the village poor nor, in particular, of the *koshchi* members.

The 'Peasants' Houses' and 'Red Tea Rooms' opened locally for cultural purposes are leading a miserable existence. Thus, the 'Peasants' House' in the centre of the Syr-Daryinsk county has been ignored by the party, soviet and other organizations, with the result that all sorts of scandals are going on there. No cultural work whatever is done. All the 'Peasants' House' did was to provide night lodgings.

School attendance by children of the village poor is far below average. In many *auls* these children do not go to school at all.

The social composition of the *koshchi* organs is as follows: of a total of over 231,000 members for the whole of Kazakhstan (268 rural district committees, and 6,652 village cells) only 54 present were village poor, the rest were medium and well-to-do farmers.

Since the organs of the *koshchi* union are infested with [class] alien elements, they are purged periodically, especially in southern Kazakhstan (Dzhetysu, the Syr-Daryinsk province). But these purges are haphazard and without the participation of the broadest masses of village poor and farm labourers. Hence the desired results are not obtained, and in several districts there are still many alien elements in the union, in some places even including chairmen of its district and village committees. The *party* element among the *koshchi* is weak. It amounts to 460 party and 3,402 komsomol members. . . .

Neither party nor co-operative organizations have paid proper attention to the collectivization and co-operation of the *koshchi* members. In the whole of Kazakhstan, during the entire period of its activity, the union has had among its members no more than about 16,000 co-operators and 36 collectives and artels.[1]

The liaison with the Committees of Mutual Public Aid and the Union of Agricultural and Forestry Workers is weak; there is no exchange of practical experience, although the Committees of Mutual Public Aid have gained a great deal of practical experience and achieved much in economic and productive work, co-operation and the collectivization of the village poor. The Kazakh and the Russian village poor are still divided by national antagonisms caused by land disputes. It has happened that the peasant committee of Mutual Public Aid, instead of giving the benefit of its rich experience to the *aul* and *koshchi* poor, has leased land from them on terms reducing them to bondage (Aktubinsk county). . . .

In the conditions prevailing in Kazakhstan the land reform is a political problem of particular importance. It would seem that, for its correct solution, the party organizations ought to draw in large numbers of the village poor; but, unfortunately, this was not done enough in the re-allotment of meadow and arable land, nor was the campaign made use of to consolidate the alliance between the village poor and the medium farmer. The result showed itself in several undesirable occurrences, such as the recent case in the town of Chimkent, the centre of the Syr-Daryinsk county. At the end of September 1928 a special meeting of the village poor, including 500 *koshchi* members, was held there to discuss the organization of land utilization by the village poor and farm labourers, and their participation in the land reform. The chairman of the County Land Administration was invited to the meeting. In the debate on how the village poor and land labourer was to get the land, and how much, the chairman of the CLA said: 'No farm labourer will receive land unless he has a certificate from the bey stating that he is, in fact, a farm labourer and has served him as such without a break for several years. A *koshchi* certificate indicating a need for land we regard as illegal; what we require is a certificate from the bey.' This statement provoked the indignation of the entire meeting, and many farm labourers made a demonstrative protest to the Executive Committee.

[1] The use of the two terms suggests that the typical 'collective' was not, as now, an *artel* but a *kommuna*, leaving members no private plots.—R. S.

The Koshchi Union in Kazakhstan

Now for the participation of *koshchi* in the most important political campaigns. Despite their weakness, the *koshchi* unions played an important role in the re-elections of the soviets in Kazakhstan in 1926, and became in some places the organizing centres of the village poor against the beys.

'Thanks to them and to the correct leadership of the party organizations, these elections were the first occasion when family and bey influence in re-allocating meadows in many Kazakh rural districts (*volost*) was overcome by the class solidarity of the village poor. This was the first time that *koshchi* really acted in these localities as the organization of the village poor.' (From the resolution of the plenary session of the Kazakh Territorial Committee of the CPSU(B), March 28, 1927.)

But there were also negative factors. It has been recorded in last year's re-elections that

'family and bey influence is still strong and that it prevailed in the elections in those rural districts (which were in the majority) where the party and *koshchi* did not exert their influence, and where neither the resolutions of the third plenary session nor the re-allocation of meadows have been carried out.'

There are also many shortcomings in the way *koshchi* participated in the present re-election campaign to the soviets. Since the party and soviet organs have not paid enough attention to its participation in the re-elections, *koshchi* owing to traditional inertia fails to fight for the election to the soviets of its candidates from farm labourers and village poor; in some places, *koshchi* representatives have not even been included in the electoral commissions.

The union's stand, however, was quite different when grass and plough-land were re-allocated in 1926–27. At that time, the party organizations noted

'on the strength of an analysis of the attitude to re-allocation taken by the two extremes of the village poor and beys, that the struggle between these antagonistic social forces did not go far enough. The class features of the struggle were often obscured by feuds among families and villages. As the class struggle developed, the distribution of forces was such that it was not possible to confront the beys by the entire village. Only in a few cases was a united front of the village poor and medium farmers organized against the beys. The medium farmers were either wavering between the village poor and the beys, or they occupied a neutral position. This attitude to re-allocation on the part of the medium farmers was basically due to the fact that their interests were not sufficiently considered. While the levelling-out principle was not designed to affect the economic interests of medium farmers by curtailing their use of land, the actual practice of re-allocation as applied in some districts, asserted the rights of the village poor to better land at the expense not only of the bey, but repeatedly also of the medium farmers. A certain proportion of medium farmers therefore suffered economic loss from the re-allocation. The mistakes committed in regard to the medium farmers have to some extent disorganized them politically.' (IVth Plenary Session of the Kazakh Territorial Committee of the CPSU (B)—October 12, 1927.)

This shows that *koshchi* did not understand how to organize the village poor; nor was it able, despite the great prevalence of medium farmers in the union, to protect these farmers on the strength of their alliance with the village poor.

A most important political campaign, recently waged in Kazakhstan, was the confiscation of the property of the beys and their expulsion from the country.

This measure of the Kazakh government, which was carried out under the leadership of the party organizations, was essentially tantamount to bringing the October Revolution to Kazakhstan or, as it was called, 'October in the Steppe'. For hitherto the Kazakh village had been left untouched; not only was its economy preserved but it had actually expanded and the Kazakh village poor lacked air to breathe. Like the medium farmers, they were enslaved and most cruelly exploited by the beys. Until quite recently they were not conscious of being the masters in their own proletarian state. They had practically no voice in the soviets which were led by the beys or their henchmen and flunkeys. The beys, not content with dominating the soviets and co-operatives, had in some places also seized control of the party organizations and completely subjected the latter's apparatus to their own interest. That is why the support given to the party in the village is still very weak. No cells have as yet taken shape in the village; nor have we any village communists at all as we would like them to be, even from the point of view of meeting the minimum requirements, i.e. communists capable of fulfilling the most elementary party duties, and not susceptible to the influence of the family and the bey. The family feud shapes all the affairs of the village. In short, in many districts of Kazakhstan, we are still faced with a patriarchal way of life and feudal relationships.

Such were the conditions leading to 'October in the Village'.

In this most important political campaign in Kazakhstan—the confiscation of the property of the semi-feudal beys—the *koshchi* did not understand how to organize the village poor, and the party cells failed to rally them around the union.

'The confiscation campaign revealed the true face of our soviet and public organizations in the village. In many places, although not everywhere, the village councillors and *koshchi* committee men did not do justice to their

The Koshchi Union in Kazakhstan

position. By force of habit, they either made an alliance with the beys or tried to be neutral.' (From the report of the Aktubinsk county.)

The beys, on the other hand, were better prepared for the confiscation campaign than the village poor. They sold off in good time a portion of their cattle and shared out another among their relatives or the villagers in order to recruit supporters. Drawing on their family connections and economic power, the beys strained every muscle to maintain their predominant position. They resorted to various methods of agitation and incited the medium farmers by telling them: 'Now it is me who is being stripped, but it will be your turn next.' The local officials, however, did not understand how to organize the medium farmers, even allowing them in some places to drift away.

The beys proved to be stronger. The various village organizations, such as the *koshchi*, soviets, komsomol and even some party cells, often fell under their influence. In some counties, notably in Semipalatinsk, it happened that the beys who were to be expelled drew up decisions in the name of *koshchi* village poor cancelling the expulsion orders. In one district, those liable to expulsion went so far as to attend a general meeting of the *koshchi*, which discussed their statements and passed a resolution requesting that the decree should not be applied to these beys. In the Chengistau, Kzyltau and Djarmin districts, the petitions in favour of the beys were signed also by komsomol and party members, not to speak of the *koshchi* members among the village poor. One of the beys collected 200 signatures including those of communists.

A characteristic case occurred in connection with the expulsion of a bey in the Syr-Daryinsk county. For some years prior to his arrest, the *ishan* as a member of the clergy, exploiting the religious prejudices of the Kazakh population, resorted to fraudulent acts designed to rouse superstitions and to propaganda aimed at undermining the Soviet state, restoring the monarchical regime and so forth. He hid systematically objects liable to taxation and incited the population to do so. He used compulsion to exact from his *aul* funds for the religious school which he had organized, and offerings, for his own benefit, for religious rites performed by him. He would threaten people who refused to submit to his demands with a weapon which he kept without the required permit. These misdeeds of Balpekov's, which fall under the articles 58–8, 58–10, 62, 118, 123, 124 of the criminal code having been fully proved, he was sentenced to three years' banishment from Kazakhstan.[1]

[1] If there was evidence for the more serious parts of the indictment, the sentence was lenient, as article 58,8 allows even for capital punishment, 58,10

Soviet Nationalities Policy under the NEP

Can it be believed that communists should intercede on behalf of that bey? Yet, there were some such petitions and not from individuals, but from entire cells: one of the komsomol, another of the CPSU(B). The petitioners, in their documents signed by 34 communists and komsomol members, state that that bey was a very good man, completely loyal to the Soviet regime, and so on. What is the explanation of two entire organizations interceding on behalf of an obvious counter-revolutionary? It appears that the bey's son was a member of that komsomol cell, and knew how to influence two cells in his father's interest.

In Syr-Daryinsk county, too, the bey who was liable to be expelled bribed with the help of the *Atkamyner* those village poor who were communists, including the secretary of the *aul* cell of the CPSU(B) and the chairman of the *aul* soviet. When the commissioner of the County Commission arrived, the village poor who had been incited and bribed by the bey protested against his expulsion. They stated that the bey was a good man and was distributing cattle among the village poor. It was discovered later that, in return for this, the chairman of the village soviet, the secretary of the cell and the chairman of the *koshchi* union had each received 100 rubles from the bey.

In the *aul* No. 5 (Syr-Darya) two of the village poor who were members of the party were invited to call on the bey Bekanov. He told them he had heard that, if the komsomol and the CPSU(B) cell should tell the confiscation commissioners that in their district there were no beys whose property was subject to confiscation, then there would be none. One of the party members replied: 'In *aul* No. 7 I met the commissioner, who told me confidentially that in our *volost* Amantayev and you are to have your property confiscated. But if the commissioner should question us about you, we shall help you.'

A candidate member of the CPSU(B), at a secret conference arranged by the bey, made a speech in which he said that, in view of the campaign for confiscating bey property, the village poor must expose the beys. He read out a whole list of beys liable to expropriation and expulsion. 'Our beys are expelled into other districts, but we, the village poor, must all support them. We will fare better if we are with the rich.'

establishes prison sentences of not less than six months, and 118 (bribery) prison sentences up to five years. But Bogdanov quotes as evidence the data of the Commission for Preliminary Investigation, not all of whose results need have been adopted even by the public prosecution: there is the strong possibility that no more than some offences under articles 123 and 124 (i.e. against the disestablishment laws), and perhaps some attempts at tax evasion were proven but that Bogdanov (and his sources) regard the very failure of the court to accept all the case of the preliminary investigation as evidence of the tendencies against which the article is directed.—R.S.

The Koshchi Union in Kazakhstan

There are many such cases.

We have also instances of other kinds of waverings among responsible officials. The county and district commissioners, coming to a village, instead of exposing the beys liable to expropriation, make deals with them and help them to hide their property.

There were also comrades among responsible Kazakh officials who far from furthering the expropriation sometimes actually counteracted it. When one of their nearest relatives was liable to expropriation, these communists pestered the secretaries of party committees and confiscation commissions with oral and written statements that their father or brother was a very good bey, a perfectly harmless bey, and by no means a big bey—could he not, therefore, be exempted from expropriation?

It is a fact that some *aul* cells and individual *aul* communists inclined towards more extensive expropriation and expulsion than laid down in the directives, and that, at the same time, they lacked party steadfastness and a firm class approach to the expulsion and expropriation of the beys, revealing thereby an obviously tendentious clan attitude and sometimes even coming out in direct defence of the beys.

The village poor and farm labourers took an active part in the campaign and helped in the detection of hidden property, so that in some places the expropriation was successful. This was the basis on which the sovietization of the *aul* gained firm support in many districts. The expropriation provoked a severe class struggle in the *aul*. The beys and the *aul* organizations of the soviet and party are engaged in a mutual struggle for the support of village poor and medium farmers. But the *aul* organizations are still too weak, they often yield to the influence of [class] alien elements, and sometimes act as direct protectors of clan interest and the beys. . . . This brings home to us the need for more serious preparation for the re-elections of the village soviets. . . .

The basic reasons for the inefficient work and the unsatisfactory state of the *koshchi* organization are the complete illiteracy of its members, and especially of the village poor and farm labourers amongst them, the prevalence of clan survivals and economic dependence on the semi-feudal beys, and a lack of appreciation, on the part of party organizations and the soviet and other public bodies, of the role of the *koshchi*. The consequence of all this is that the *koshchi* have not enough influence on the public and political life of Kazakhstan. Neglect of the union by organs of the People's Commissariats of Education and Agriculture, the co-operatives and others is another cause of these shortcomings.

In this connection, it is not without interest to ascertain the state of organization of the village poor in the other national Republics. The available data show that the work among the village poor is no better than in Kazakhstan. In the Crimea, for example, the power of former landlords and kulaks is still preserved. Their land has not yet been properly nationalized, the village poor have not been given land, they remained oppressed and exploited by the kulaks. The soviet and co-operative organizations were infested with alien elements, nor were the village poor represented in them. It was only after an investigation by the CC of the CPSU(B) that an end was put to this disgusting state of affairs. The village poor in the Republics of Central Asia have not been organized either. The *koshchi* union, which should have brought them material benefits and extended their influence on the soviet and co-operatives, was ignored by the party leadership. Some comrades went so far as to wish to do away with the *koshchi*. . . . Without entering into the details of the union's work it is at least necessary to state that the social composition of *koshchi* in Central Asia is far from satisfactory.

'The *koshchi* union, as an organization of the indigenous village poor, is strongly infested with alien social elements. With a membership, after the reorganization and purge of 1927, of about 200,000, it consists of 46 per cent of farm labourers and village poor, 34 per cent of medium farmers and 20 per cent of well-to-do and beys. As a result, the union has been transformed from the class organization of the village poor into a national peasant organization.' (*Izvestiya CC CPSU(B)*, January 6, 1929.)

This most unsatisfactory phenomenon is due to lack of leadership by the party. In Uzbekistan, although the plenary session of the Central Asian Bureau of the CC had decided to intensify the work of *koshchi*, the county committees left this question in abeyance for four months.

In Turkmenia the *koshchi* consisted of 46 per cent of village poor, 50 per cent of medium farmers and 4 per cent of well-to-do, though here, too, in some places the union was led by beys and well-to-do elements.

In the Kirghiz Republic, the position of the *koshchi* is somewhat better. After the purge and reorganization, the share of the village poor in its social composition has been increased to 63·25 per cent, while the farm labourers amount to 22·54 per cent, the medium farmers to 13·98 per cent and employees to 0·35 per cent. In the purge, 12,247 beys and manaps were expelled from the union. Nevertheless, we find here that in individual cantons the percentage of village poor sifted out is high: 26·50 per cent of the village poor

The Koshchi Union in Kazakhstan

in the Dzhalal-Abed canton and 43 per cent in the Osh canton have been expelled from the union. In Kirghizia, too, we are faced with great shortcomings in the practical activity of the union (weak mass work, poor participation in political and economic campaigns, collectivization, co-operation, and so on). This does not mean that the *koshchi* union is wholly ineffective, that it has outlived its time, lost its value and should be wound up. The above-mentioned negative features merely show the likely result of our indifference and failure to give guidance and assistance to the various links in the machinery of our political and practical work. There are, after all, a great many cases to show that, owing to the failure of the party to provide leadership, our Russian groups of village poor, too, exist only on paper. . . .

That is why we must be quicker in fulfilling the party directives, especially those of the XVth Party Congress. We must push this matter through now, because the re-elections to the soviets and other political and economic campaigns (state procurements of grain and so forth) have directed the whole attention of the party to the conquest by the village poor of the key place in building up the economy and the soviets in the USSR.

First of all, it is necessary to decide as a matter of principle, whether we need the *koshchi* union, and whether it fulfils its functions as a form of organization of the village poor supporting the party in the village. The answer is yes. The *koshchi* union must continue its work. At the XVth Party Congress, Comrade Molotov said succinctly:

'The *koshchi* union, too, has historical roots in our Eastern Republics and it arises from their peculiar conditions illustrated . . . by the fact . . . that in many districts the task is not to revive the soviets, but to establish them. We need this special organization of the village poor. We must support it in every way because it furthers the work of establishing the soviets. We must support it in every way because it is still very weak. But in the conditions prevailing in the Eastern Republics of Central Asia, especially Kazakhstan, there can be no doubt about the great importance of the *koshchi*.'

The union, as it is now, must be thoroughly purged of alien elements; it must be radically reorganized in regard to its functions with a view to assuring the position and leadership of the farm labourers and village poor inside the organization. Such is the requirement of the present phase of the socialist reorganization of agriculture and the tasks arising from it. It is necessary to adopt urgent measures which will ensure that this historical organization of the village poor does, in fact, justify its existence as a class organization. This must be done now, for, if we are able to restore the efficiency of the union as a class organization and to organize the village poor around it, it will be easier to achieve the desired political results in the re-elections to the soviets, whereas last year's re-elections produced many negative features.

The *koshchi* union must be given such independent economic and productive tasks (productive assistance to the village poor, unification of the village poor and small peasant holders in artels, associations, collectives and so forth) as to enable it to promote, after the model of KKO and DOV (dekhan societies of mutual help), the collectivization and co-operation of the households of the village poor, and the organization of the entire agriculture on the basis of socialist principles.

The work among the village poor must not be treated as a general and abstract question, but it has to be properly co-ordinated with the class line of soviet, party and other organizations. Moreover (after preliminary practical experiments in some districts), efforts should be made in the village to hold village poor meetings and conferences. In the end the *koshchi* union must become a really powerful organization supporting the party in the village, capable of organizing the village poor and the farm labourer, and of conducting, on the basis of a firm alliance between them and the middle farmer, a resolute struggle against the offensive of the kulak and bey, whose power and influence in the *aul* are still very considerable.

It is necessary to bring about a change in the party leadership, seeing to it that the party organizations should have a different perception of, and give better guidance to, the work with the village poor and especially the *koshchi* union. To underestimate the political importance of the organization of the village poor, of its work and alliance with the middle farmer, is dangerous and harmful to the policy of the party.

DOCUMENT NO. 8

THE LAND AND WATER REFORM IN THE SOVIET EAST[1]

by V. NODEL

... In the Soviet East, the solution of the bourgeois-democratic tasks of the proletarian revolution and the transition to the socialist tasks were naturally much more protracted than in the conditions of Russia where the village poor and the bulk of the medium farmers had a considerable experience of mass risings, had passed through the phase of struggle against the landlord and received their class training at the front. The basic reason [for this delay in the East] lay in the 'under-development, backwardness and obscurantism of the poorest peasants, the absence of a national proletariat and the lack of experience in the class struggle.' In the prevailing correlation of class forces, Turkestan, Kazakhstan and some other Eastern Republics were not only unable to solve independently the tasks of the socialist but even of the bourgeois-democratic revolution.

... [yet] it is incorrect to assert, as is currently done, that the revolutions in the East 'are eight years too late', that 'the economy in the Central Asian village has preserved its old physiognomy in the eighth year of the revolution', and that 'the social relationships in the Eastern village have hardly changed during the years of revolution', and that 'economic restoration has proceeded on the pre-revolutionary basis.'

The socialist nature of the revolution in the East manifested itself, above all, in the fact that it was led by the proletariat of Russia who helped the working peoples in the former colonies to reorganize their economy on socialist principles, by-passing the capitalist stage of development, owing to the ever-increasing assistance from the proletariat of the former metropolis.

It is a mis-statement of the problem to say that the socialist stage of the revolution does not start until after the land and water reform. This would be an essentially mechanical approach to the revolution. It would amount to severing the former colonies from the common economic system of the USSR and to denying the measures taken for the socialist reconstruction of economy during the whole past

[1] *Revolutsia i Natsionalnosti*, 1930, No. 1 (slightly abridged).

period. The organization of the *Chief Cotton Commission* as an organ representing the all-Union industry and linking the latter with the individual native peasant, illustrated the impact of socialism on the petty peasant economy, even though the beys or kulaks have, to some extent, preserved their role of middlemen (which, it is true, had declined from year to year already prior to the land and water reform).

Although the village poor did not succeed in taking over the land immediately after the October Revolution (yet such attempts had been made), and even though the land seized by them was often returned to the landlords and beys, great and decisive changes have nevertheless taken place in the political organization of the masses and in the economic system of the Soviet East during the period of 1917 to 1925 (the beginning of the land and water reform on a mass scale).

The peculiarity of socialist construction in the East was the foundation of socialist economy and of socialist relationships that had been laid *before* the tasks of the bourgeois-democratic revolution were finally solved. Precisely because we were able to accumulate a certain proportion of socialist elements in our economy and, by using them as a basis, to organize, on this basis, the village poor and the middle farmers, we could accomplish the land and water reforms with comparative ease.

... The reform of 1920–21 was successful mainly because its sharp edge was directed against one of the most blatant legacies of colonialism. When *we solved the task of the bourgeois-democratic revolution by the reform in the Semirechi region, we marched in step with the entire Kirghiz peasantry against the Russian kulaks.* A simultaneous struggle against the representatives of the colonial regime, i.e. the Russian kulaks, and against the Kirghiz national bourgeoisie was obviously impossible. It was only in the struggle against the Russian kulaks [in Kirghizia] and their liquidation as an independent political force that the conditions were established for the process of internal differentiation, for the liberation of the village poor from the influence of their own national kulaks. Although mistakes were committed in the reform of 1920–21, it would be incorrect to deny its political and socio-economic importance. It is no exaggeration to say that, without the reform of 1920–21, we would not have had the reform of 1925. It was a necessary stage in the historical development of the Soviet East.

Water and land-and-water reforms had also been attempted before 1925. As a rule they petered out, mainly because of the wrecked state of economy and of the economic isolation of

The Land and Water Reform in the East

many Eastern districts, especially in Central Asia, during the civil war. With the practical cessation of cotton sowing, and a sharp drop in the ratio of commodity production to total output, the influence of feudal and capitalist elements increased and the struggle for land relaxed.

. . . Certain delays in the land reform (such as took place in some districts and Republics, for instance in Daghestan and the Crimea) were due to the fact that the leading cadres were, to some extent, out of step with the class differentiation in the village. The weakness and numerical inferiority of the national proletariat compelled, during the first period of the development of the soviets, the use of the petty bourgeois and partly bourgeois intelligentsia in order to establish contacts with the national peasantry. The replacement of these cadres by cadres originating from the basic mass of the peasantry and the urban proletariat naturally met, and is still meeting, with considerable resistance. The fact that the Soviet apparatus was infested and socially heterogenous resulted even in occasional return to capitalist and feudal elements of portions of the land taken from them in 1920–21.

The following two quotations illustrate the tremendous advance made by the oppressed peasantry which had been suffocating in the nets of the Moslem clergy:

'Our Shariat does not permit any violation of anyone's property rights. If someone encroaches on somebody else's rights without the owner's permission, then Lord God—the Creator of eighteen thousand worlds—will not forgive that. . . . We must not demand the distribution of land and kindred objects.' (Reply of a Moslem representative to the First Central Asiatic Territorial Congress of Peasants.)

'Rather than settling us into the plain, take away the land from the kulak landlord and big cattle breeder, and give it to us. If you give us the kulak land in our own mountains, this will be the real October Revolution.' (From a statement of the mountain peoples of Daghestan at a peasant gathering in 1927.)

. . . The agrarian revolution in the form of land-and-water reforms has [now] been basically completed in the cotton-growing districts of Uzbekistan, Turkmenistan, Kirghizia and Georgia; it is being carried out in the Crimea and Daghestan and in preparation in the southern part of Kazakhstan, Karakalpakia, Tadjikistan and the cattle-breeding districts of almost all the national Republics. A reform of cattle breeding was carried out only in Kazakhstan, where as many as 700 households of big feudal manaps have been wound up.

The land-and-water reform in Uzbekistan has removed more than 200,000 hectares of land from the landlords, big merchants, administrations of religious institutions and so forth. In Turkmenistan alone more than 20,000 hectares of land were obtained.

The land and land-and-water reforms have considerably diminished the land hunger of the village poor by placing at their disposal large land funds and to some extent the implements of production. In Uzbekistan, 28,853 *chairiker* tenants, 26,525 native peasants without land or short of land, and 5,625 farm labourers, i.e. 10 per cent of the total number of the households, have been allotted land. In Turkmenistan, 32,778 households, including 10,056 landless households and 22,721 households short of land, have received allocations.

Let us examine the basic economic results of the land-and-water reforms in the Uzbek SSR (the results of these reforms in the other Republics have not yet been worked out).

The exploitation of land by the individual groups has undergone a sharp change.

The investigation held in 1927 (two years after the reform) by the Central Statistical Office of Uzbekistan in 11,710 households which had been allotted land, and the analysis of a census covering 10 per cent of the households have revealed, in the Ferghana, Tashkent, Samarkand and Zarevshan provinces, a *sharp decrease* (from 4·3 per cent to 0·5 per cent) *of landless households, a fairly considerable reduction of the number of households short of land* (possessing approximately one hectare) (from 38 per cent to 34·3 per cent) *and a reduction in the group of kulak exploiters* (from 6 per cent to 3·8 per cent).

The economy of the village poor has undergone a considerable change and reconstruction.

After the reform, the number of those renting land among the households which had received land has decreased by almost eight times (in Andizhan from 72 per cent to 6·59 per cent, in Ferghana from 53·3 per cent to 9·03 per cent, in Khodzhent from 64·6 per cent to 8·04 per cent); the average number of cattle per household has more than doubled; the hire of cattle has considerably decreased; 15 per cent of the households which have been allotted land hire cattle, but of the remaining households 35 per cent. The tilling of land with draught animals belonging to different peasants but harnessed together for the work is twice as frequent among households which had been allotted land as among the rest—46 per cent and 20 per cent respectively. The local equipment is being more rapidly replaced by European equipment, the use of tractors by households which have been allotted land is growing (in Andizhan, before the reform, 1·72 per cent of the households used tractors; after the reform,

The Land and Water Reform in the East

10·36 per cent; in Ferghana the figures are 1·3 per cent and 5·72 per cent respectively; in Khodzhent 0·78 per cent and 3·1 per cent; in Tashkent 1·5 per cent and 11·96 per cent). The proportion of land under exploitation has risen on the allocated land to 80 per cent and the average sowing per household has grown from 0·97 per cent to 2·4 per cent. The proportion of cotton sowing has considerably increased on land taken from the beys and handed over to the native peasantry: before the reform, the cotton fields occupied 35 per cent; in 1926–27, on the land now allocated to the village poor, they expanded to 52 per cent.

The village poor have freed themselves from the need to pay the landlords and feudal elements tens of millions of rubles in rent.

In Central Asia alone, the abolition of absolute rent[1] has saved the peasantry 25–28 million rubles per year.

The land-and-water reform has ensured the development of the productive forces in agriculture.

In Uzbekistan, in the course of two years, the land allocated to the native peasantry has yielded an additional output worth 14 million rubles.

The objective conditions for a more rapid socialist reconstruction of economy have become favourable.

Prior to the reform, Uzbekistan had only 85 kolkhozy, in 1926 it had 189. Of these, only 14 kolkhozy have been established on peasant land, while the rest had developed on land which used to belong to the landlords, beys and the administration of religious organizations.

The expropriation of 700 large-scale private cattle-breeding farms in Kazakhstan resulted in the establishment of as many as 300 kolkhozy wholly or partly given to cattle breeding (25·7 per cent of the cattle were allocated to the socialized sector).

One of the fundamental reasons why in several Republics and provinces the economic development has been delayed, is that they have not completed the agrarian revolution. In this respect it is interesting to compare the structural changes in the economies of Uzbekistan and Azerbaidjan. Whereas the cotton-growing area of Uzbekistan in 1929 had already reached 120 per cent of the pre-war area, Azerbaidjan had a fall in the proportion of technical crops from 12·5 per cent to 12·1 per cent and, in particular, of cotton from 12 per cent to 11·3 per cent, because not enough attention was paid to the problems of the struggle against the survivals of feudalism and

[1] Nodel apparently regards the abolished feudal rent as 'absolute' rent in terms of Marx (*Capital*, Vol. III, Chapter 45—the differential rent, from especially favoured land, is claimed by the Soviet state in the form of taxation and/or higher delivery quotas). According to Marx (*ibid.*, Chapter 47) rents of the type formerly current in Central Asia comprehend all, or nearly all, the surplus product.—R.S.

serfdom in agriculture (the specific forms of land tenure and so forth).

However, even in those districts where the land-and-water reform has been carried out, there are still obstacles to the rapid socialist transformation of these Republics and districts.

The land-and-water reforms had been basically directed against the landlords and semi-feudal elements. Only the upper layer of the kulaks has been affected.

At present the position in most of the Eastern Republics and districts is acute, because the proportion and influence of the capitalist elements is still much greater than in all the other districts of the Soviet Union. According to the data of the Central Statistical Office of the Uzbek SSR, 7·6 per cent, forming the upper strata of the peasantry, have concentrated in their hands 26 per cent of the sowing area, 20 per cent of the draught animals and 44 per cent of the small cattle, whereas the 39 per cent poor households have only 12 per cent of the sowing area, 14 per cent of the draught animals and 10 per cent of the small cattle. In Kirghizia, the upper 10 per cent of the peasantry have 23 per cent of the sowing area, 29 per cent of the draught animals and 50 per cent of the small cattle, whereas the 43 per cent of the households of the village poor have 20 per cent of the sowing area, 19 per cent of the draught animals and 8·3 per cent of the small cattle.

The differentiation is still sharper in the cattle-breeding regions. In Turkmenia, the upper 10 per cent of the cattle breeders have 39 per cent of the large cattle and 42 per cent of the small cattle. In the Kenimekh district of Uzbekistan 9·3 per cent of the households have 41 per cent of the Persian lamb herds.

The basic forms of exploiting the village poor are land leases, primarily in the form of *chairiker*-tenure and *randzhibar*-tenure [crop-sharing and labour rents]. The difference between the Eastern Republics and all the other districts of the USSR[1] consists in the fact that here *the beys or the kulaks are the principal landlords, and the village poor the tenants.*

The data of the investigation of 400,000 households held by the Chief Cotton Administration in 1927 show that (in some districts of Uzbekistan) the households using less than one hectare rent from 57 to 76 per cent [of land] in addition to their own land. Among this group, the percentage of non-utilized land is insignificant,

---

[1] Because of the land distribution by the village community (*mir*) in Russia, as distinct from Western Europe (and, as the article shows, Asia), it was in the typical case the *poor* who leased his land (which he could not cultivate himself because of lack of implements of production) to his richer neighbour.—R.S.

while among the higher groups a considerable amount of land is not used in their own household. This is confirmed by the results of a systematic investigation of seven *kishlaks* [hamlets] in the Assakin district.

Relations of Lease and Letting (data for 1928 in %)

	Up to 1 ha.	Up to 3 ha.	Over 3 ha.
Proportion of sowings to one's own land (in % of the latter)	177	94	79
% of tenants in the group	54	15·5	2
% of letters in the group	0·87	11	29
% of all the leased land the group occupied	67	32·5	0·5

A great evil consists in the retention of lease forms in kind: 94 per cent of the entire land leased in return for labour service fall on the village poor, while the beys lease land mainly for money. Eighty-two per cent of the poor households renting land in return for labour service, are getting less than half of their harvest, 15·5 per cent are getting half, and only 5·2 per cent more than half of their harvest. In many districts, credit usury which levies 300 per cent per annum is strongly entrenched (an investigation in the Trotsky credit association in Uzbekistan produced evidence of an average rate of annual payments of 288 per cent).

The offensive against the kulak is not sufficiently developed. The work with the village poor is weak, and the Soviet apparatus is largely infested. All this naturally impedes the general rate of the socialist offensive. In the Assakin district—a typical district—of every 100 village poor only 0·4 were on the staff of the soviet and co-operative apparatus; every 100 well-to-do had two people. Of every 100 employees, 33 were from the well-to-do. Among the elected personnel, every 100 village poor had only 0·9 representatives of their own, the medium farmers 1·3, but the kulaks 3·9 (data for 1928).

In almost all the National Republics and districts the process of completing the agrarian revolution is opposed and resisted, with exceptional force, not only by the feudal and capitalist elements (which is natural) but at times also by a section of the party and soviet apparatus, which defends and represents the interests of those elements. In Uzbekistan, the so-called 'group of the eighteen', which consisted mainly of leaders of the soviet apparatus, operated actively against the land-and-water reform. In Kazakhstan, the group of Khodzhanov-Sadvokasov struggled against the expropriation of the big feudal cattle breeders. In the Crimea, it was the group of

Ibragimov, in Daghestan—a considerable part of the soviet and party leadership.

Only by resolutely overcoming the bourgeois influences and the right-wing deviations in the individual links of the party and soviet apparatus is it possible to organize and accomplish the agrarian revolution in all seriousness. Wherever the struggle was protracted, wherever—owing to specific local conditions—it was not possible quickly to overcome the influence of the bourgeoisie and right-wing deviationist elements, the land reforms were either completely wrecked, or they did not basically affect the capitalist upper strata.

In the Crimea the bourgeois kulak elements have exploited their influence on the soviet apparatus in effect to the point of interfering with the CC of the CPSU(B), and nullifying the land reform, since the norm of land to be retained was fixed at 57 hectares. In Daghestan, the first project of the land reform left the land relationships in the mountain villages unchanged by reducing the reform to moving the village poor from the mountain districts to the plain.

Despite the great diversity of conditions and tasks facing the individual Eastern Republics and districts at the present time, the basic [tasks remain]: resolute and implacable struggle against the capitalist elements, sweeping expansion of sovkhoz and kolkhoz construction, gradual transition to complete collectivization on a mass scale and liquidation of the kulak on this basis, elimination and destruction of kulak influence on the party and soviet apparatus, expulsion from the party and the soviets of socially alien elements, an extensive effort to organize the village poor, resolute and consistent struggle for the Leninist principles of national policy against the deviations from it, and in the first place against the right-wing deviation.

DOCUMENT NO. 9

THE ROLE OF THE ETHNOGRAPHER IN SOVIET CONSTRUCTION IN THE NORTH[1]

by A. LINEVSKI

For historical reasons, the only socialist state in the world consists, according to the academic record, of 169 nationalities, which are divided into twelve basic national groups: three Slav (91 million) and four related peoples (460,000), two Baltic (160,000) and seventeen Iranian (2,240,000) peoples, eight tribes representing Indo-European (800,000), thirty-nine Japhetic (5,730,000), five Semitic (1,955,000), twenty-seven Finno-Ugro-Samoyed (2,910,000) and forty-seven Turkic (25,115,000), three Mongol (362,000), six Tungus-Manchu (80,000) and nine Paleo-Asiatic (35,000) tribes; and 150,000 people belonging to the Far Eastern civilizations—altogether 133 million people belonging to 169 nationalities.

Owing to the multi-national composition of the population of the Soviet Union, the ethnographer has to play a most important part in Soviet construction. He must be able to combine the directives of the state with the habit of mind of the natives, and the interests of the state with the interests of the native masses, so as to adapt the native population to the life of the whole Union.[2] . . . Hence it is clearly impossible to speak of the apolitical or [purely] academic function of ethnographers in the Soviet Union.

To enable the ethnographer to do his work well as a builder of socialism, two basic principles must, in my opinion, be observed:

I. In these days when we are changing from one epoch to another, one tends (and it is quite obvious why) to divide all peoples into 'our own' and 'not our own'. To a certain extent, every man is a representative of either the new or the old epoch. This change from one epoch to another among the indigenous mass is quite different from the way it occurs in our society.

---

[1] *Sovietskoye Stroitelstvo*, 1929, No. 8 (slightly abridged).
[2] It would be highly desirable for local officials from the national minorities or people graduating from higher educational establishments to be assigned, if only for a year, to the Ethnographic Department of the Leningrad State University in order to acquire practical experience of ethnography in the work of Soviet development.

Soviet Nationalities Policy under the NEP

'There are people of alien nationality working in the apparatus of village Soviets who ... often know neither the conditions of life (*byt*) nor the language of that nationality; every member of that nationality approaches such officials with great distrust. They say: "He's not one of ours." When you begin talking in their native tongue [they say]: "It is our man ... he's one of ours." But when a Russian instructor or even a member of the Praesidium of the Provincial Executive Committee arrives, they say: "A stranger has come." ' (Speech of Comrade Shaposhnikov at the Conference of Commissioners for National Minorities, p. 86.)

That is why any incoming official, with the best intentions but unfamiliar with the local language, will remain 'a stranger', whilst say what you will, any kulak ... who speaks the common language is regarded as 'our own' man. Words spoken to the native in his own language are generally more convincing than the same thought expressed in a foreign tongue. Hence to do Soviet work without a knowledge of the native language will be very difficult if there are opponents of a certain measure among the natives. Unfamiliarity with the native tongue is a most serious obstacle, impeding proper work on the part of the Soviet ethnographer. But this difficulty may be mitigated by the native youths who have, to a certain extent, been sovietized.

II. What is still more important, if the work is to be a success, is the exercise of tact by the official. Even though he may have a most thorough knowledge of the local language, the newcomer will always for a time be met by the population with reticence and reserve. It rests with him either quickly to dissipate that veil of strangeness or, on the contrary, to thicken it. Success or otherwise depends on whether the newcomer revives the methods and errors of the Tsarist officials, or whether he will be careful to avoid them. By bringing home to the population the difference between himself and the former authorities, the ethnographer (and any Soviet official) will lay a firm foundation for successful work.

The same contrast must be continuously underlined in day-to-day activities. The guiding motive of the Tsarist regime was the absolute subjection of the natives. Such tactics must be rejected once and for all. They must never be adopted when sovietizing the indigenous tribes.

'Formerly it used to be the duty of the population to drive about free of charge all kinds of authorities in the district; this duty has been abolished' (report by the Olsk District Executive Committee of the Far-Eastern Province). It would be the grossest possible mistake to adopt this proposal from one of the committees of the North: 'If travelling expenses cannot be obtained, then it is possible to get a

The Ethnographer in Soviet Construction in the North

meeting of Samoyeds to resolve that they should drive a militia man for nothing.'

If a militia man drives up to the dwelling of a suspected native and, after the investigation, forces the men to drive him back free of charge, how can the Samoyed discriminate between the Tsarist village policemen and the representative of the Soviet Government?

Absolutely inadmissible, too, is the forcible subjection of the native to some official order. Here is a glaring example of such political illiteracy:

'I proposed that a hundred to two hundred head of reindeer stricken with mange should be sold (for the purpose of experimental cure.—A.L.). "Selling is all right," replied the rich reindeer breeder. "We'll sell twenty reindeer." The chief of the Turin cultural base insisted on a hundred. The Tungusi did not agree. There was nothing to do but to get the compilation of orders issued by the Krasnoyarsk Provincial Executive Committee, and to tell them that if they refused to sell the mangy reindeer and deliver them for cure, we would take all the mangy animals without their consent on the strength of this particular order, and cure them. This turn of the conversation had its effect, and the breeders at once agreed to sell a hundred head of reindeer chronically affected by mange.'

Such action by the chief of the Turin cultural base must be denounced as anti-Soviet. To tell a native that if he does not give up something on his own, it will be taken from him by force on the strength of an order, means to blur in his mind the difference between the Tsarist and the Soviet regimes.

The chief of the cultural base committed another serious offence:

'We celebrated the 10th anniversary of October by inaugurating the House of the Native. After the official part of the celebrations the Tungusi were treated to food and drink. They had been invited beforehand and told that there would be refreshments. All those living nearby, about thirty people, came. We treated them to food and drink in the same way as ourselves. The Tungusi were very pleased, and when we commemorated the death of V. I. Lenin, on January 22, a great many of them, to our astonishment, came to the first memorial evening. That evening passed off without refreshments, and the natives were terribly aggrieved; not one of them remained for the second day. It became clear afterwards that they love celebrations with refreshments.'

To call the natives together and then let them go hungry means utterly to misunderstand their psychology (and not only native psychology). When this is the approach to the natives, the question arises: what is the use of spending 30,000 rubles a year on maintaining that 'cultural base'?

In contrast to this, we find in other reports from officials of the

North examples of a different approach. Thus in the county of Nikolayevsk-on-Amur, the village librarian, Comrade Chaplinski, displayed a correct ethnographic approach:

'The day of the October Revolution and the 1st of May were spent in festivities; apart from talks on the significance of these celebrations, shooting competitions and boat races for prizes were arranged. The whole population (Golds) attended the celebrations.' (Report on the work of the Bolon native reading hut of the Lower Tambov District.)

That the successful sovietization of the natives depends on the correct organization of the officials' work is shown by the reports[1] of the commissioners for native affairs to the local committees of the North. The commissioner for the upper Amur, Comrade Kozin, writes:

'The village librarian Chaplinski has aroused the interest of the native population in the work of the village Soviet; from 40 to 80 natives from all the nomadic camps in the district are present at the sessions of the rural Soviet.'

The state spends substantial amounts on the work among the natives. For instance, the three schools in the Khatangsk, Jassovoi Stan and Cheranda villages, which are attended by 15 pupils, cost the state 73,260 rubles a year. This circumstance is bound to place purely civic duties on the ethnographer, for the following factor must be taken into account as one of the elements complicating the rapid sovietization of the native masses:

'After the October Revolution the Russian population received the land of the landlords, but the national minorities did not get such land' (Comrade Shaposhnikov, Conference of Commissioners, p. 85). The fact that the Nentsi[2] have always lived on state land (and sometimes on Privy Purse land) must invariably be taken into account when the Soviet official has to explain the significance of the October Revolution for the toilers.

That is why it is more difficult for the Soviet official to do successful work among the native population than among the Russians. Hence it is necessary to study the mentality of the native so as to be able to explain to him the difference between the policy of the Soviet and the Tsarist regimes. This must be done in such a way as to make the difference concrete and obvious: 'In reply to the question whether the Committee for the North has done well by building in the tundra a hospital, a medical centre and a school, a Tungus said: "All the

---

[1] The Russian word *oklad*—rate of pay or tax—is obviously a printer's error, for *doklad*, report.—Tr. N.

[2] Translator's note: the word *nemtsy* (Germans) is obviously a printer's error.

The Ethnographer in Soviet Construction in the North

buildings are all right inside and outside, they are big, but of what use they will be, I cannot say." ' (Report by the Turin cultural base No. 2 for 1927–28.) This example shows that every word, every promise must be fully implemented. Unless this happens, the confidence of the natives will be undermined.

But it is not enough to do something that is useful to the public. Even such a harmless matter as an ABC can suddenly become a public evil if it has been composed without the ethnographer:

'A Mordvin comrade told me that their ABC contains the words "Mama" and "Papa". But they refuse to pronounce the word "Papa" because, in the Mordvin language, it is an indecent word. A young Mordvin girl came home and said: "You know, father, our teacher makes us read indecent words." There are also such oddities in the Kazakh ABC. The book must be checked not only from the political and technical viewpoint but also in the light of public life and environmental conditions.' (Dosov, Conference of the Commissioners for National Minorities, p. 415.)

Without such checks, which basically amount to ethnographical supervision, the result may be to tempt the boys and embarrass the girls, and as for the outcome: 'Imagine—says Comrade Dosov (*ibid.*)—a conservative old man of the East hearing that his children in the Soviet school are taught indecent words, and you will see that this is not a trifling matter. Such is the position of the work in popular education, which is supposed to be a purely academic business.

Here is another example of how Soviet reality is reflected in a distorting mirror when native education is undertaken without an ethnographer:

'Latvian and Jewish children attend Russian schools; when it comes to public anti-religious work, the only matters discussed are the Christian Easter or the Christian Christmas, and the Jewish child gains the conviction that the Christian Easter is a bad thing and that Christ has never lived, but that "our" Moses, of course, did since "my Daddy believes in him, and has great respect for the Rabbi".' (Garfunkel: from the Briansk province, Conference of Commissioners for National Minorities, 1928, p. 342.)

In consequence of such an approach, the entire anti-religious work comes to nothing; the Latvian and Jewish beliefs retain their hold and among the Russian population there develops the most infamous anti-Semitism and chauvinism with everything that this implies. . . . In the field of public health, the ethnographer's first task is to explore what forms of medical treatment are most widespread among a certain population, and what are the reasons for it; in the second place he must ascertain what drugs are most acceptable to the natives and which ones must still be regarded as premature, and why; thirdly, he must find out how to co-ordinate popular lore with scientific medicine; fourthly, how to explain to the masses a given method of treatment; and fifthly, how to interpret in the easiest and simplest way accessible to native understanding the medical results achieved.

Nor can the ethnographer overlook some questions relating to the co-ordination of preventive medicine with environmental conditions. The abolition of popular customs which are inadmissible in medicine is to some extent also the duty of the ethnographer, but the full burden of the practical execution of that task must be placed on the native official.

By May 30, 1928, the RSFSR alone had 2,930 national village soviets, 110 national *volosts*, 33 national districts and 2 national counties, apart from autonomous provinces and Republics. Approximately half of all the tribes of the Union live in the remaining 5 independent Republics.

The task, to-day, is to continue the demarcation of districts (*rayoni*).... The whole of this immense work which is still in full swing, is far from completed. There can be no doubt that everything done hitherto will periodically be re-done, since the work has often been allowed to drift, and the definition of tribes and particularly the demarcation of national frontiers was often based on data provided by *volost* Executive Committees. I know from personal experience that some Chuvash settlements were listed, not in the Chuvash but in the Tatar Republic, 'thanks to the patriotism' of the administrator of the given locality.

In most cases administrative officials regard language as the criterion for defining national frontiers, and ignore the most interesting factor of *denationalization*—the imperceptible crowding out of the native tongue by a more powerful and stronger neighbouring people (for instance, the Tatarization of the Chuvashs). That is why the ethnographer who is called upon to take part in the work of district demarcation will naturally not be content with mere language. Frontiers, I should think, must be delimitated on the basis of the self-determination of a certain population, taking into account moreover the question of the geographic direction in which the *economic interests* of a certain group are tending. The following is a characteristic instance of an incorrect administrative division: 'The frontier along the Dzhup-Dzhur ridge divides the Tungus clans into two, causing serious economic injury to one of them; one gets its supplies

The Ethnographer in Soviet Construction in the North

from Alna, and the other from Nelkan, where average prices are 200 per cent higher.' (The Committee for the North attached to the Far-Eastern Territorial Executive Committee, February 22, 1928, on the demarcation of national districts of the native population.) It is the duty of the ethnographer in such a case to insist that the protest of the clan be taken into account. It is also his task to suggest the setting up of village soviets with a mixed population. Who but an ethnographer can handle such a job, considering that there are in the district 5,000 Russians and 4,000 natives roaming about the territory?

How is one to organize clan soviets among the Laps if their clans are completely intermixed with other nationalities? This is the situation: 'There are no district Lap soviets, since the Laps have no majority in any of the districts. The Lavozer district Executive Committee includes Lap representatives, but its active officials are Zyrianye-Izhemtsy.' (The Murmansk Committee of the North, Report for 1928.) Can one consider such a position as satisfactory? Obviously not, since there is no guarantee that the fragmentized Lap tribe will be thoroughly protected against exploitation. That is why the Committees of the North are installing in such places representatives for national minorities with the rank of commissioners for native affairs.

Cadres of indigenous officials whose job is to assist these representatives are being trained in the Northern faculties in Leningrad, Khabarovsk and in other places. That indigenous officials are best suited to solve the national contradictions is illustrated by the following report:

'The reason for all the fulmination of the Russian trappers against Vylko is the fact that, as chairman of the Soviet, he protects the Samoyeds whom the Russian trappers are used to boss. This practice isn't over yet: at a meeting in Maliye Karmakuly, inhabited predominantly by Russians, they raised the question of evicting a Samoyed camp. Vylko gave them a proper rebuke.' (Archives of the Committee of the North of October 16, 1928, No. 22.)

The ethnographer will never allow the tribes to be unified indiscriminately merely on the grounds that they have a common form of culture. The Committee of the North attached to the Komi province is perfectly correct in stating: 'If the Zyrian nomads are registered with the Samoyed native soviet there arises the danger that the Zyrians may exert influence on Samoyed affairs.' It is obvious that Zyrian officials, as members of a more civilized nationality, are in a position to violate some of the fundamental principles of sovietization.

Often the population itself adopts measures of self-defence. Thus the Kiren Committee of the North records the exclusion from the native soviet of russified citizens exploiting the native population. It is for the ethnographer to decide the complicated question as to when a denationalized element becomes a public danger to the native life, and when, on the contrary, it helps, by its presence, to raise the cultural level of the mass by which it is surrounded.

Thus the ethnographer infuses socialist principles into the solution of the national question. As long as the shortage of native officials remains so acute, he represents the most reliable safeguard guaranteeing to some small nationality an existence with equal rights in the socialist state.

The ethnographer also plays a responsible part in devising the administrative apparatus. About 100 tribes in the Union have still retained some clan conditions of life, which introduce various additional requirements into the work of sovietization. It is the duty of the ethnographer to be able to harmonize often contradictory principles.

So long as the administrative apparatus of the native district is in the hands of people shaped in pre-revolutionary times, astonishing echoes of feudalism are likely to linger on:

'The existing inequality arising from clan principles is complicated by survivals of slavery. These survivals are expressed, for example, by the fact that in the encampment of Dolon, the son of the Iagu Veldi was not elected to the native soviet because he was by origin a slave. The way a dispute is solved depends on whether a man is either one of the slaves or one of the slave holders. When it comes to abuse, one often hears: "Who do you think you are? Only a slave. Don't raise your voice too much, or I'll lock you up." The lock-up is the stocks through which the arms and legs of the offender are pushed. The stocks are still kept somewhere in a shed, to prove, when necessary, that one is not a slave by origin. These environmental peculiarities (*byt*) of the native population were not taken into account in the work of the local apparatus.' (Report on the investigation by the Commissioner for Native Affairs in the upper reaches of the Amur, Comrade Kozin, for 1928.)

It is possible that the above example is unique and does not apply to other places (it is evidently a survival of Manchurian feudalism). Instead, we often find that a clan which is strong in numbers strives after power. Thus the same commissioner writes:

'The tribes are not intermixed, and the organization of clan soviets is impossible. Nevertheless, a feature of the clan feud has been preserved— the struggle for influence, for leadership in public and Soviet work.'

This continuous internal struggle for power is a veritable scourge for the scattered clans which are numerically inferior and therefore weaker.

'The native court, the *baita*, which still functions in remote districts, is often biased and unfair to the numerically weak clans. This can be clearly observed, particularly in clan feuds when the victorious clan inflicts heavy punishment on the defeated. The oppressed and down-trodden clan, therefore, looks to the Soviet organizations for protection, but since the native Soviet consists mostly of representatives of the strong clans, such protection is not forthcoming.' (Report by the Commissioner for Native Affairs in the upper reaches of the Amur.)

... Customary law, i.e. the law hammered out by the people itself, has always been the basis and determinant of the public life of the masses. Hence, by exerting a cautious but persistent influence on the customary law of the natives, it is possible to have a direct influence on their conditions of life. The ethnographer is faced with an entirely new task in public work, that of studying the customary law of the native tribes and discovering what it has in common with the Soviet code. Various particles of fundamental clan principles coincide in many ways with socialist justice. An attentive study of the mental make-up of the natives will make it possible thoroughly to sovietize their customary law.

The problem of rooting out environmental crimes is far more complex because of their complete divergence from those of the Europeans. Since there are almost no cases at all of theft or murder for gain, the Committee of the North attached to the Krasnoyarsk County Executive Committee has reduced native crimes to the following: (1) payment of the *kalym* (ransom for the bride) and forcing a girl into matrimony; (2) bigamy and polygamy; (3) contracting or enforcing marriages of persons who have not yet reached puberty; and (4) the kidnapping of women for enforced marriage.

Such infringements of the law occur almost exclusively in provinces with a mixed population:

'According to the report by the Commissioner for the North in the North Baikal district, only one unimportant civil case came up among the local Tungusi in eighteen months, after they had been organized in a separate native district. For, owing to their nomadic life, they have very few contacts with the settled population.'

Comrade Eisenberg, who as chairman of the Central Government Commission had been sent to investigate the Bautov native district at the end of 1926, writes:

Soviet Nationalities Policy under the NEP

'We have not been able to establish a single case of theft among the Orochoni, not even of food of which, at times, they are in acute need. But there is a different crime rate among the settled immigrant Russian population in these districts. During the first half of the current year, 90 criminal and 46 civil cases came before the People's Court of the 19th district (in the Chichevka settlement). The Commissioner for the Bautov district, which had no District People's Court, reports that the District Executive Committee is swamped with civil and other cases.' (The Buryat-Mongolian Committee of the North, Report for 1926–27.)

Bearing in mind this circumstance, it is particularly important to check how the local administration copes with the national problem:

'We list as Kamchadals those inhabitants who are local aborigines representing a mixture of Tungusi, Yakuts, Koriaks and former Cossacks, deportees, as well as Japanese and Americans who had come here at the time when the wealth of Kamchatka and the Okhotsk shore was being plundered.' (Report by the Olsk District Executive Committee to the Organization Department of the County Executive Committee of Nikolayesk-on-Amur for 1927–28.)

What is the result of such a mixture? Above all the predatory exploitation of defenceless Tungusi and Koriaks by such 'aborigines' as Russian Cossacks, deportees, Japanese and Americans.

If it is not possible to have ethnographers everywhere, then it is at least necessary to give the people going out to work among the natives some ethnographical experience, some ethnographical training in their approach to the population.

This applies largely to the agents of Gostorg [the State Trading Organization] and the co-operatives. We often find in the reports of the local committees of the North astonishing illustrations of evil intentions or of a criminal and intolerably negligent attitude on the part of these officials. The natives are tempted to eat chocolate, while not enough grain is being brought in, and so forth. Thus, in the North-Baikal district the import of grain products amounted to 62,000 rubles (17 per cent) and of groceries to 42,000 rubles (12 per cent). The import of cloth totalled 77,000 rubles (22 per cent) and that of other goods apart from tobacco and hunting weapons, 87,000 rubles, or 25 per cent of the entire import of commodities.

This has an extremely perilous effect on the population.

'The decline of reindeer breeding is caused in particular by an excessive consumption of the reindeer as food. Some families have eaten 21 out of 35 reindeer. Several causes compel the Tungusi to eat up the last reindeer. One is insufficiency of food supplies brought into the Ilimpeisk tundra by

The Ethnographer in Soviet Construction in the North

the trading organization. Every Tungus tries to eat the maximum amount of meat. Even in cases of extreme poverty, he will try to avoid spending money on bread, particularly rye bread, and spend his last kopek on the finest wheaten flour. (Report by the Head of the Turin Cultural Base No. 2 for the year 1927–28.)

There can be no doubt that it is one of the duties of the ethnographer to study native requirements, particularly in the sphere of food. Considering what the Buryat-Mongolian Committee of the North described as 'the native's complete insouciance about the future', the ethnographer must discover the reasons for the preference for the most expensive and finest flour rather than for black bread. If this is merely a matter of taste then the import of the finest flour can simply be stopped. The local authorities often attempt to stop the scandalous activities of the agents.

'Last year and in 1927–28 the supply was extremely bad. In the first place, there was absolutely no co-ordination in the import of commodities between the fisheries on the one hand and Daltorg [the Far-Eastern Trade Agency] on the other. . . . In the second place, when the District Executive Committee compelled the local agents to draw up the commodity estimates with the co-operation of the local population, and to pass these estimates through the rural soviets and the District Executive Committee, it appeared that the opinion of the local population and the local authorities was not taken into account. Of the commodity estimates for 1927–28, which had been co-ordinated with the District Executive Committee, goods worth 30,000 rubles have not been reported, so that the population went short of absolute necessities (flour, groats, tea, sugar), and a lot of fur skins will be smuggled abroad.' (Report from the Olsk Executive Committee for 1927–28.)

Nor can the ethnographer overlook the element of class struggle. The exploiting strata represented by buyers, middle-men and so forth are still very strong in eastern Siberia. Thus one of the reports says: 'The vital interests of the bourgeoisie which has survived in the North have been so strongly affected by *Dalgostorg* [Far East State Trade Organization] that it will not yield without battle. We must be prepared for the sharpest and most unexpected forms of struggle.' Elsewhere we find this situation:

'The general indebtedness of the population to state and co-operative trading organizations in the three northern counties amounted to 786,000 rubles by October 1, 1926. From the debtors' registers of the Baun county one can conclude that a very considerable proportion of the credits has been distributed, not directly to the population, but to various contractors, middle-men or simply speculators. How much the population has actually received through the latter is unknown. They are still "collecting" those debts from the population and have thereby gained control over the state trading agencies and co-operatives.' (Summary Report of the Yakutian Committee of the North for 1925–28.)

'The debts are inherited and paid from generation to generation. One of the rich native households is not only the creditor of the households in its own nomad camp but also of the nomad camp nearby.' (Report on the Investigation in the Upper Reaches [of the Amur] for 1928.)

The contractors and buyers, having become middle-men between the state trade organs and the natives, saw to it that the debts were cancelled by the Revolution; by retaining these moneys and at the same time collecting the old debts, they enriched themselves at the expense of the state. And the wealth thus acquired produced new elements of the rich, replacing those ruined by the Revolution.

The head of the Turin Cultural Base, who has confined to the rich the propaganda for the treatment of reindeer suffering from mange, has committed a serious political and sociological error. An ethnographer would, of course, take into account that the owner of 2,000 reindeer, even if 1,000 of them are sick, is less affected by the affliction than a poor man half of whose herd of 20 is stricken with mange, and who can be more easily convinced that it is necessary to treat the sick animals.

There is evidence that administrative officials do not take into account the mentality of the native. The nomadic way of life has put a stamp on their mentality which is diametrically opposed to that of the city dweller.

'The peculiar psychology of the Tungus is expressed by his absolute lack of concern for the morrow. Hence his scorn for any kind of work that ties him to one place. He will willingly accept an advance on his fur skins, as he knows that he will get the animals in the taiga. But he will not be in a hurry to go out hunting, so long as, owing to the advance received, he has, for the moment, everything required for life. The officials of *Dalgostorg* had to beg the Tungusi, who had received advances, to make haste lest they miss the best time of the hunting season which had already begun.' (The Buryat-Mongolian Committee of the North, 1926–27.)

The above facts show that the officials of *Dalgostorg* included no ethnographers. Even the greatest solicitude for the native and the most sincere desire to help him are bound to do harm if the approach is clumsy.

The same committee writes:

'Several organizations have simultaneously given advances to the same Tungusi, as a result of which the advances became so considerable that the Tungusi had no hope of clearing them. Nor did they give much thought to it; they simply took what was offered. Owing to such absurdities, the

The Ethnographer in Soviet Construction in the North

Tungusi ... have not only failed to improve their economic conditions, but have, on the contrary, worsened them by falling into irredeemable debts.'

The Buryat-Mongolian Committee of the North insisted that only one organization should undertake the provisioning of each district.

The study of native mentality is urgent. Owing to the incessant decline of reindeer breeding several native units will soon have to change their customary occupation: in some places they will have to settle as agriculturists, and in others as fishermen.

'Hunting predominates in the entire Okhotsk native district.... With the destruction of the reindeer herds, the importance of fisheries grows from year to year.' (The Committee of the North attached to the Executive Committee of the Far Eastern Territory on the Regionalization of the Native Population in the Okhotsk Sea Area, 1928.)

It is the duty of the ethnographer-economist to investigate what kind of fisheries are most rational in local conditions. The vital task is to train the natives at once in the most advanced methods, without tolerating extensive, grossly primitive fishery. The question becomes even more complicated when the state intends to settle nomadic reindeer breeders. It is clearly up to the ethnographer, and no one else, to work out the most painless forms of transition which will accelerate the process.

'Immediate preparations must be made for the transition of the natives from the nomadic to new forms of economy, to start with stock-raising and agriculture. At the same time, they must be drawn into the fishery on Lake Baikal by organizing purely Tungus co-operative fishery *artels*.' (The Buryat-Mongolian Committee of the North for 1926–27.)

But while the ethnographer by virtue of his functions is in some ways the representative of the interests of the tribe which he is studying, he is, at the same time, as a citizen of the Union, bound to protect the interests of the whole state.[1]

The Yakutian Committee of the North writes:

'The assistance given to the natives by the centre, and the measures taken by the latter in the North ... have revealed a definite deviation in the direction of cultural parasitism amongst the natives. This diminishes to a large extent the economic stimuli and produces among them dangerous inclinations towards independence.'

[1] At present several dozen ethnographers, both graduates and students of the Ethnography Department of the Leningrad State University, are working for the purpose of acquiring their practical experience [as prescribed by the academic curricula] in the field of Soviet construction mainly under the Committee of the North attached to the All-Union Central Executive Committee.

Soviet Nationalities Policy under the NEP

There is a potential and real danger of going too far in this direction, i.e. of accustoming the native to live at the expense of the state instead of helping him. This danger of developing parasitism sets the ethnographer additional tasks. It is his duty to our socialist state, to have a proper understanding of the forms and extent of the assistance required by a particular tribe, combined with a sober appreciation of the danger of producing an inclination towards dependence.

The honourable function of the ethnographer is all the more important and prominent in that: 'the position of national minorities in our country is watched with some vigilance by people abroad. Some national minorities are of special importance for us, as they live in frontier districts.' (T. Dimanshtein, Conference of Commissioners for National Minorities, 1928.) In this way, the services of the ethnographer as the transmitter of socialism to ordinary people of different cultural levels assumes an importance extending beyond the borders of our Union.

That is not to say, of course, that the ethnographer in our country is the centre of everything! A sober appreciation of the facts shows that it is the function of the Soviet ethnographer to grasp the mentality of the native population he is dealing with. His fundamental task is to be able to give socialist enactments such forms as are accessible to the understanding of the native masses. . . .

There remains one last question. The Commissioner for Native Affairs investigating the upper reaches of the Amur, Comrade Kozin, says in his report: 'A group of ethnographers in Goryun is wrecking the progressing work of the village soviet and the District Executive Committee by fostering among the natives the conviction that it is necessary to preserve social survivals such as the payment of ransom for a bride, the cult of magic, and so forth.' I should think that it is possible to study the surviving old forms of environmental life and, at the same time, to be active in developing new ones. This must be particularly obvious to ethnographers of the Shternberg-Bogorazov school. By continuing their efforts to raise the level of the natives to the present-day civilization, we shall prove that, instead of academic science being apolitical as maintained in the West, there exists a direct and living link between science and life.

DOCUMENT NO. 10

EXCERPTS FROM: THE VICTORY OF THE LATIN SCRIPT . . .[1]

by V. ALIYEV

(The introduction of the Latin script) 'is a great revolution in the East.'—
LENIN

Many peoples of the East, submerged by the fiery current of Islam and subjugated by the Arab conquerors, have experienced, since the sixteenth century, all the 'charms' of the Arab culture of Islamism and of the Arab script.

The essentially theocratic teaching of Islam with its fatalism, its injunctions to the faithful to adhere, in every question, to the letter of the Koran, its absolute denial of free will, its acceptance of man's complete dependence on divine predestination (*Kadar* in the theological book *Laukhul-Makhvuz*), and the rejection of all innovations (*kullubidgatin kharamun*) has crippled the human will.

The most powerful instruments for moulding the minds of the culturally backward and fanatical masses—the school and press—were a monopoly of home-bred religious leaders, the sheikhs and scholastic mullahs, who had lorded over the minds and property of the masses for a thousand years.

Already in the middle of the nineteenth century it became evident that the Arab script did not correspond to the spirit and the language of the numerous peoples conquered by the Arabs and forcibly converted to Islam. Among the Turko-Tatar peoples, in particular, the adoption of the Arab script evoked strong protests.

In the middle of the nineteenth century, in Azerbaidjan, one of the prominent and most enlightened Turkic writers, Mirza-Fatali Akhundov, made the proposal to replace the Arab script by a new latinized alphabet on which he had worked for many years. However, under the conditions of pre-revolutionary oppression Akhundov could not achieve tangible results. . . .

Closer to our days, yet still in pre-revolutionary times, this

[1] *Revolutsia i Natsionalnosti*, 1930, No. 7, pp. 19–28. In the title of the article the words 'the best monument for Comrade Agamaly-Ogly' are added. In our translation the first two pages of the article, which represent an obituary of the leader of the latinization movement, are omitted.—R.S.

question received much attention from Mahmed-Aga Shakhtakhtinski, one of the prominent old Azerbaidjani publicists who spent his whole fortune on publishing a paper entitled *Shark Rus* (the Russian East). Back in 1912–13, the prominent Tatar writer Said Ramiyev also endeavoured in the columns of the paper *Idyl* (Volga) to popularize the idea of replacing among the Tatar population the Arab alphabet by the Latin script.

As early as 1912 the Albanians had substituted the Latin for the Arab alphabet; the Cherkessy and Abkhaztsy in Turkey, too, had already before the Revolution tried to reform their own written languages in this way. . . . The Caucasian missionary society, which practised the Russification policy among the mountain peoples of the Caucasus, tried in every way to introduce them to literacy by means of a script based on Russian. The more liberal Moslem clergy, starting with the Shamilian Naib Lechinalau, sought to counteract the Russian missionary alphabet by using a reformed Arab script. Neither met with support among the broad popular masses, and the drafts of the Russian as well as Arab national alphabets remained, in fact, on paper.

It was only the October Revolution which inaugurated the sweeping cultural and economic development of the formerly oppressed nations of the East, and cleared the road leading to the creation of a national literature and national written language for those people who had had none before. . . .

. . . As early as 1920 in the city of Vladikavkaz, the centre of the mountain republic, courses were inaugurated to instruct members of the various nationalities in the new latinized script. In 1922, by decree of the Board of the People's Commissariat of Nationalities, a special commission consisting of Comrades Guseinov, Dutei, Djadivev and Umar Aliyev was established at the Commissariat for the purpose of devising a national script based on the Latin alphabet. At the same time, in Azerbaidjan too, a special commission was set up under the chairmanship of Comrade Agamaly-Ogly and attached to the Azerbaidjan Central Executive Committee, for the purpose of latinizing the script in the Azerbaidjan SSR. Referring to these measures, the late Nariman Narimanov said there and then: 'Now I am convinced that the new alphabet will come to life.'

By decree of the Azerbaidjan Central Executive Committee of October 20, 1923, which was signed by Comrade Agamaly-Ogly, the new alphabet was recognized on equal terms with the Arab alphabet, and by decree of June 27, 1924, the new alphabet was recognized as the only alphabet in the state and compulsory for general use. . . .

The Victory of the Latin Script

Simultaneously with Azerbaidjan, among the mountain peoples of the northern Caucasus, too, the idea of latinization was inculcated with varying degrees of success.

Finally, in 1926, the Resolution of the First All-Union Turkological Congress, which met in Baku, noted:

'... the tremendous positive significance of the adoption of the new Turko-Latin alphabet by Azerbaidjan and [various] Provinces and Republics of the USSR (Yakutia and the Ingush, Karacheyevo-Cherkess, Kabardin, Balkar and Ossetian Autonomous Provinces). Recognizing and warmly welcoming the immense positive achievement of the above Provinces and Republics of the USSR in introducing the new Turko-Latin alphabet, the Congress recommends to all Turko-Tatar nations to study the experience and method of Azerbaidjan and the other Provinces and Republics in order to decide about its applicability in their own midst. . . .'

. . . .

... The practical application of the new latinized alphabet, and its substitution for the Arabic alphabet in all the National Republics and Provinces of the Soviet Union—from the Caucasus, Azerbaidjan, Tataria, the Crimea, Central Asia to the Altai and Buryat-Mongolia and so on—has provoked a class struggle so sharp and embittered that the acuteness and scope of this ideological clash probably exceeded that accompanying any other social reform in the Soviet East. . . . The resistance of the Azerbaidjan Arabists to the latinization of the alphabet was backed in every way by the Mussavatists in their mouthpiece *Eni-Kavkazia*, published in Constantinople.

The same resistance to latinization emanated also from the homebred sheikhs, murids and mullahs in Daghestan and among the mountain peoples of North Caucasia. The latter, led by Sheikh Ali Mitayev [and] using hired bandit elements, met literally with daggers drawn the first copies of the Soviet alphabets in the new script which appeared in the mountain villages. The hunger strike proclaimed by the Chechen mullahs in protest against latinization was a characteristic token of this opposition.

The same resistance was put up by the movement of Ibrahim-Valiyev in the Crimea—which sabotaged in every way, and tried to discredit, the idea of latinization.

The counter-revolutionary Sultan-Galiyev movement and the chauvinist Tatar national-bourgeois intelligentsia were headed by Alimdjan Sharaf in Constantinople whose pamphlets against the Latin alphabet resisted in every way the introduction of the new alphabet in Tataria. At that time, Kazan was about the centre of Arabism. The Tatar Arabists, in their desperate struggle against the new alphabet, went so far as to demand, in the famous 'Petition of the 82' to the Central Executive of the party, that the Arab alphabet should be recognized as the official one in Tataria.

For the chauvinist national-bourgeois intelligentsia in Kazakhstan, struggling against the new and for the Arab alphabet, Bairursunov, from the platform of the first All-Union Turkological Congress, proclaimed a near Kadet programme on the development of national culture.

It is equally important to note the part played by the national right-wing opportunist elements who, under all kinds of plausible pretexts, stood out against the idea of latinization and sabotaged its practical application. We find the same picture of the class struggles also in Central Asia, where a counter-revolutionary group led by the Munavar-Kariyev movement—i.e. representatives of the *Milli-Isteklal* group[1]—also endeavoured to wreck the introduction of the new alphabet by every means.

The revolutionary significance of the new alphabet extends far beyond the confines of the Soviet Union. The movement for latinization in India and in Arabia is persecuted as a Bolshevik epidemic by the 'cultured' colonizers of the East. . . .

. . . To-day the new alphabet embraces the following peoples, speaking:

Turko-Tatar languages: (1) Azerbaidjani, (2) Crimea-Tatars, (3) Nagais, (4) Kumyks, (5) Turkmens, (6) Uzbeks, (7) Kirghiz, (8) Kazakhs, (9) Bashkirs, (10) Tatars, (11) Yakuts, (12) Oirats, (13) Khakass, (14) Shors, (15) Uigurs, (16) Karakalpaks, (17) Karachais, (18) Balkars.

Mongol languages: (19) Buryat-Mongols, (20) Kalmyks,

Japhetic languages: (21) Avars, (22) Dargins, (23) Laksis, (24) Lezgins, (25) Chechens, (26) Ingush, (27) Kabardins, (28) Adygeis (Kiakhs), (29) Abkhazi, (30) Lazi.

Iranian languages: (31) Ossetians, (32) Tadjiks, (33) Bokhara-Jews, (34) Kurds, (35) Mountain-Jews (Tats), (36) Talyshs.

Far-Eastern languages: (37) Dungans (Chinese).

A characteristic indication of the ease with which the new alphabet is assimilated by, and diffused among, the broad masses is the fact that, within a few years in most of the Republics and Provinces where the new alphabet has been adopted, the percentage of literacy in the new alphabet has exceeded many times the literacy in the old Arabic alphabet. The latter moreover embraced primarily the well-to-do bourgeois and kulak elements, the clergy and so forth, whereas the

[1] See below, pp. 176 ff.

The Victory of the Latin Script

literacy in the new alphabet expands mainly among the proletariat and working peasantry.

Approximately four million people have already learned to read and write in the new alphabet. Meanwhile there has been a considerable expansion in the publication of the periodical and non-periodical press.

At the present time, more than a hundred papers and journals are published in the new alphabet, and a hundred million sheets of printed books have been issued in more than 40 languages of the Soviet peoples.[1]

[1] For the further facts of latinization see above, p. 23.—R.S.

PART III

The Crisis in the Village and the Struggle for the Collectivization of Agriculture

DOCUMENT NO. 11

EXCERPTS FROM: THE CLASS STRUGGLE IN THE AZERBAIDJAN VILLAGE[1]

(Summing up the Elections to the Soviets)

by I. SVIRIDOV

I

The election campaign in Azerbaidjan took place in a setting marked by the difficulties encountered in economic construction, a sharpening class struggle, a growing complexity in the social relationships of the village due to the transition to extensive co-operation and collectivization, increased activity of the village poor and farm labourers, the expanding work among women and the transition to the new Turkic alphabet.

The development of the campaign was shaped by the finely clear-cut and exhaustive directives to consolidate, by means of organization, the work of the block of village poor and medium farmers; to wage a resolute struggle against the kulaks and complete their political isolation; to broaden Soviet democracy and self-criticism; to renew completely the soviets and to expel from them the people who have assimilated themselves to the kulaks, morally degenerate and other anti-Soviet elements; to draw the toiling masses into the practical work of the soviets; to promote the rural *aktiv* [the body of those participating in civic activities] extensively to leading work; to increase the rate of kolkhoz construction, to struggle for an advanced (*kulturnoye*) development of agriculture; and to expand the cultural development in the village.

The election campaign was so organized as to draw into it right from the start the Soviet general public, the workers, and the social, trade union and state organizations from those at the centre down to the lowest.

During the preparatory period it was the task of the leading organizations in Azerbaidjan to train special cadres of local workers for the purpose of holding the electoral campaign in the village. This training was absolutely imperative under the conditions prevailing in the country, with illiteracy affecting the overwhelming bulk of the

[1] *Sovetskoye Stroitelstvo*, 1929, No. 5 (abridged).

rural population and reaching 80 per cent among the members of the local soviets. Considering moreover the insufficient training of the local *aktiv* and the weak [manifestation of] initiative among the local officials, it becomes evident how important it was to train the cadres before the election campaign. Five thousand district and rural activists could pass through the seminaries organized for this purpose in all *uyezds* and districts. The union of land and timber workers, the komsomol and the peasant committees for mutual assistance also organized the training of their cadres.

The Central Electoral Committee, the Praesidium of the Central Executive Committee and the *uyezds* introduced into this campaign some organizational innovations which did much to further the success of the work and to enliven the report-making campaign at the elections. These innovations included special propaganda bullock carts designed to serve remote settlements and areas inhabited by nomads; information desks at the rural electoral commissions; wall newspapers; exhibitions by the People's Commissàriats illustrating the state of production; meetings of women delegates; meetings and conferences of groups of village poor on the problems of organizing rural electoral committees, reviewing the lists of the disfranchised[1] and studying the directives for new deputies (*nakazy*) and the nomination of candidates to the soviets; reports from members of soviets to their own organizations such as peasant committees, co-operatives, komsomol cells and so forth; reports from rural organizations at the plenary sessions of the soviets; early displays of the lists of candidates to new soviets; the personal delivery of electoral notices and, particularly, to women by women only; competitions between *uyezd* and *daira* rural districts on how best to arrange the campaign and organize the workers; the provision of means of transport (carts) for women attending the meetings; the despatch of voluntary workers' brigades to the village (65 brigades including 380 workers); visits to conservative housholds by women delegates and women activists on the eve of the elections to remind the women to attend; and, finally, the separate treatment of all crimes committed by kulaks and [other] anti-Soviet elements over land questions and for environmental reasons, and the hearing

---

[1] Before 1936, certain groups of citizens regarded as potential enemies of the Soviet regime were disfranchised. These included the highest officials of the Tsarist regime, active participants in the civil war on the anti-Soviet side, unless they had mended their ways, ministers of religion, persons exploiting labour (the capitalists admitted by NEP, and in the village the kulaks). The activity of a rural electoral committee in reviewing the lists of the disfranchised concerned mainly the question who of the more prosperous peasants should be classified in the last-mentioned category. See the following page.—R.S.

The Class Struggle in the Azerbaidjan Village

of such cases out of turn by travelling sessions of the people's courts on the days when report-making gatherings and electoral meetings are held.[1]

The campaigns for casting off of the veil, and the introduction of the new Turkic alphabet which was connected with the elections, enlivened the whole election work and made it possible to get the rural working masses to pay greater attention to the problems of deepening the cultural revolution.

II

... The reduction in the percentage of the disfranchised from 7·8 per cent (in 1927) to 5·6 per cent (in the present year) is the result of a more matter-of-fact approach to one of the most important elements of the campaign—the classification by social qualifications, and a more expert classification compared to previous elections. It is the result of correcting the errors committed in previous elections [restoring] the medium farmers wrongly disfranchised in the past, and granting voting rights to local clerks [*yuzbashi*] and policemen of the Mussavat government with less than six months' service, and to village judges.[2] The more correct classification of the disfranchised and the prevention of abuse of disfranchisement for settling personal accounts were much furthered by the Baku, Gandzha and Nukhin workers who had travelled to the villages under their patronage to take part in the electoral campaigns. The workers' brigades have largely secured a correct interpretation and application of the electoral instructions, especially regarding the medium farmer. Nevertheless, in some places, serious mistakes were made and had to be corrected later. Mistakes were made by the village and district electoral commissions. Thus, in the Autonomous Province of Nagorny Karabakh, it was necessary to restore the rights of 1,100 people who had been wrongly disfranchised (33 per cent of the total).

III

... The report-making stage of the campaign, when the chairmen of village soviets and the soviets as a whole were reporting on their work, attracted the attention of the broadest strata of workers. This

---

[1] See the following document.

[2] Evidently Moslem religious judges (*Kadis*) on the lowest level, who had been disfranchised before because of a broad interpretation of the disfranchisement of ministers of all denominations. The (bourgeois-nationalist) Mussavat government ruled from the fall of the Soviet regime, under foreign intervention, in 1918 until early 1921.—R.S.

was considerably furthered by the campaign for self-examination on the part of the village soviets, the preliminary examination of the reports of the village soviets at their plenary sessions, the pre-campaign reports of people's courts, co-operatives and peasant committees, reports of the government in large centres, the participation of representatives of organizations, departments and institutions directing rural work, and a maximum fragmentation of the electoral districts (3,200 report-making 'places' against 2,000 in 1927).

The direct participation of the Baku workers in the report-making gatherings brought about a great deal of activity, especially among the village poor and farm labourers. No less than 25 speeches were made at these gatherings. Very often report-making gatherings lasted a whole day, and sometimes two to three days.

The reports revealed the shortcomings in the work in the village. The work of rural soviets, co-operative organizations, courts, administrative authorities and so forth was much criticized.

The report-making campaign revealed that in some places the soviets lacked authority as cultural and economic entities. The village soviet does not yet function as the central source of the measures which are to bring about the cultural and economic development of the village. The village soviet has still an insufficient grasp of such problems as a proper tillage of the fields, better sowing of grain and valuable technical crops, harvest yields, pests in agriculture, building schools and hospitals, contacts between the soviets and peasant masses, organization of clubs and reading huts. Even where these problems are being appreciated, the soviets have not worked them out properly or handled them in a practical way. The peasant committee, the people's court, the State Insurance Agency, the system of agricultural and consumers' co-operatives and the meliorative and cattle-breeding associations have very often been left without the required leadership or the direct and immediate influence which should have emanated from the village soviet. Whilst these organizations carried out their functions, the village soviet willy-nilly stood apart. It also happened that when the soviet displayed initiative its decisions were ignored. In some places, the class line of the co-operatives was distorted (their administration was infested with people alien to the Soviet regime, there were cases of embezzlement, misappropriation, credit grants to the well-to-do and so forth). In some *uyezds* intolerable distortions occurred in the assessment of the agricultural tax; anti-Soviet elements got into the peasant committees; the courts, too few in numbers, understaffed and swamped with cases, developed bureaucracy and red tape. The fact that the People's Commissariats did not give enough directions to the soviets, that the reading huts were poorly serviced and that soviet chairmen were often replaced, impeded the practical work in the village.

The report-making campaigns boiled down to an extensive self-examination by those active in the village. This has thoroughly shaken up the local officials and given them definite lines along which their village work can be made more sound, especially in promoting agricultural co-operation and more scientific methods among the village poor and medium farmers and more definite work by the soviets amongst the masses. The transition to advanced methods of agriculture requires more expert management than has been available hitherto. The report-making campaign has increased the authority of the rural soviet and raised the question of entrusting it with the entire operative work in the village. The report-making campaign has definitely established that it is necessary to organize village courts, to introduce a rural budget for planned training of the officials of the soviets, to hold *daira*—study meetings for the officials of peasant committees, rural courts, the State Insurance Agency and so forth, to abolish the general and political illiteracy among the members of soviets (which amounts to 70 per cent), to provide departmental literature ... and to organize special women's courses....

V

... The activity and increased attendance of women at report-making and election meetings were much enhanced by the campaign for throwing off the veil; special meetings of women delegates during the organization period; the organization of the village poor in co-operatives; the intensified work among women for the last two years; despatch of women's brigades and women workers into the *uyezds*; the inclusion of schoolmistresses in the work; the filmshows by mobile cinemas, dealing with issues of everyday life; the provision, in some *uyezds* (Geokchai, Nukha), of special carts for the transport of women to the election meetings; the delivery of election notices to women, exclusively by women activists and women delegates; and the repeat notices issued to the women on election day.

The meetings of women's delegates were not confined to the narrow framework of the election problems. Apart from the basic political tasks (the elections, the veil, and transition to a new alphabet), these meetings discussed the women's work and conditions of daily life and the degree to which their needs and requirements are served by the soviets and the public organizations in the village. They also

The Struggle for the Collectivization of Agriculture

arranged for reports to be given by women members of the soviets, and examined the draft instructions for the new soviets.

Whilst in the electoral commissions of 1927 barely 2 per cent were women, 1,154, i.e. 12·5 per cent, have now been elected to the commissions. Everywhere the women candidates to the electoral commissions were first discussed at women delegates' meetings, and then adopted at report-making gatherings.

The maximum fragmentation of the report-making and electoral sectors has resulted in doubling the attendance of women at report-making gatherings in this campaign. Of the 395,154 women electors, 145,315 took part in the report-making gatherings, i.e. 36·7 per cent (against 18 per cent in 1927). This is a substantial figure for Azerbaidjan. Of the 145,315 women attending the report-making gatherings this year, 5,646 (3·9 per cent) spoke. The women criticized frankly and boldly the work of the soviets and individual Soviet officials.

Whilst until quite recently the women did no more than attend women's meetings, the peasant woman is now taking a direct part in the class struggle which is blazing up in the village. In Kurdistan, the women forcibly evicted kulaks who had burst into a meeting of village poor in order to wreck it. In the village of Kishlag of the Kasumkend *daira* of the Salyansk *uyezd*, they called on individual households, agitating for attendance at the elections. In the Nukhin and Gandzhin *uyezds* women on horseback, braving frost and mud, visited the most conservative households, summoning and persuading the women to attend the report-making gatherings.

The kulaks and clergy made every effort to suppress the activity of the women, by resorting to agitation, persuasion, threats and physical violence. Growing insolent in the course of agitation, the kulaks tried first to play on '*namus*' (honour). They dinned into the ears of the medium farmers: 'Why do you allow your wives to attend the meetings? Don't follow the farm labourers; they've long since lost their wives.' Having failed to achieve anything by these means, the kulaks incited the village elements who lacked class-consciousness to physical retribution. Women taking part in the meeting were beaten up, maimed and driven from their homes.

At their pre-election meetings, the women electors examined quite thoroughly the candidatures to the soviet, the names of young and energetic women from the village poor and medium farmers. At the electoral meetings, they prevented the well-to-do polygamists from beating up their wives, and the drunkards and suchlike from standing as candidates.

Apart from Zakataly, where joint meetings could only be held in

The Class Struggle in the Azerbaidjan Village

17 places (out of 107), and some villages in other *uyezds* (Saliany, Lenkoran and others), the women everywhere attended the joint meetings voluntarily, often arriving there before the men. Zakataly lagged behind because it is an *uyezd* where the Lezgin mountain people still cling strongly to their way of life and religious fanaticism. This is why some women in Zakataly refused to attend election meetings and even to receive electoral notices.

The success of the campaign for throwing off the veil can be gauged from the fact that in many villages crowds of women without the veil attended joint meetings with men—whereas in the earlier elections it had been necessary to hold separate meetings. According to preliminary data, more than 20,000 veils were cast off at report-making and electoral gatherings during the election campaigns.

The campaign for throwing off the veil covered the whole of Azerbaidjan. In Nakichevan, where exceptional attention was paid to it, more than 3,000 women cast off the veil at the meetings; in the Bash-Norashen *daira* 1,650 Turkic women did so. In the Kasum-Ismailov and Dalmamedli districts (Gandiha), where the influence of the clergy and the kulaks is strongest, there are several villages in which all the women came to the elections without the veil. In the Nidzh *daira* of the Nukhin *uyezd* more than 200 women cast off the veil. In the villages of Chukhur Kabla and Tevlia (Nukha) literally all women came to the elections without the yashmak [veil].

... The [electoral] instructions contain the following women's demands: speedy promulgation of the decree abolishing the veil[1]; supply of village co-operatives with ready-made women's clothes to replace the veil; evening classes for illiterates; cultural institutions for women and co-operatives; an increase in the number of women in the administration of consumers' and agricultural co-operatives; the admission of women to co-operatives for training purposes; the fullest use of funds available for organizing the village poor and farm labour women in co-operatives; the inclusion of women in the work of rural public organizations; the establishment of crèches in various artels; more midwives and personnel in the medical services for women; greater attention to women's complaints; the termination of the abuses occurring in the registrars' offices; the abolition of marriage of twelve-year-old girls, and of bigamy; a widespread and continuous popularization of Soviet legislation; resolute measures against husbands beating up their wives and against village

[1] No such decree—which, indeed, would have contradicted the Party's concepts on the methods of fighting religious prejudices—has ever been promulgated. From the above passage it appears that the Women's Department, and perhaps also the P.C. of Justice of the Azerbaidjan SSR, supported, for some time, a more radical course, similar to that taken in Kemalist Turkey.—R.S.

The Struggle for the Collectivization of Agriculture

hooliganism; an intensification in the work of women's delegates; and a closer link between the *uyezd* and the village.

VI

The resolutions of the report-making and electoral meetings that mosques and churches must be handed over to cultural and educational institutions mark an event of exceptional political importance for Azerbaidjan.

The tendency to close the mosques which actually manifests itself on the spot is due to the growing cultural requirements of the village and the acute need for accommodation for cultural purposes. Transfers of mosques to cultural purposes have occurred not only in places where the public, cultural and educational work is well organized, but also in the most backward villages, where the influence of the mullahs is still strong. Mosques in the Zakataly *uyezd*, the Khillin *daira* of the Salyan *uyezd* (15 in the latter) and the Geokchai *uyezd*, the huge 'Dzhume-Mosque' in Salyany, and the mosques in Agdash, Diyally and Geokchai have been handed over for schools, clubs, cinemas, red corners and reading huts, by request of the general gatherings.

During this campaign the mass of the workers have dealt a crushing blow to religious fanaticism and the influence of the mullahs, priests and other clergy. . . .

VII

The results of the elections to the soviets in Azerbaidjan are best illustrated by figures.

This year, of the 838,671 electors, 606,741 took part, i.e. 73 per cent against 60 per cent of the total in 1927; of the 398,140 women electors, 243,740 attended, i.e. 61 per cent against 36 per cent in 1927. Compared to previous re-elections this shows a 13 per cent increase in the general attendance and a 25 per cent increase in that of women. In the soviets, the women constitute 18·5 per cent (against 13·7 per cent in 1927).

. . . The social composition of the soviets, compared to 1927, is as follows (in percentages):

	1927		1929	
Farm labourers and workers	15·4	} 56·7	16	} 51
Village poor	41·3		35	
Medium farmers	32		37·7	
Handicraftsmen and artisans	1·4		1·4	
Teachers, doctors, agronomists and other employees	9·9		9·9	

The Class Struggle in the Azerbaidjan Village

This table shows a growing percentage of medium farmers at the expense of the village poor, and stability of all the other groups. Owing to the increase in the number of members, in some soviets to as many as sixty, the numerical strength of the farm labourers and workers in the new soviets has risen to approximately 2,000 and that of medium farmers to over 5,000.

In regard to party membership, the composition of the new soviets is as follows: Communist Party, members and candidate members, 11·2 per cent (10 per cent in 1927); komsomol members, 12·4 per cent (9·3 per cent in 1927); non-party people, 76·4 per cent (80·7 per cent in 1927).

The percentage of literate members of the soviets has also risen— from 31·9 per cent in 1927 to 36·6 per cent in 1929. New members of the soviets comprise 59 per cent of the total.

Still more characteristic are the data on the village soviet chairmen, 53 per cent of whom were elected this year. In 1929, 116 women chairmen of village soviets were elected (23 in 1927). The percentage of literate chairmen of village soviets has increased from 48·8 per cent in 1927 to 53 per cent. . . .

DOCUMENT NO. 12

REVOLUTIONARY LEGALITY PROTECTING THE ELECTIONS IN AZERBAIDJAN[1]

by N. SELIMKHANOV

The elections of the soviets in Azerbaidjan were marked by a greater activity of all the social groups of the peasantry and a sharpening of the class struggle.

The organized action of the village poor and farm labourers in alliance with the medium strata of the village has provoked stubborn counter-action on the part of the hostile elements—kulaks, mullahs, former policemen and so forth. Having lost the material basis of their power and finding themselves driven from their positions, the kulaks in the Azerbaidjan village tried, by various devices, to retain their influence on the more backward strata of the toiling peasantry. Where this did not work, they resorted to more overt action, wrecking meetings and beating up individual active workers, in some cases without shrinking from causing them injury or death.

The attempt on the life of a member of the electoral commissions in the highland districts of the Lenkoran *uyezd* compelled the Azerbaidjan Central Executive Committee to adopt various measures safeguarding the undisturbed and businesslike work of the electoral apparatus, and guaranteeing the quick and resolute dissolution of all activity by anti-Soviet elements. Immediate investigations of cases of wrecking the campaign and attempted assassinations, the adoption of appropriate counter-measures, demonstrative trials on the spot coinciding with village poor gatherings and report-making and electoral meetings—these were the basic means of protecting the interests of the electors. The further development of the campaign proved how very expedient and timely were the measures taken by the Central Executive Committee of Azerbaidjan and the Council of People's Commissars of the Azerbaidjan SSR.

According to preliminary data, 95 cases directly connected with the elections were tried, apart from those of environmental (*bytoviye*) crimes, and 277 labour and land cases the hearing of which was timed to coincide with the campaign.

Most of the cases were concerned with beating up farm labourers,

[1] *Sovetskoye Stroitelstvo*, 1929, No. 4.

Protecting the Elections in Azerbaidjan

armed attacks on meetings and individual workers, and illegal meetings, and such environmental crimes as not admitting women to meetings, beating them, breaking up women's meetings, and preventing the work of women activists and women delegates.

In almost all the *uyezds* of the Azerbaidjan SSR, farm labourers were beaten up or killed. There were nine such deaths, and also assassinations and attempted killings of chairmen of village soviets and active women. The Soviet court treated these anti-Soviet attacks with maximum revolutionary severity, passing six sentences of death by shooting, which were carried out, and eight sentences condemning 36 people to imprisonment from one to 10 years; in the remaining cases the prison sentences were for shorter periods or there were fines of varying amounts.

The following are the most important and characteristic cases in some of the *uyezds*: in the village of Krasnoye in the Gandzha *uyezd*, a certain Manatsakov, having been disfranchised, attempted to murder the secretary of the district committee of the komsomol. The court, assisted by public prosecutors from the electoral commission and the komsomol, sentenced the accused to five years' imprisonment.

In the Shemakhin *uyezd*, the citizen Bagi Mahmed Ogly was sentenced to 10 years' imprisonment for assassinating the farm labourer Baba Ali Baba Ogly. It should be stated that all the murders of farm labourers and other activists were committed because they had exposed kulaks' frauds and caused them to be disfranchised. Kulaks who had been denounced by their labourers for fraudulently suppressing their property status from the financial, administrative and other authorities resorted to violence and arms.

The Supreme Court held a special travelling session in the Kubin *uyezd* to try the case arising from the assassination of the chairman of the village soviet and the secretary of the party nucleus, and sentenced three kulak assassins to death by shooting. In the Kubin *uyezd*, too, 13 kulaks were sentenced to varying terms of imprisonment for attempting to break up meetings, hooliganism, violating the decrees of the local authorities on electoral campaigns, and so forth.

In Tazakend of the Kurdistan *uyezd*, the session of the people's court examined on the spot by order of urgency a case arising from an illegal meeting of kulaks for the purpose of putting up their candidates to the soviet. Each of the eight participants was sentenced to six months' imprisonment.

In the Agdam *uyezd*, one kulak was sentenced to 10 years for killing a farm labourer, and six kulaks and mullahs were tried for attempting to wreck the preparatory work for the elections.

The Struggle for the Collectivization of Agriculture

In the Lenkoran *uyezd*, two members of the village electoral commissions were killed. One of these cases was heard at a special travelling session of the Supreme Court, and the accused, Bakhman Bek Ali Bek Ogly, was sentenced to death. Two analogous cases took place in Salyani and one in Nakhichevan.

In the Kariagin *uyezd*, in particular, farm labourers who took part in electoral campaigns were often beaten up, although the Azerbaidjan government, by special decree, had released them from work on the days of farm labour, village poor, report-making, election and other meetings. All these cases were heard out of turn despite the shortage of people's courts in that *uyezd*.

It is particularly interesting to follow up the so-called 'women's cases'. In the village of Togan in the Gandzhin *uyezd*, a certain Khalil Namaz Ogly was tried for preventing his wife—a schoolmistress—from doing election work among the Turkic women. The party's call to cast off the veil was widely taken up by the Soviet village public. The ignorant, down-trodden Turkic woman discarded the veil and went to the meetings in order to exercise her electoral right, despite the threats of the kulaks and the counter-action of the clergy. This was the background of a sanguinary tragedy in the Kubin *uyezd*: the kulak Ali Geidar Abas Kuli Ogly killed his wife and mother-in-law for throwing off their veils and attending an electoral meeting. He was sentenced to death, in conformity with the criminal code of the Azerbaidjan SSR dealing with crimes against the liberation of women. In Kurdistan, citizen Akhmedov was sentenced to forced labour for again beating up his wife, who had attended a women delegates' meeting.

On the whole, despite its numerical limitations, the judicial apparatus took a fairly active part in the election campaign, especially in its report-making stage. In many villages law officers gave reports on revolutionary legality. In almost all those places which have people's courts, 'question and answer' meetings were arranged to popularize Soviet law, and particularly the electoral law. In some districts, by request from the electors, reports on the work of the people's courts were made at report-making gatherings. The information desks set up at the village soviets at the very beginning of the campaign were often served by people's judges, examining magistrates and members of the Board of Defence Counsels. Although certain deviations occurred in the preparatory period—in some *uyezds*, such as Nukha, Lenkoran and Zakataly, the judiciary failed to take an active part in the work—the legal apparatus nevertheless became very active during the report-making campaign owing to the resolute measures taken by the Central Electoral

Commission and the People's Commissariat of Justice of the Azerbaidjan SSR.

It should be said in conclusion that, despite some inevitable errors, the Soviet judicial apparatus, by taking part in the election campaign, has done much to bring the state apparatus close to the broad strata of the toiling peasantry.

DOCUMENT NO. 13

CLAN SURVIVALS AS A FORM OF CLASS STRUGGLE IN NORTH OSSETIA[1]

by K. KULOV

... In North Ossetia to-day, socialist construction is impeded by the fact that clan survivals have still a considerable influence on the consciousness of the masses. The expanding socialist offensive provokes to a rabid and desperate resistance the kulaks and their agents the clergy, who, though crushed, are not yet completely beaten.

The kulaks in North Ossetia are waging the class struggle cleverly under the guise of national idiosyncrasies and clan survivals. . . .

Prior to the complete collectivization, the reactionary clan survivals particularly prominent in North Ossetia were: clan enmity which found its most violent expression in blood feud; bigamy and polygamy; the bride's ransom [*kalym*]; and kidnapping of women. Until recently all these reactionary survivals have played a considerable part in Ossetian life. Every year the blood feud claimed dozens and hundreds of victims; at best it served to enslave for many years, by means of *kompozitsia* (blood ransom), the members of the economically weak clans, placing them in a state of dependence on the wealthy families, who mercilessly exploited the 'guilty' clan. With the break-up of the Ossetian clan as a definite group of people linked by common blood origin, property and labour, the blood feud lost its social and economic 'justification'. In clan society, the blood feud was a manifestation of the inter-clan struggles in cases when the integrity of a clan was infringed by hostile external forces. Thus, the killing of one member of the clan injured the common economy of the clan, in which each worker represented a definite value, so that the interests of the whole clan were affected. The purpose of revenge was to cause the same injury to the clan of the assassin. That is why the blood feud extended to all the members of the clan. In most recent times, the number of people in a state of blood feud with another clan has sharply declined, while the blood feud itself, owing to the changes which have taken place in its economic basis, has assumed different forms—mainly the payment of ransom for the blood which has been shed.

[1] *Revolutsia i Natsionalnosti*, 1933, No. 2, pp. 55–60 (slightly abridged).

Clan Survivals as a Form of Class Struggle

The Ossetian clans, as such, have broken up long ago, but some of their reactionary customs have survived up to the days of complete collectivization and of the elimination, on the basis of collectivization, of the kulaks as a class.

The Soviet Government, guided by the correct Leninist nationalities policy, has denounced all the reactionary clan survivals as criminal, and is waging a fierce struggle against them. But, basically, these survivals are being overcome by the whole course of socialist construction and the merciless struggle with the class enemies.

Three years of complete collectivization in North Ossetia have yielded great results in the matter of eliminating many clan relationships and clan survivals which had prevailed until recently. For instance, national, and especially clan and family, seclusion is rapidly coming to an end. It is being broken down by kolkhoz production, in which hundreds of people of different clans are taking part side by side. Owing to collective work in the kolkhoz fields of North Ossetia, the clan feud is gradually dying out. In the village of Khumalag, in one of the brigades of the *Stalin* kolkhoz there are working together the members of three clans, who prior to collectivization not only did not speak to one another but were in a state of downright mutual enmity.

During the last two years there has not been a single case of bigamy or polygamy in North Ossetia.

No less significant are the developments in the custom of abducting women, the paying of bride's ransom and other reactionary survivals in the treatment of women. Whereas, as late as 1930-31, 66 women had been forcibly kidnapped and 176 people had received sentences for these crimes, during the whole of 1932 only one woman was abducted in the entire province, and moreover the crime was prevented on the spot by kolkhoz guards, who rescued the woman and handed over the kidnapper to the organs of criminal investigation. The *kalym*, changing its form even before the kidnapping of women, has gone underground, but it is still causing us much harm, especially in the highland belt. Since the establishment of the Soviet regime in North Ossetia the *kalym* has changed its form several times. At present it continues in the guise of, for example, a list—agreed upon beforehand—of things bought by the bridegroom 'for his bride', but most of which remain with the girl's parents or relatives.

The blood feud, too, is often manifested in the class struggle against the successful socialist construction and certain particular measures of the Soviet Government.

By exploiting kinship and family relations the kulak, [as] the class enemy, often succeeds in wrecking certain measures of the Soviet state. Let us quote some examples which confirm that clan survivals in North Ossetia represent a special form of the class struggle.

Kerim Smailiyev, a dispossessed kulak, having exploited kinship and family relations to organize a bandit group, engaged for two years, but especially in 1932, in systematic looting of kolkhoz property, as well as in open armed robberies of the workers of the Baslanov starch and treacle combine. Smailiyev and his group stole from the kolkhoz of the village Tulatovo six horses, a cart with two horses and a great deal of other property. The gang committed these acts of loot and plunder almost before the very eyes of the population, but—because of kinship and family relations—the collective farmers kept silent and the gang went unpunished. Smailiyev was hiding continuously with some of his numerous relatives. Almost all of them were aware of his criminal activity, but out of 'clan solidarity' they housed and concealed for a long time, often against their will, this obvious criminal and enemy of the Soviet regime.

... Before the Revolution, at the time of Russian Tsarism, [Ossetian] banditry and the related theft of horses and cattle were an expression of the class struggle and the national liberation movement. Banditry (*obrechestvo*) under Tsarism consisted in regular raids by individual groups of mountain-people against the institutions and property of the Tsarist administration and the property of individual representatives of the Russian and Caucasian exploiting classes. Banditry as an elemental movement against predatory Russian Tsarism was supported by the goodwill of the working masses. At the present time, [however,] to resort to banditry means to conceal the actions of the class enemy directed against the interests of the workers and damaging their economy.

With the final break-up of clan life, with the stratification of the Ossetian peasantry into social groups—kulaks, medium farmers, village poor and farm labourers—and the intensification of the class struggle in the Ossetian village, banditry attracted the declassed and anti-social elements who, exploiting the survivals of the past, have started to carry off cattle and horses from the working population....

A characteristic example was the robbery committed at the dairy of the kolkhoz in Khumalag village. One night, 36 milch cows were stolen from the farm. Some of the criminals were arrested, and it was ascertained that one of the leaders of the gang was Baskayev, a declassed element who had been continuously prosecuted for various crimes. It was Baskayev who, having tied himself up with people who had formerly engaged in cattle and horse theft, had robbed the farm. And the day after, the kulak class enemy started an intensive

Clan Survivals as a Form of Class Struggle

propaganda: 'Well, you see? It took the communists and collective farmers a whole year to set up a dairy farm, but in a single night our good lads have driven off all the cattle and wrecked the farm.'

Needless to say, the Soviet Government's decree of August 7, 1932, on the protection of public (socialist) property was applied to the criminals in all its severity.[1]

Until recently, theft of cattle and horses made up a considerable proportion of the crimes committed. Thus, in the Ordjonikidze District, during four months in 1932, the militia dealt with 67 cases, of which 19 were cases of horse and cattle theft. From August to October 1932, 45 horses and nine head of cattle were carried off from the collective farms in the Right Bank District. On the whole, it was the collective farms from which cattle were carried off. The plunderers were led mostly by former kulaks. For example, in September 1932, in the village of Kardzhin, former kulaks who were on the fugitives' list were exposed as horse and cattle thieves. They were regularly stealing kolkhoz horses and light carts. The dispossessed kulaks Itarov and Mitilov had many kinsmen in the village of Kardzhin, and by virtue of clan solidarity they succeeded in winning over some of them to their side. This is how, by exploiting the survivals of clan seclusion, the kulaks organized the systematic looting of kolkhoz property.

. . . .

The examples quoted show that the kulak is cleverly taking advantage of the historical and traditional forms of banditry and horse and cattle theft in order to undermine and wreck the collective farms. This kulak manœuvre has been exposed in good time. At present, the judicial organs of North Ossetia are applying the full severity of the decree of August 7, 1932, to the class enemy—the kulak trying to camouflage his counter-revolutionary activity by environmental and national peculiarities.

We have dwelt so far mainly on the clan survivals, which are exploited by the kulaks in their open struggle outside the collective farm. Let us try now to show the negative effect of the environmental survivals on relations outside the kolkhoz.

In collective farm life to-day there are still many survivals from clan life which have an adverse effect on kolkhoz production. At times kulaks succeed in creeping into the collective farms to organize sabotage, the loot of kolkhoz property, of the harvest and so forth. Thus the dispossessed kulak Bedoyev crept into the *Molotov* kolkhoz and obtained, within a month, the post of brigade leader. From the

[1] Presumably this means that they got the maximum sentence, execution—R.S.

The Struggle for the Collectivization of Agriculture

very first, he began to organize the most backward collective farmers, who were his kinsmen, for thefts of maize directly from the field. He organized his group in utmost secrecy; when four of its members were subsequently caught with the stolen kolkhoz maize, they stubbornly concealed the identity of the organizer of the thefts—their kulak kinsman Bedoyev, who among them enjoyed the authority of a clan elder.

In the judicial practice in North Ossetia, cases were very frequent when a witness at court retracted from his original testimony exposing a kinsman 'of his own', for fear of bringing upon himself the censure of the clan, and also owing to ideological persuasion by the 'honoured' elders claiming to be the exclusive guardians and interpreters of the customs and traditions of the past.

These dark reactionary forces have still such an effect on the backward collective farmers that these sometimes retract at court from their earlier truthful evidence. This cultivates perjury, impeding the application of the most important Soviet laws. The kulaks make wholesale use of it. Thus a former kulak of the Nogir village, having crept into the kolkhoz, stole a bullock cart, and this was confirmed at court by the witness Abayev and several others. But when the ex-kulak was sentenced to 10 years' imprisonment, his kinsmen were seized with excitement; day and night they were calling on the witnesses, 'persuading' them that, by relentless force of custom, they must resolutely retract from their evidence, or else, it was said, they could not escape the blood feud. All this was done in extreme secrecy. [And] the witnesses, unable to withstand this reactionary pressure, informed the provincial judicial authorities that their evidence before the court of the first instance had not been true, and asked for the abrogation of the sentence.

It is clear, therefore, that during the last years the kulaks have made use of perjury as a definite form of class struggle. And that is why the struggle against clan survivals in the human consciousness, i.e. the socialist re-education of the collective farmers, is so important in the socialist offensive in the village.

In the conditions of North Ossetia, the prevalence of survivals of clan relationships cannot but affect the problems of organizing labour in consolidating the collective farms.

... There were cases when individual brigade-leaders or time-keepers were pursuing a policy entirely for their own personal or clan interests. These kolkhoz 'workers' paid exceptional attention to their kinsmen, allotting them, more often than to others, horses for their personal needs; distributing to them grain more quickly and in larger quantities; and, above all, crediting them, on some pretext

Clan Survivals as a Form of Class Struggle

or other, with more labour days. However, in relation to other clans, especially 'hostile' ones, brigade-leaders at times pursue a line sharply infringing their interests. Thus it came about that hundreds of labour days earned by a 'hostile' clan were lost without a trace. Sometimes it is not merely a matter of simply denying the use of the kolkhoz horse or reducing the number of labour days, but of direct provocation, loot and theft of kolkhoz property. For instance, a brigade-leader would allow the collective farmers of the 'hostile' clan to take a certain amount of maize from the field. But after some time he would himself inform the [kolkhoz] administration and the judicial authorities that these collective farmers 'have stolen kolkhoz maize', in order to reduce his 'enemies' to the category of criminals under the law of August 7, 1932.

These survivals of clan relationships are a great obstacle to kolkhoz development. By fanning and playing them up, the kulak class enemy sometimes succeeds in disguising his wrecking activity, and diverting the attention of the workers so as to engage with greater impunity in sabotaging kolkhoz construction. It happened also that individual communists were taking the lead in arousing the survivals of clan relations. In the Digor district, the ex-chairman of the Novo-Ukhur kolkhoz *Kommunist*, the party member Tegayev, organized the loot of kolkhoz property. Tegayev gave to his kinsmen assignments for whole bags of grain. To the women he allotted *a whole kolkhoz bull for a clan funeral repast*!

Another kolkhoz chairman, Baimatov, celebrated his brother's wedding at kolkhoz expense.

No less characteristic are the survivals of clan relationships in the Nart village in the Ordjonikidze region. This village arose in the plain after the sovietization of North Ossetia. All its inhabitants are from the highlands, and the survivals of clan relationships are particularly strong. The village had about ten hostile clans which, though formerly reconciled in the way prescribed by custom, nevertheless continued to nurse mutual ill-will. With the complete collectivization of the village, the clan survivals did not, of course, vanish automatically, but assumed different forms. For a time the kolkhoz was managed by members of a clan which was in a state of feud with two other clans. This 'clan' management directed the sharp edge of the repressive measures of the Soviet regime (in their full severity) against the 'hostile' clans! It denounced individual representatives of the 'hostile' clans as mere sham collectivists and embezzlers of public property and, in the end, as counter-revolutionary agitators. The persecuted clans, for their part, were repaying in kind, conducting an intense campaign against the hated management of the kolkhoz and denouncing the entire kolkhoz work and even the kolkhoz organization as a whole as the handiwork of the 'hostile' clan. This clan struggle permeated every sector of work in the collective farm. And the tense atmosphere did not relax until a change of management was made, i.e. until a chairman from a neutral clan was appointed.

The kulaks did not hesitate to make use of the clan struggle. While the kolkhoz managers were wrangling with their clan opponents, the class enemy organized, among a section of the backward collective farmers and aggrieved clans, counter-revolutionary activity against the foundations of collective farm construction.

The survivals of clan relations have also a negative effect on co-operative work. Almost all the crimes committed in the co-operatives of North Ossetia were connected, in one form or other, with survivals of clan life. Thus in the consumers' [co-operative] society of the village Karg-kokh, the shop assistant L. Gabisov regularly served his kinsmen and friends with the bulk of manufactured goods which were in extremely short supply and earmarked for diverse state procurement campaigns. When his 'own people' came into the shop, they obtained what they wanted out of turn, while the remaining mass of the workers, after queuing for hours, received either that which it 'pleased' Gabisov to give them, or mostly nothing at all. In some rural consumers' societies the shop assistants organized, side by side with the general queue, a special one for their 'own people'. A kolkhoz woman, in a complaint to the prosecuting magistrate about the scandalous action of a shop assistant, stated that she had stood at the counter of the consumers' society, i.e. under the very eyes of the shop assistant, from morning until evening, without getting anything, whilst he was uninterruptedly serving 'his own' kinsmen and acquaintances. Embezzlements in the co-operative system, too, are often closely connected with survivals of clan relations. In Khumalag village, in the consumers' co-operative, the shop assistant Kozayev, by making gifts to his bride and her kinsmen, embezzled almost 5,000 rubles—a kind of *kalym* at the expense of the Soviet co-operative movement. He sent the better part of the manufactured goods, products and so forth to the kinsmen of his bride. This criminal embezzlement of co-operative property occurred almost before the eyes of the whole population which displayed a great deal of tolerance towards it. . . .

The apparatus of the soviets, especially on the village level, is also occasionally adversely affected by clan survivals. . . . The survivals of clan relations often assume the form of unprincipled wrangling or of ganging-up of individual clans: these survivals are particularly

Clan Survivals as a Form of Class Struggle

noticeable in the conduct of economic-political campaigns (grain deliveries to the state, sowing, the mobilization of [agricultural] resources and so forth). Certain campaigns might be carried out by individual members of the soviet apparatus by means of mere administrative injunctions against members of clans which they regard as 'hostile'. Cases of such injunctions purely for the benefit of narrow clan interests, and for the purpose of injuring the interests of 'hostile' clans, occurred in the villages of Zilgi, Nart and others. The influence of clan survivals on certain links in the soviet apparatus has continued until quite recently. Dispossessed kulaks, owing to the support of 'high-placed' kinsmen, were often removed from the kulak register and restored in their rights.

It also happens that individual officials, in pursuit of clan feud, see to it that the most active members of a clan they regard as 'hostile' are entered in the register of kulak households, although in fact their households are by no means subject to dispossession. Thus in the village Olginsk, Kundukhov and Dzantiev by 'clan' management saved a substantial number of their relatives who were subject to immediate dispossession, but dispossessed those who were by no means liable to it.

All this shows clearly that, basically, in the present state of the national development of North Ossetia, the relationships arising from clan life have assumed a peculiar form of class struggle. Yet until recently many people, especially from the Ossetian nationalist intelligentsia, regarded the socialist re-education of the collective farmers and the struggle against the survivals of clan life simply as cultural work divorced from politics (*kulturnichestvo*).

These opportunists, who plead that the economic basis of clan relations has been eliminated, are denying the necessity for an active struggle against the survivals of clan life and treating it as a secondary matter. Thereby they are playing into the hands of the class enemy— the kulak. A systematic and active struggle must be waged every day against the survivals of clan life, while at the same time relentlessly rebuking the opportunists of all brands who reduce this [aspect of the] class struggle, waged on principle, to mere haphazard cultural work divorced from politics.

DOCUMENT NO. 14

EXCERPTS FROM: COLLECTIVE FARM WOMEN OF TATARIA[1]

by A. NUKHRAT

At the first All-Union Congress of kolkhoz shock-workers Comrade Stalin said: 'The kolkhoz women members represent a great force. To keep it back would be a crime. It is our duty henceforth to promote the women in the kolkhozy so as to release that power for action.'

The women of Tataria have displayed real Bolshevik power in collectivization. Their contribution to Tataria's victory in socialist agriculture has been far from negligible. Already in 1932, according to the calculation of labour days earned, female labour in the Tatar kolkhozy amounted to 37 per cent—against 31 per cent in the Russian kolkhozy. That year the Republic had 162 women tractor drivers, dozens of brigade-leaders, and several women were chairmen of the best kolkhozy.

... The victory of collectivization, a factor of the greatest significance in Tataria and due to the active participation of the women, has radically altered the status of the peasant woman, especially among the Tatars.

What was the position of the Tatar woman in the past?

The lot of the Tatar working woman was the same as that customary to all the women of the East. There was the yoke of poverty without means of escape—for the woman's path into the world, to independent life, was blocked by the interdictions of religion and the Shariat laws. There was the yoke of spiritual darkness and illiteracy—the power of superstitions, mullahs and quacks. The arbitrary rule of the father and husband to which the woman had meekly to submit—the docile submission of the woman. The joyless, unprotected toil for the kulak, the mullah and huckster. Child-birth in the bath-house, illness and death of the children. Clandestine or open sales of women, when their fate, their marriage was decided by the *kalym* (bride money), when women, like cattle, had a price. Bad harvests and famine generally led to overt sales of Tatar women. They were taken to market to Bokhara, Azerbaidjan, and, via the

[1] *Revolutsia i Natsionalnosti*, 1933, No. 11.

Kolkhoz Women of Tataria

Crimea, to Turkey. Was there a harem of khans, beys, merchants and industrialists without Tatar women? They were sold literally for a pood of flour.[1]

But the past has gone for ever—our victories are a pledge of that. The kolkhozy have introduced a new way of life, in which labour has become a matter of joy and honour, the guarantee of prosperity, and the source of equal rights for women. Kolkhoz farming is crushing the mullah, the quack and the Shariat laws. In the kolkhoz is no place for the *kalym*, for the people here are linked by socialist labour.

This has been beautifully expressed by the Tatar poet Akhmed Erikeyev. His poems express man's new attitude towards women, the truth of the new life.

KALYM

Ransom for the bride?—'What nonsense.'
Bridegrooms do not pay it nowadays.
Your customs of life, granddads, fade like smoke.
We have done with your kalym.
I will no longer buy for money
The girl I love.
If she will marry for money
She is not worth a farthing.
If you want to marry me,
And your kin expect the kalym,
Tell them that the great kalym
Has been paid by the one you love.
My kalym is not silver coin.
It is the lead that riddled me,
Lead from the rifles of the Basmachi.[2]
It is well worth silk and brocade.
My kalym is not added up in cash.
The Soviet passport is my kalym.
It is contained in the shock-work I do.
It is in my fight for the new life.
It is in the dozens of textbooks
Whose great wisdom I have grasped.
In our days even the best girl
Can expect no finer kalym.

(*Komsomolskaya Pravda*, October 8, 1933.)

'... The kolkhoz movement has advanced to leading posts a great many remarkable and capable women' (Stalin). Let me

---

[1] The author has knowledge of a case when a Tatar orphan girl from Bashkiria was sold in Bokhara for one pood of flour and 20 pounds of rice.

[2] Translator's note: counter-revolutionary bands in Central Asia during the Civil War.

introduce the remarkable women of Tataria—the best of the best—kolkhoz chairmen and village soviet chairmen.

The whole of Tataria knows the chairman of the kolkhoz *Gigant*, in the Nizhny Chelnin district—the komsomol member Gaisha Shamsutdinova. Her kolkhoz has been entered on the red board. She was the first in the Republic to complete the grain delivery.

Here is the chairman of the Russko-Krasin village soviet of the Aksubiisk district—Varvara Yefimovna Vanchurina. Let her tell us her own story:

'I have been chairman for two years. Our men [first] called me "Fortnight". You won't, they said, work on for more than a fortnight: this is not a woman's job. But here I am at it already for two years, and my village soviet, formerly the most backward, has become the leading one in the district.

'In my village soviet, the kolkhoz *Komsomolets* had 24 households which did not own cows, but now there are only three, and they too have received assistance from us in the form of permanent work throughout the year that they may be able to buy cows. In my kolkhoz, members who are fit to work are allotted at least 200 labour days each. My husband, for instance, has received 280 poods of grain, i.e. 180 poods of wheat, and 100 poods of rye. And this does not include vegetable crops. There can be no argument about it: we are leading a prosperous life.

'Our living conditions, too, are changing. Our kolkhoz has two crèches for 60 children, a canteen for 130 people, and field canteens for each brigade.

'In my village soviet, since I am there, almost all the officials are women. My deputy, Comrade Anna Petrina, is a good activist. The chairman of the group assisting the Public Prosecutor, Comrade Pelageya Zakharova, too, is working well. The chairman of [the group] assisting the Workers' and Peasants' Inspectorate, Mariya Vladimirova, is one of the best women activists. The chairman of the finance section, Tatyana Kozlova, is an untiring worker. I am saying this because, before I came, there was not a single woman in the village soviet.

'As for myself, I have worked for the kulaks from the age of ten. After the Revolution, I took a charwoman's job in the office of the elevator. Here I learned to read and write. In 1929, from the moment our kolkhoz was organized, I was the first to join it. My husband, Comrade Vanchurin, did not want me to work in the village soviet. Yielding to kulak propaganda, he began to demand that I should give up the work. But I called him to account in the kolkhoz wall newspaper. He recognized his error and admitted that he had fallen into the trap laid by the kulaks. By now Comrade Vanchurin has become a good shock-worker and communist.' (*Rabotnitsa* [The Woman Worker] 1933, No. 29, p. 4.)

In 1933, approximately 10 per cent of the tractor drivers were women, i.e. 220 (against 162 in 1932). Combine-harvesters [too] were

Kolkhoz Women of Tataria

introduced in Tataria, and to-day the Republic has already 38 women combine operators (out of a total of 232); in the Sarmatov district, four women kolkhoz members served as senior combine operators.

'Nine women tractor drivers are working in the Tumutuk Machine Tractor Station (Aznakai district). Nine pairs of strong women's arms are driving the steel horses confidently over the spacious kolkhoz fields. The tractor of Zigan Shakirova works better than all the others: having completed the spring sowing plan three days before the appointed time, she has worked 32 hectares "in excess".

'During the harvesting, the *Inter* driven by Zigan has threshed the grain, all the time exceeding its quota: instead of 200 centners it threshed 300–350 centners per day. At the same time, the steel horse "did not eat up" the food norm allotted to it: 2·5–3 kilograms of fuel per hectare were saved where it did the work.

'Shakirova's tractor was never idle. There were no cases of breakage during the whole spring and summer. Zigan knows the minutest detail of the interior, all the habits and caprices of her *Inter* tractor. It obeys the slightest movement of her strong small hand.

'Zigan Shakirova is quite young. She is only 19, but already she wears the shock-worker's badge, and tucked away at the bottom of her little camping trunk is a diploma. She received both tokens of honour at the 1st All-Tatar Congress of kolkhoz shock-workers. By September 1, she had already earned 220 labour-days. For every labour-day she will receive 10 kilograms of grain crops—138 poods of grain! Zigan had never seen such wealth before. Last year she had received only 32 poods[1] for the whole of the twelve months.' (*Krestyanka v Tatarii*, [The Peasant Woman in Tartaria] No. 1, p. 2.)

. . . .

... Tatar women work in pig farms (how long did they regard the pig as the most unclean and sinful animal!). Kaliullina Gulsum has been working as a pig breeder in the kolkhoz *Magarif* from February 1933. The farm has achieved great successes. The number of its pigs has increased from 226 in 1932 to 542 in 1933. Kaliullina intends to earn as much as 400 labour-days.

Here we have one more woman shock-worker—Praskovya Antonovna Kuznetsova. She is forty years old and the best stable

---

[1] I.e. 5·4 centners (1,190 lb.). At that time the bread ration for industrial workers doing heavy physical work amounted to 640 lb. per annum; Shakirova's earnings were not so much higher if it is kept in mind that she is unlikely to have had resources for covering her other needs other than sale, or use for feed, of part of the grain received on her labour days (no distributions other than of grain are mentioned, as would surely have been the case if they had been important). Conditions in the Tatar village are sufficiently characterized by the terms in which Shakirova's earnings of 1933, the fourfold of her near-subsistence minimum earnings of 1932, are described in a publication with obvious propagandist intentions.—R.S.

attendant of the kolkhoz *Na Shturm* in the Spasski district. Before collectivization, the Kuznetsov family had never had a horse of their own; they 'were always kow-towing before the kulaks', working all their lives, yet never able to escape from poverty. How can a peasant do without a horse? But now, in the kolkhoz, this is the third year that she is looking after a dozen horses, sparing neither strength nor time. . . . By September 1, 1933, Comrade Kuznetsova had earned 250 labour-days, and her husband and young son 220. For every labour-day they will receive half a pood of grain, including six pounds of wheat. And the family has only five mouths to feed.

Kuznetsova has been awarded five prizes, a diploma and the shock-worker's badge. She was a delegate to the 1st Congress of shock-workers, and has travelled to Moscow to report to Comrade Kalinin. She has achieved a good and prosperous life, (and) her only concern now is to *buy spectacles and to learn reading and writing*, so as to improve further the care of kolkhoz horses.

Among the working women of Tataria there are still many illiterates, which causes us great concern. All the kolkhoz women have now been given the task of spending the winter on study, and study is a must. The whole Republic has taken up Comrade Krupskaya's slogan: 'The shock-workers of the socialized agriculture must become the shock-workers of proletarian culture.'

The activity of the kolkhoz women was brought on primarily by the mass work among the women undertaken by the party organization of Tataria, and by the provision of crèches and playgrounds for the children of the kolkhoz women. This received a great deal of attention in Tataria. . . .

During the harvesting campaign alone, 179,867 kolkhoz children have been admitted to the crèches (against 150,000 provided by the plan); 18,837 children (against 3,000 provided by the plan) have been admitted to mobile and field crèches, and as many as 4,000 people were trained to serve as staff in the kolkhoz crèches. The development of kindergartens presents the following picture: in 1933 the Republic had 1,216 permanent kindergartens with 64,750 children (including 34,059 Tatar children). Five thousand six hundred and eighty-nine playgrounds were used by 170,690 children (including 95,454 Tatar children). As many as 5,000 people were trained as kindergarten and playground staff.

The crèches and playgrounds are greatly effective in facilitating women's labour in the kolkhozy. Let us illustrate this by referring to the field camp of the Krasnoznamenski kolkhoz *Alda*, in the Aktinsk district (in the sector of the Machine Tractor Station). Here every brigade had its crèche. The labour-days put in by women whose children were in the crèches have considerably increased. Thus, at harvesting, the kolkhoz woman Gubaidullina has earned 41·19 labour-days, Sirazeyeva 46·30, and Sibirzianova 42·23.

On the other hand, of the women who did not have their children in the crèches, Mukhametsianova earned [only] 13 labour-days, and Akhmetova 10.

This is why the party organizations of Tataria, at present, are raising the question of establishing children's institutions permanent in every respect with a permanent and well-trained staff. They are most energetically supported in this programme by the prosperous kolkhoz members, who desire their children to be given proper education and to grow up in good health, with bright and active minds that are not poisoned by religious dope. . . .

DOCUMENT NO. 15

EXCERPTS FROM: SETTLING THE NOMADS IN KIRGHIZIA[1]

by A. MUKHAIDZI AND NAZAREVSKI

... A Republican committee has been organized for the purpose of directing the settling of nomads in Kirghizia. Its plan provides for the settlement of approximately 40,000 households in 12 districts earmarked for that purpose by the summer of 1933 (10,000 in 1931 and 30,000 in 1932). At present settling proceeds in approximately 150 areas in 12 districts.

The principal efforts to settle nomads were made in the northern districts of Kirghizia ... in the south only in the Alai-Gulchin district.

In 1931, 300,000 rubles for settling the nomads were assigned by the People's Commissariat of Agriculture of the RSFSR, and 70,000 rubles were allotted in the budget of Kirghizia. ... An average of as much as 80 hectares of land suitable for agriculture was contemplated per household, allowing 63 hectares for pasture, 12 hectares for hay making and 5 hectares for tillage. This draft calculation, serving as a rough guide, was based on the fact that each household, under the approved norms, could have up to 12–20 head of livestock evaluated in standard cattle.[2]

To fix such scales for each household means to allot for land utilization an area of approximately one million hectares, including also the agriculturally unsuitable lands such as rocks, steep precipices, stone deposits, clay beds, glaciers and so forth. Since an average of some 30 kopeks was all that was available per hectare, the organization of land utilization boiled down simply to instructions on land exploitation. These instructions were of very poor quality, especially as Kirghizia was, and still is, suffering from an acute shortage of cadres of organizers of land utilization (in the whole Republic only

[1] *Revolutsia i Natsionalnosti*, 1933, No. 12.
[2] These standards in 1948 were:

Adult cow, horse, bull, ox	1·0
,, sheep, goat	0·1
,, pigs over 4 months old	0·25

See *Slovar Spravochnik Sotsialno-Ekonomicheski Statistiki*, p. 218, 1948—Translator's note.

Settling the Nomads in Kirghizia

six of them had higher education). Moreover, the available cadres of organizers of land exploitation were utterly unprepared for tackling the most important tasks of preparing the territories and the sectors to be settled. In practice, poorly qualified land-organizing officials had to solve . . . questions such as the selection of economic centres and their internal organization, the parcelling out of land plots, ameliorative work and so forth.

The insufficient study of the agricultural territories of Kirghizia, the lack of agricultural plans for the individual districts, and the actual absence of agronomists caused serious delays and reduced, in places, the effectiveness of the work of organizing land utilization.

As a result, the population was dissatisfied with what had been done. The defects in the organization of land utilization were at times exploited for anti-Soviet agitation by the beys and manaps. As an illustration of the tenseness of that agitation the example of the Atbash district may be quoted. The population which was settled there showed its dissatisfaction with the land demarcation by destroying the demarcation signs, so that the work had to be done anew.

In 1932, owing to the liquidation of the class enemy, and the correction, in a Bolshevik way, of the errors committed earlier in this sphere, the masses evinced considerable enthusiasm for settling. Unfortunately, the lack of material resources, the shortage of cadres, and the weak leadership in the centre and in the districts made it impossible to draw fully on that enthusiasm. One of the biggest mistakes, in particular, was the attempt to service in 1932 the greatest possible number of households, without considering what material possibilities and cadres were available. A plan was adopted to transfer to a settled way of life 30,000 households instead of the 10,000 proposed by the People's Commissariat of Agriculture of the RSFSR.

The Council of People's Commissars of the Kirghiz ASSR, by decree of February 23, 1932, confirmed the following measures for settling the nomadic and semi-nomadic population:

1 In the first place to consolidate the settlements of 1931, by providing the people concerned with buildings for industrial, living, cultural and social purposes.

2 To settle 30,000 new households in 12 districts of the Republic in such a way that their needs were catered for by organizing land utilization, prospecting for amelioration, irrigation and road building, and preparing building for productive and dwelling purposes in regions where it would be facilitated by local conditions and the initiative of the settlers.

The operational plan for 1932 as confirmed by the Republican Nomad Settlement Committee amounted to 2 million rubles from the

The Struggle for the Collectivization of Agriculture

budget of the RSFSR (credits for settling purposes), 5 million rubles from the budget of Kirghizia (out of which sum 2,968,000 rubles were assigned directly for settling and the rest for cultural development), 2,024,200 rubles from the agricultural credit, 588,000 rubles from co-operative funds, and 9,531,000 rubles from the population's own resources in cash and labour. The total amount of the operational plan, therefore, exceeded 19 million rubles.

On completion of the finance plan, it was discovered that there was a gap in the local budget section, which threatened to derange the work already in hand. In order to curtail the finance plan as painlessly as possible, the works of melioration and organizing land utilization were simplified.

This kind of 'simplification' is wholly inadmissible, but it mitigated, to some extent, the consequences of the gap. However, owing to the fact that funds allocated by the RSFSR were short of 150,000 rubles, the reduced plan was not fulfilled either.

The following table illustrates the fulfilment of the plan for settling the nomadic and semi-nomadic population in 1932 as reflected by the expenditure on some measures:

Description of the measures	Total cost
Organization of land utilization	1,526,184
Melioration	397,428
Irrigation	145,440
Road building	544,308
Housing	6,847,200
Construction of buildings for productive purposes	2,327,550
Hospital building	325,950
School building	1,838,005
Co-operative development	36,800
Training of cadres	32,000
Scientific research work:	
(a) the issue of an agricultural map and investigation of land resources	97,000
(b) making inventories of fodder land	21,500
Expenses for economic administration:	
(a) wages for work in connection with agricultural settlement	14,140
(b) expenses on economic organization	16,899
(c) inspection travels by various people, apart from the apparatus for work in connection with agricultural settlement	13,295
(d) other expenses	17,912
(e) credits closed owing to the fault of the Kirghiz State Bank	47,182
Organization of land utilization and the apportioning of land by settlement	3,721
The surveying of territory in connection with the organization of land utilization by the settlers	20,000
Total	14,822,515

Settling the Nomads in Kirghizia

... It is significant that almost half of the total of all these measures went for housing. The bulk of this expenditure was covered by the population, i.e. 6,105,000 rubles out of a total of 6,847,000 rubles; the remainder was provided in the budget of the RSFSR and the budget of Kirghizia. The construction for productive purposes was financed by agricultural credits and the resources of the population. Schools were built at the expense of the Kirghiz budget and by means of labour supplied by the population, in some places the whole of the construction cost being covered by the latter (for example, the Atbash district).

The organization of land utilization was mostly covered by the budget resources of the RSFSR and the Kirghiz Autonomous Socialist Republic.

Road-building costs were borne mainly by the population, which provided 483,000 rubles out of a total of 544,000 rubles.

Meliorative and irrigation works were largely covered by budget provision, although the population too had a share in melioration costs (approximately 50 per cent of the total).

Hospital building proceeded solely at the expense of the budget resources of the Republic.

The following table shows the fulfilment of the finance plan:

	Budget of the RSFSR	Budget of the Kirghiz ASSR	Agricultural credit	Co-operative resources	
	Budget of the RSFSR	Budget of the Kirghiz ASSR	Agricultural credit	Co-operative resources	Resources of the population (in cash and labour)
Provided for by plan	2,000,000 (for settling nomads)	5,000,000 (for cultural construction in the years of settling)	2,024,200	588,000	9,531,000
Actual fulfilment	1,850,000	2,366,000	130,000	98,000	8,164,000

We see, then, an immense gap between plan and fulfilment.

It is significant that the committee in charge of settling the nomads was not even able to mobilize agricultural credit. This but shows that the committee failed to secure the active participation of the organizations whose job is to provide direct services to the agricultural population, and which have financial resources required for it (for example, the Agricultural Bank and the co-operative movement).

The negative features, which could have been avoided had the committee been better organized and shown greater activity, include:
1 A failure to allocate from the budget of the Kirghiz Republic more than 2½ million rubles out of the 5 million rubles provided by the plan for settling purposes. Moreover the existing method of paying out the budget sums was such that each district, instead of receiving cash, had to obtain by and for itself the funds for school and hospital construction from local taxation, charging these funds to the account of the People's Commissariat of Finance of the Republic. As a result, these funds came in so irregularly that in some places work defined in the plan as obligatory was frustrated.
2 A lack of building materials for constructions connected with the settling process and a failure to assure in the plan the provision of materials in short supply. This made it necessary to obtain through the co-operatives building materials in short supply on account of consumers' goods, and prevented the settlers from receiving sufficient window panes. Nor did the Nomad Settlement Committee do enough to counter the squandering of building materials in short supply which were delivered to the district. Hence most of the buildings remained half-finished and unsuitable for occupation.
3 The muddle in the work of the People's Commissariat of Finance and the People's Commissariat of Agriculture of Kirghizia. Since the budget funds for settling purposes, which were allocated from the budget of the RSFSR, were handed out by the People's Commissariat of Finance, without making anyone responsible for their proper use, they were used for purposes other than those intended. That is why money regularly arriving from Moscow was held up in the till of the People's Commissariat of Agriculture of the Republic, instead of being sent to the districts of settlement.
4 The unsatisfactory work of the Central Administration for kolkhozy, as shown up by the ill-conceived selection of officials—building technicians, foremen and so forth.
5 The slackness in serving the districts of settlement on the part of the People's Commissariats of Food and Health, the Central Administration for kolkhozy, and most of the central institutions of the Kirghiz Republic. The decree of the Council of People's Commissars of Kirghizia of January 23, 1933, which made it obligatory to supply the settlers' households with manufactured goods, has not been complied with. The Commissariat of Health, instead of fulfilling the

plan tasks of hospital construction to the amount of 1,200,000 rubles, spent only 325,000 rubles on new hospitals in 1932. The Central Administration for kolkhozy has completely failed to provide agronomical services for the kolkhozy formed by the settlers. Nor has the Central Tractor Administration of Kirghizia hitherto done anything in this respect, apparently because of its failure to realize the great political importance of the settlement.

6 The insufficient organization of scientific research in aid of the settlement, despite the fact that many problems of the greatest importance for the settlers are still obscure, and although Kirghizia has a scientific research institute for cattle-breeding, which could have given a start to the study of these problems.

It must be noted that the central Nomad Settlement Committee has still not understood what important services the scientific research institute could render.

7 Finally, the lack of co-ordination between the work of nomad settlement and sovkhoz construction and the failure to make use of the experience of sovkhozy in the sphere of cattle-breeding.

The socialist reconstruction of the economy of the former nomads which arises from their new settled way of life requires a scientific foundation. Yet problems which are of the greatest importance in nomad settlement and which could further its accomplishment have not yet been clarified. In cattle-breeding—which, according to the instructions of the leading [party and state] organs, is basic to the settlers' households—even such important questions are still unclear as, for example, the problem of how to organize the fodder base; the problem of the rational upkeep of cattle during different seasons, arising from the transition from nomadism to a settled way of life; the problem of how to increase the productivity of cattle-breeding; of how to reduce production costs and so forth.

Scientific research work is particularly urgent in regard to setting up the fodder base.

In former times, the cattle herds were provided with the necessary fodder by driving them to new territory when the grass was eaten up in the places where they had roamed before. For every season there was a definite sector of grazing land. In winter, the cattle were kept in the valleys free from, or with very little, snow. In the spring and summer, the cattle gradually climbed higher into the mountains under the snow line. In this way, during the whole summer, the beasts had access to the young, freshly growing grass. In the autumn, seeking protection from the bad weather, the cattle started on the descent again, so as to spend the winter in the sheltered valleys, on the so-called winter grazing lands. Such a regime, however, subjects the cattle to the permanent threat of fodder shortage and *dzhut*, i.e. the threat of mass extinction.

From the standpoint of the struggle for socialist cattle-breeding, such fodder resources cannot be regarded as satisfactory. It becomes imperative to assist the population—apart from introducing a rational use of natural pastures—in establishing also artificial fodder resources (fodder gathered from the threshing floor, fodder concentrates, siloing and dried meadow fodder, fodder roots and so forth).

Up to the present, the absence of a clear and well-considered plan for the use of natural pastures in the event of large herds being driven to the grazing lands has, in particular, led to a gross overexploitation of some sectors of the grazing land. The result was that the cattle not only grazed the grass down to the ground, but stamped it out altogether. Large bald patches of 0·5 hectares or more appeared. Such a way of exploiting pastures is, of course, incompatible with properly organized cattle-breeding.

Yet—apart from individual attempts such as, for example, that made by the kolkhoz Ak-dzhdar in the Atbash district—the kolkhozy have not yet realized that there is such a problem as the correct organization of the use of fodder resources.

This is the main reason why the steady numerical increase of the cattle is accompanied by a deterioration in quality in some districts, although these districts are enjoying preferential treatment.

The enthusiasm shown by some district officials for an excessive extension of the grain-growing area is another impediment to the establishment of a rational fodder basis and the consolidation of cattle-breeding. The error inherent in such a deviation is underlined by the fact that, according to the directives from the party and the government, these are basically cattle-breeding districts.

Practical tests have shown beyond doubt that it is possible to increase considerably the productivity of the local cattle, even with the simplest improvements in its upkeep. But to introduce—as some utopians recommend—trough feeding into the settlers' kolkhozy, although good natural pastures are available, would obviously be inexpedient, for it would cause a sharp rise in production costs. However, it would be equally inexpedient to retain the present methods of driving the cattle to grazing land, allowing them to roam the whole year under the open sky without getting additional fodder.

The establishment of proper conditions for the upkeep of cattle appropriate to settled households would have a great effect on the numerical increase of the cattle, and even more so on its quality and productivity.

Settling the Nomads in Kirghizia

The increase in the productivity of cattle cannot be discussed without reference to the question of cross-breeding.

Despite many most valuable achievements in the cross-breeding of Kirghiz cattle with Shvyz bulls in the Alamed sovkhoz, the possibility of improving the quality of the bulk of the cattle by cross-breeding has not yet been fully explored. The same applies to the question of cross-breeding Yaks with Shvyz bulls.

This is true also of cross-breeding of sheep by infusing fine-fleeced breeds, as practised, for example, in the Tamchi sovkhoz in the Balykchi district. But the usefulness of introducing this method, instead of importing into Kirghizia Merino sheep of the new Caucasian type, requires a most thorough investigation of its economic effectiveness.

As regards other branches of agriculture for consumption purposes, such as the introduction of grain, vegetable and garden crops, it is necessary to ascertain the concrete possibilities of implanting them in the settlers' kolkhozy, for it would be undesirable and even impossible to base the latter solely on cattle-breeding.

Unfortunately the planning authorities of the Kirghiz ASSR are paying little attention to this problem, although the settlers themselves are showing the desire to cultivate such crops.

Thus, in the Atbash district the population received no seed potatoes at all. Even the Akdzhar kolkhoz, which is considered a model, had great difficulty in getting a small quantity of onion seeds for demonstrative sowing.

In the Naryn district, too, there is still scepticism in regard to vegetable cultivation, although the subsidiary farms of the Commandatura of the OGPU are growing cabbage heads weighing approximately 16 kg. each and potato tubers weighing about 2 kg. each.

One could cite many such instances. But those mentioned are quite sufficient to demonstrate the need to study the whole complex of problems facing the former nomads in connection with their new settled life and their transition to a higher stage of economic development.

. . . .

The needs of the settlers are attended to in the districts by the district settlement committees, set up by decree of the Council of People's Commissars of Kirghizia, of December 17, 1931, and attached to the District Executive Committee. They are directed by the deputy chairman of the District Executive Committee, in cooperation with the appropriate district organizations (the land, water and other departments).

The Struggle for the Collectivization of Agriculture

... The district settlement committees are limiting their work to a formal application of party and government directives. There were cases when the basic tasks of the settling process were ignored. Not enough is done to struggle, as Bolsheviks should, against the pilfering and misuse of building materials in short supply sent to cover the needs of the settlers. It happens, too, that the committees slur over the struggle against the misdeeds of the wreckers (for instance, in the Stalin district).

There is no systematic plan for the organization of building for housing and agricultural needs, for economic reconstruction in the districts of settlement, melioration, irrigation, the organization of land utilization and so forth. Thanks to the great enthusiasm of the population, the work is taking its own course. That is why, though good in places, it is mostly unsatisfactory.

The scales of the standard plan for living houses, as laid down by the central Settlement Committee of Kirghizia, do not always satisfy the population. Instead of fixing a building standard in accordance with local conditions, the district leadership allowed the matter to drift. The result is not only that the houses differ in size, but also—and this is the main thing—in building technique, with a general tendency to fall below the norm. Almost no attempt was made to establish a close link with the settlers by giving them the necessary guidance. This naturally gave the class enemy an opportunity for agitation against the settling of nomads especially in the first stage of the work (the Atbash, Naryn and Stalin districts). . . .

During the first stage of the work, the district settlement committees also failed to see to it that the kolkhozy should be supplied with basic building materials (timber, nails, glass) and the simplest building tools (axes, cross-saws and so forth). These simple tools are still lacking in some of the settling places. Since the nomads did not know how to use these tools, it was sometimes necessary to organize special courses to train the indigenous population in the use of the axe, the saw or the plane. The kolkhoz settlers are showing great interest in this training and are displaying great abilities. If the work of the district settlement committees were as it should be, we should have already had considerable cadres of relatively well-trained builders from the indigenous Kirghiz population.

The district settlement committees failed to assist the settlers in forming their own building cadres and made no efforts to organize the technical management; the available specialists were ignored. All this accounts for the bad quality of many buildings in all the places of settlement.

Many of the newly built houses had cracks and faults in the

Settling the Nomads in Kirghizia

incline of their walls. The foundation was often only 15 cm. deep, instead of 70 cm.; sometimes there was no foundation at all; and so forth. Another cause of the building defects was, of course, a lack of energy on the part of those doing the work, who failed, for example, to oppose the illegal instructions of the local managers, who were trying to build the greatest possible number of houses at the expense of quality.

In this respect one ought to mention a feature which is highly characteristic of the attitude taken up by leading district officials to the settling of nomads. Lacking a proper understanding of the whole political and economic importance of this process, many leading officials tried to embellish the real state of affairs, instead of honestly revealing all the shortcomings and fighting for their elimination, as would befit Bolsheviks.

Carried away by their enthusiasm for house-building, the district settlement committees did not give the population enough aid in the construction of farm buildings. That is why, in places, the cattle had to spend the winter in the open fields, for even simple enclosures were lacking (the Atbash, Naryn and Stalin districts).

But in some districts, such as Karakol, where the settling process has extended over a longer period and where it benefits from the experience of neighbouring European settlements, there are buildings for the cattle. Many of the stables built in the Kirghiz kolkhozy of that district are so good that they could serve as models even for the kolkhozy of Moscow province (for instance, in the Zyndan, Chon-Dzharges, Isayev, Urazbekov kolkhozy and others).

It is significant that the Chon-Dzharges kolkhoz should now wish to rebuild the first living houses of the settlers, which had been constructed in 1924, as they no longer meet the growing cultural requirements of the population. But before improving its living houses the kolkhoz built, in the first place, very good stables for the kolkhoz horses. This shows, in some places, a growing understanding among the settling Kirghiz population of the importance of improving the care of the animals as a pre-condition of raising its productivity. It is necessary that these tasks should be generally understood and duly supported also by the leading officials in charge of settling the nomads.

As a rule, nothing is done by way of melioration in the settling places. Failing to grasp the importance of melioration, district officials did not try to obtain the funds required for it either through budget allocation or through agricultural credit. The need for it is immense, and at times melioration works at relatively low cost could greatly increase productivity.

The Struggle for the Collectivization of Agriculture

The organization of land utilization was unsatisfactory mainly because of the shortage of cadres and the immensity of the tasks placed on the officials in this field.

The hurried organization of land utilization in the Atbash district in 1931 had to be almost completely changed in the subsequent years. According to the candid admission of the very organizers of land utilization, the work undertaken there in 1932–33 was not of much use, for although the land was cut into strips, the kolkhoz members did not apply crop rotation. . . .

The selection of bad [land] sectors can have serious effects on cattle raised in the settlers' kolkhozy, and endangers the very idea of nomad settlement. A correct distribution of their cattle requires very thorough scientific research. The work of organizing land utilization is impeded also by causes which are relatively easy to remove, if only the district leaders paid greater attention to the matter. These causes include: (1) the absence of permanent workers—the kolkhozy are always allotting new people, and their training takes time; (2) shortage of horses; (3) irregular allocation of money to the organizers of land utilization (delays of several months have become the rule); (4) irregular supply of food for specialists and workers.

We have already mentioned errors in the selection of settling places from the point of view of the comfort of the settlers. The greatest shortcoming in this respect was the lack of water for irrigation and even drinking. Such a state of affairs causes justified discontent among the settling kolkhoz members and discredits amongst the population the idea of settling the nomads. That is why the irrigation and water supply of these places ought to have been introduced as a matter of special urgency. . . .

. . . .

. . . The above facts show that a great deal of work has still to be done in the settlers' kolkhozy so as to provide them with a firm material basis: cadres, building materials, means of transport and appropriate funds. . . .

The organization of labour in the settlers' kolkhozy, which still retains many survivals of the former nomadic system, is not yet properly established. The accounting of the work performed is extremely bad. There are no cadres of reliable workers. The available kolkhoz *aktiv* requires a thorough check from the point of view of class attitudes.

There is still an acute need for educational work and the diffusion of culture and enlightenment among the kolkhoz members and particularly among the kolkhoz *aktiv*. It is also necessary to introduce into agriculture technical skill and up-to-date methods of cattle-breeding under kolkhoz conditions.

As for housing in the settling places which we have investigated, it must be recognized that, despite the various shortcomings mentioned, it is nevertheless in the process of improvement. Already the planning of the settlements, where the houses are built in regular rows and, sometimes, with trees planted along the broad streets, represents a great achievement. It is an achievement not only in comparison with the Kirghiz winter camps in the mountain districts, but even with the Asian cities in the valleys, with their narrow streets between houses clinging tightly to one another. The schools, clubs, hospitals and bath-houses already built in many settling places are causing a radical break in the cultural and day-to-day life of the Kirghiz nomads.

When discussing the growing economic power of the settlers' kolkhozy, it is necessary to bear in mind that a radical reorganization of the entire agriculture has taken place in the Atbash district during the last few years. For example, land tillage, which covered a grain area of only 300 hectares in 1927, had 15,600 hectares under grain cultivation in 1933. It is interesting, moreover, that the Atbash district shows not only a quantitative increase in the sowing area but also a radical change in agricultural technique. Thus, two years ago, the archaic *omach* was in general use. But now it has been completely displaced by the plough.

Side by side with the expanding grain crops, vegetable cultivation is being gradually introduced, despite the specific obstacles such as shortage of seeds and lack of experience in vegetable cultivation (so that, when weeding, carrots are pulled out instead of weeds) and so forth. The amount of vegetable cultivation introduced into the former nomadic districts is inconsiderable. But the very fact that the indigenous Kirghiz population is growing and consuming vegetables is significant.

An immense amount of work has still to be done in rationalizing the branches of cattle-breeding and, particularly, in developing its fodder base. But one notes already an advance in hay-making and beginnings of siloing. In the Karakol district, some kolkhozy this year even practised some experimental sowing of fodder beet for cows.

School building and the struggle against illiteracy have greatly improved the cultural level of the kolkhoz members. The age-old Eastern slavery of the woman, in particular, is receding more and more into the realm of legend. Not infrequently, women from the settling population become members of the kolkhoz administration and team leaders, or take charge of Red corners[1] and so forth, and play an active part in social and political work, in economic organization and in production work.

All this is an indication of the important changeover taking place in the settlers' kolkhozy to a new way of life and new forms of production.

[1] Small libraries associated with occasional lectures, classes, folksong and drama circles which serve, in the smaller kolkhozy and factories, as substitutes for clubs.—R.S.

DOCUMENT NO. 16

THE PRACTICE OF CHAUVINISM AND LOCAL NATIONALISM[1]

by P. RYSAKOV

Facts are indeed stubborn. Only facts could induce a bourgeois politician like Voldemaras[2] to state during the autumn session of the League of Nations that, owing to 'the lively activity of Soviet Russia in the field of reviving and supporting the National Regions ... the League of Nations will probably in the near future be faced with a serious problem which is maturing without its being aware of it. ...'

We shall quote only some particular examples, illustrating the achievements of our national policy. ...

Take *Uzbekistan*. Before the Revolution that country, stripped by autocracy of its national physiognomy, had no industry of its own. But during the last three years, the industrial investments alone amounted to almost 50 million rubles. The investments in popular education and health services for 1927–28 and 1928–29 reached 89 million rubles. Whereas before the Revolution the Republic had less than 10 secondary schools, attended by the offspring of the colonial officials, it now has four higher educational establishments, which train dozens of indigenous engineers, doctors, chemists, agronomists and so forth. Fifty per cent of the workers of Uzbekistan are from the indigenous population. Bled white by autocracy, Uzbekistan was not able to develop its basic production—cotton growing and processing. At present the economy of the country has been switched in that direction, and already in 1931 Uzbekistan will gather from its fields 400,000 tons of cotton and build a network of cotton-processing works. ...

Take *Kazakhstan*, the land of 'barbarians and bare steppes', as [it was] described by the Tsarist colonizers. That very country has already ploughed up over 4 million hectares of 'bare steppe', to be followed by as many as 20 million more. In 1915, Kazakhstan had 1,825 schools with 89,000 pupils (of whom 13,000 were Kazakhs), but in 1930 the Republic had 8,834 schools with 334,500 pupils

---

[1] *Revolutsia i Natsionalnosti*, 1930, No. 8 (slightly abridged).
[2] Lithuanian dictator from 1926 to 1929.—R.S.

(3,454 Kazakh schools with 130,000 pupils). The people, which had been downtrodden by autocracy, has founded its own university and reared hundreds of indigenous specialists. But recently a country without roads, Kazakhstan now has 1,452 kilometres of the Turksib [railway], and is building 2,042 kilometres of new railway lines. In the leading enterprises of the Republic, the indigenous proletariat now occupies a dominant position (Karsakpai—63 per cent and so forth).

All these are quantitative achievements. The qualitative achievements are no less instructive. The liberation from the colonial yoke of autocracy and the privileges it was establishing for the kulak settlers, the land-and-water reform in Central Asia,[1] the confiscation of the property of the big semi-feudal beys in Kazakhstan and so on, and finally, the mighty wave of collectivization which embraces ever new strata of the village poor and medium farmers—all these factors are making for the socialist transformation of the backward Republics of the Union. Already 23 per cent of all the households in the National Republics and Provinces have been collectivized.

This is the basis on which the culture of the nationalities, which is national in form and proletarian in content, is growing and developing. This is the basis on which national antagonism among the individual nationalities is being effaced. . . . But this is also the background against which Great-Russian chauvinist and local nationalist distortions, errors and direct counter-revolutionary acts are often manifested. The socialist offensive calls forth the counter-attack of the class enemy, which shows itself particularly in the weakest links of the party.

The activity of the class enemy in the national sector of our socialist construction has increased a great deal lately. Showing itself, as it does, in the weakest links of our party, it assumes the form of deviations towards (Great-) Russian chauvinism and towards local nationalism. Let us analyse some of the most striking manifestations of either type of deviation—the 'creeping deviations', as Comrade Stalin defined them at the XVIth Party Congress.

. . . .

'. . . I do not understand the formulation: national in form and international in content. I can understand the second half—international in content—but the first half—national in form—is unintelligible to me. I do not know national culture. I know bourgeois culture, I know proletarian culture, but I do not understand national culture.'

This quotation has not been taken from the Trotsky-Vaganyan files. Its author is a member of the Association of Proletarian Writers of

[1] Cf. Document No. 8, pp. 103 ff.

Georgia, Rozenfarb, who asserted at one of the *recent* plenary sessions of the Association 'that it was a reactionary idea to create a culture which is national in form and proletarian in content.'[1]

Unfortunately his is not an isolated case. Now and again, despite the magnificent declarations on 'internationalism', 'the struggle for culture and progress' and so forth, Great-Russian chauvinism shows its cloven foot. Take, for example, the teachers of Polotsk (Belorussia), who refuse to conduct the lessons in the Belorussian language under the pretext that 'knowledge of the Belorussian language dooms the pupils to ignorance.' Take the 'internationalists' of Baltin (Moldavia), who are declaiming against switching to the Moldavian language the work in the institutions of the Autonomous Moldavian Soviet Socialist Republic on the ground that it would allegedly separate Moldavia from the USSR and arrest cultural progress. Take the school official Krinkov in Buryat-Mongolia, who is telling the children that 'it would be good if there were no Buryats in the world.' Take the communist cell of the Simferopol City Department for Education which listens to melancholy theories alleging that 'it is necessary to close down the Jewish adult schools for literacy', and that 'in the Tatar schools, at least 30 per cent of the teaching must be switched to the Russian language.' Take ... but the above examples (from) the experience of *the last few months* are sufficient to convince us that the Great-Russian chauvinist deviation in the question of national cultural development has been intensified. What is the essence of that deviation? It is to deny the possibility of, and the need for, developing, in Soviet conditions, a culture which is national in form and proletarian in content. It is not necessary to restate Comrade Stalin's criticism, at the XVIth Congress, of the anti-Leninist nature of this kind of denial. It is obvious that that criticism has either not yet penetrated the consciousness of a certain section of officials in the national districts, or that their consciousness is completely subjected to the influence of the hostile classes. In either case, it is our task to struggle, with all the resolution and consistency at our command, against the attempts to distort the basic line of the party in the questions of developing national cultures.

But the intensification of Great-Russian chauvinism is not confined to the front of cultural development. Great-Russian chauvinism is still more active in the other fields of our work in the Republics and Provinces. Here are a few characteristic examples.

The Assistant Public Prosecutor of Kvyl-Arvat (Turkmenistan), Telyatnikov, wrote the following profound resolution on the case of a Russian foreman who had indulged in gibes at the expense of

[1] I.e. rejected the official party formula, as elaborated by Stalin.—R. S.

The Struggle for the Collectivization of Agriculture

Turkmen workers: 'In the conditions of the National Republics, it can only be a question of chauvinism on the part of the indigenous nationality.' The timber-floating managers in the districts of Buryat-Mongolia are setting lower wage rates for Buryat timber floaters. In the Sevastopol naval yards, the non-fulfilment of the industrial finance plan is being justified by this—to put it mildly—'peculiar' argument: 'How can one fulfil the industrial financial plan with Tatars working the lathes?' In the northern districts of Kazakhstan, especially on the Turksib railway, Kazakh workers are badly received because 'one has to do the work for them'. On the Turksib railway, too, Kazakh workers are often given the worst accommodation. In the Kazan fur factory, the senior staff was baiting and trying to discredit the only Tatar woman engineer, but for a long time the party cell 'did not notice' it. In the 'First of May Workshops' (Tashkent), with the silent consent of the party cell, specially extended delays were introduced for the admission of Uzbek workers to the trade union. In Tashkent, too, in the *Ilyich* factory, the wage rates for Uzbek workers are lower than for Russian workers of equal skill.

We shall pass over the cases when people of the Black Hundred type beat up and bait the indigenous workers. But the picture of the growing Great-Russian chauvinism would remain incomplete if we did not quote some facts from the practice of the *korenizatsiya*[1] of the apparatus and the efforts to raise cadres of the indigenous proletariat in some national districts. In these fields, the tendencies of Great-Russian chauvinism are most glaring, even though they are carefully concealed by reference to 'objective causes'.

The picture of the indigenization (*korenizatsiya*) of the central apparatus in the *Crimea* is as follows: in the People's Commissariat of Finance, only seven of the 107 officials are Tatars; in the People's Commissariat of Agriculture, 46 of 606 officials are Tatars; in Soyuzkhleb, only two of 66 employees are Tatars, and both are . . . messengers. In the other central institutions, too, we get almost exactly the same picture. Matters are no better regarding the development of cadres from the indigenous proletariat: the Crimean industries employ 27,210 workers, but these include only 1,806 Tatars. The metallurgical plant in Kerch (the largest undertaking in the Crimea) has only 416 Tatars (5·3 per cent) among its 8,103 workers.

[1] Verbally 'making indigenous'—i.e. appointment or employment of members of the locally predominant nationality instead of Great-Russians or members of other more developed nationalities. This measure, implied already in the decisions of the XIIth Party Congress (1923), was strongly emphasized in that of the XVIth (1930): see Document No. 20 below. On excesses of this policy see Document 6 above, and the next document.—R.S.

The Practice of Chauvinism and Local Nationalism

Even though the indigenization of the apparatus in the Tatar Republic compares favourably with that in several other autonomous units, the data illustrating the development of Tatar proletarian cadres are nevertheless very alarming. In the textile industry the proportion of Tatar workers by April 1, 1930, reached 30·3 per cent, but at the beginning of October it dropped to 27·3 per cent. In railway transport, the Tatar workers amounted to 12 per cent of the total; in water transport, to 10 per cent.

In Uzbekistan, by March 1, 1928, the apparatus of the principal organizations had been 23·5 per cent uzbekized The Central Asian Bureau of the Central Committee of the CPSU(B), the Central Committee of the Uzbek CP(B) and the Central Executive Committee of Uzbekistan decreed that the apparatus of all these organizations must be 100 per cent uzbekized by September 1, 1930. It appeared, however, that at the appointed time the percentage of Uzbekization had fallen to 22·6 per cent. In the People's Commissariat of Agriculture of Uzbekistan, which deals exclusively with the indigenous peasantry, 80 per cent of the correspondence is conducted in the Russian language. In several enterprises of Uzbekistan the percentage of workers from the indigenous population has fallen lately. Thus in the Ferghana plant, in May of this year, 62·5 per cent of the workers were local people, but by August their number had dropped to 51 per cent.

These computations and figures do not, of course, depict the general state of the indigenization of the apparatuses in the National Provinces and Republics, nor of the development of indigenous proletarian cadres in these Provinces and Republics. In the last few years, considerable achievements have been made in this sphere. The indigenization of the [Soviet] apparatus and of cultural and educational work in the Ukraine, Belorussia and several Transcaucasian Republics has entered the final stage. The development of non-ferrous metallurgical industry in Kazakhstan, the building of the Turksib line and the railway to Stalinabad, and so forth have laid a powerful and concrete basis for the efforts to raise cadres of the indigenous proletariat in the Eastern districts. In the course of the last year the indigenous proletariat has risen by 60 per cent. At the same time, the decisions of the XVIth Congress on the shift of industry to the East and the intensified industrial development in Eastern districts, based on local resources of raw materials (textile, non-ferrous metallurgical industry and others)—these decrees are holding up splendid perspectives for the development of the indigenous proletariat in the Republics of the Soviet East. However, the above-mentioned facts and computations prove once again that the struggle against the manifestations of Great-Russian chauvinism is not yet waged systematically, and that in several places its political significance is not yet sufficiently appreciated.

In his definition of the nature of the deviation towards Great-Russian chauvinism Comrade Stalin said at the XVIth Congress:

'The essence of the deviation towards Great-Russian chauvinism consists in the tendency to gloss over the national differences of language, culture and daily life; the tendency to prepare for the abolition of the National Republics and Provinces; the tendency to undermine the principle of national equality and to debase the party policy of making the [Soviet] apparatus a national one, nationalizing the press, the schools and other state and public organizations.'

Our leading local organizations often fail to see the political essence of Great-Russian chauvinist manifestations, since they consider these individual manifestations outside the common political framework of the Great-Russian chauvinist tendencies. Precisely herein lies the basic defect of our struggle against Great-Russian chauvinism. While successfully bringing to light and revealing the individual sallies, we seldom draw political conclusions from them. For example, it is not enough to dismiss the Assistant Public Prosecutor of Kvyl-Arvat and to reveal him as a blatant chauvinist. It is necessary to show by his example where the political roads of Great-Russian chauvinism are leading to. . . .

. . . .

The growth of the National Republics and Provinces and their socialist transformation is accompanied by the sharpening struggle not only of the dying-off classes of the former ruling nation but also of the exploiting classes of the nationality in question. Penetrating into the party organizations, those struggles assume the form of anti-party nationalistic groupings which frequently link up with direct counter-revolution, as was shown by the Sultan-Galiyev movement.[1]

Lately, the local nationalistic elements have considerably revived. This is proved by many cases. Let us dwell on the most striking examples on which no light has been shed as yet in our leading press.

Quite recently the counter-revolutionary nationalistic organization *Milli Istiklal* (National Independence) was uncovered in Uzbekistan. Continuing the programme of the other counter-revolutionary organization *Milli Ittikhad* (National Unification), which also has been liquidated recently, the *Milli Istiklal* pursued the aim of overthrowing the Soviet regime and setting up a bourgeois state.

[1] See above, p. 19.

The Practice of Chauvinism and Local Nationalism

In the expectation of [foreign] intervention, the organization was training cadres and conducting counter-revolutionary sabotage in the People's Commissariat of Education, the juridical organs of Uzbekistan and the party organizations. The leaders of the organization were prominent officials of the People's Commissariat of Education and the Supreme Court and made use of the soviet apparatus in order to train, inside it, cadres of 'future administrators of the state' and to discredit the Soviet Government and the party. With the same aim in view, *Milli Istiklal* strove to seize control of many public organizations, in particular the society *Kzyl-Kalyam* (The Red Pen), whose tasks included 'the strengthening of proletarian ideology in artistic literature'. The counter-revolutionaries were successful in the society *Kzyl-Kalyam* which came to be led by a member of *Milli Istiklal*.

Of course, that organization cannot be regarded as representing one of the types of nationalistic deviation in our party. It was a *direct counter-revolutionary organization* which had penetrated the ranks of the party. But its discovery is a sign not only that our internal enemies are reviving their counter-revolutionary efforts, but also that the nationalistic deviation in the ranks of the party is becoming more active. *Milli Istiklal* subjected to its influence the nationalistic elements of the Uzbek CP(B), guiding their work to its own counter-revolutionary purposes.

The party organizations of Uzbekistan, like true Bolsheviks, reacted to the discovery of *Milli Istiklal* with the required severity and firmness. But in some of these organizations this was accompanied by plain nationalistic demonstrations. Thus, at a meeting of the Samarkand party *aktiv*, which discussed the report of Comrade Ikramov (the secretary of the CC of the Uzbek CP(B)) on the uncovered counter-revolutionary organizations, the speaker was handed the following note: 'Our Uzbekization proceeds in such a way that Uzbeks sit at the head of the institutions, and Uzbeks are the coachmen: some are riding, some are driving, but the work is directed by the Russians. Is this Uzbekization? Is this not [rather] colonization by the Russians?' At the same meeting, a certain Ayupov asserted that the CC of the Uzbek CP(B) is an 'incubator of colonizers'. These statements betray not only a pathetic identity with the ideas of the well-known counter-revolutionary Chokayev, who had written that 'the only function of the highest Uzbek officials is to act as rubber stamps while the actual policy and work are directed by the Russians.' Stemming from a plainly infamous slander of the party, they show that there are grave nationalistic inclinations in the ranks of the Uzbek CP(B). This obliges the party to observe maximum vigilance towards every kind of deviation in the national question, and to step up, in every way, the struggle against Great-Russian chauvinism, as the most dangerous [deviation], and also against local nationalism.

An organization in many ways identical with *Milli Istiklal* was discovered recently also in the Tatar Republic—the organization *Diidigyan* (Great She-Bear). It is true, that organization did not yet pursue such aims as *Milli Istiklal*. But acting underground, and having selected literature as the arena for its activity, *Diidigyan* set itself the task of an organized struggle against the leadership of the party in literature, against proletarian literature. Not content with activities within Tataria, *Diidigyan* extended its activity also to Bashkiria. The organization was able to secure considerable influence on individual communists and even the party organizations concerned. This is proved *inter alia* by the fact that the communist Seifi, one of the prominent Tatar men of letters and editor of the journal *Yanalif*, began to assert that '99 per cent of the Tatar nation are working people' and that, consequently, the class struggle in the Tatar village was 'an invention', and so forth. These very tenets were points of the propaganda of *Diidigyan*. It is true, in this case, that Seifi's assertions can be related to his right-wing opportunist views. But this is another proof that the ideology underlying the deviations in the national question is closely mixed up with the opportunist deviations in party policy.

There is no need to quote further examples showing the revival of local nationalism (national democratism in Belorussia and so forth). We shall merely note that that revival is typical not only of the National Republics and Provinces, but also of nationalities who have no autonomous units of their own. Thus, in the Polish press (*Kultura Mass*) some comrades have expressed the idea that it is impossible to develop a Polish proletarian culture in the conditions of the USSR, and that it is necessary 'to orientate the course towards Poland'[1] and so forth.

We shall not analyse the above-mentioned examples, nor the nature of the reviving local nationalism. They speak for themselves: the nationalistic elements, reflecting the hopes of the dying-off exploiter classes in the national districts, have become considerably more active, in some cases (Uzbekistan, Belorussia) growing into direct counter-revolution, and assuming the tactics of wreckers'

[1] While Rysakov, writing in 1930, described this view as a serious deviation (his reference to 'comrades' shows that its representatives had a future communist Poland in mind), in 1946 indeed an exchange of populations was arranged between the Ukrainian and Polish Republics, with the evident implication that either culture should develop in its own national territory.—R.S.

The Practice of Chauvinism and Local Nationalism

organizations of the type of the 'Working Peasants' Party' and the 'Industrial Party'. The best and only method of fighting local nationalism is to fulfil the directives of the XVIth Congress: while conducting a resolute struggle against Great-Russian chauvinism, as the chief danger among the national deviations, we must also activize the struggle against the deviation towards local nationalism, *'and, at the same time, do more to apply the Leninist national policy in practice, to eliminate the elements of national inequality, and to develop the national cultures of the Soviet Union.'*

. . . .

... A review of the practice of 'the creeping deviations' cannot be complete unless we dwell on one more type of nationalistic local deviation—i.e. the master-race chauvinism and contempt displayed towards the smaller nationalities by the stronger ones. A striking manifestation of that deviation could be observed in the recent dispute between Georgia and Soviet Ossetia on the question of exploiting the marble quarries in the vicinity of the village of Tsnelisi.

A few years ago, South Ossetia had begun to exploit these quarries. When it was discovered that they yielded marble and talc of very high quality, the Building Trust of Georgia began to dispute South Ossetia's right to work the quarries, on the 'formal grounds' that the mountain in which the work was done is situated on the Soviet frontier between Georgia and South Ossetia. Trying to prove the exclusive right of Georgia to exploit the quarries, the manager of the Building Trust of Georgia, Comrade Kalanadze, resorted to the following arguments: 'This part of the mountain is absolutely and unreservedly ours, for, according to historical data, the frontier between [the lands of] the Princes (!) of Amirabzhibi and Palavandov used to run here.'

Thanks to the intervention of the Transcaucasian party organs, the dispute was solved in favour of South Ossetia. But that prolonged dispute gave rise to persistent talk of depriving South Ossetia of its autonomy, of 'curtailing and gradually winding it up'. This in turn begot nationalistic sentiments in South Ossetia.

This is the most striking example of a series of chauvinist attacks against the weaker nationalities and national minorities. These attacks sometimes read like anecdotes.

For example, the following case happened in the town of Kuba (Azerbaidjan). A member of the staff of the Regional Educational Committee, an Armenian woman, refused to speak Armenian with Armenian callers, and demanded that they should speak to her in

Turkic. When she was asked for the reasons she said: 'If I should talk to them in Armenian, I shall be immediately dismissed for nationalist deviation.' Evidently in Kuba there were reasons for such an assertion. Examples such as this seem to dwarf the dozens of cases when the cultural, economic and day-to-day amenities of the national minorities are ignored outright: the need for a Ukrainian newspaper was stubbornly overlooked in the Kuban; when the cultural five-year plan was drawn up in Azerbaidjan, educational work among the national minority was 'forgotten'; in Kazakhstan, despite the repeated decrees of the territorial committee, almost no special cultural and educational work is done among the indigenous peasants; in some districts of the Ukraine the need for Jewish schools is disputed for 'objective reasons', and so on and so forth.

All these occurrences made it an urgent need to shake up thoroughly some stale 'minds' who regard the work among the national minorities as secondary, and indulge in master-race attacks against the small and weak nationalities. This task is being considerably facilitated by the delimitation [of the territories] into districts which is now nearing completion.

. . . .

The struggle against the increasingly active deviations in the national question and the correct application of the Leninist national policy are the most important conditions of the success of our general socialist offensive. That is why we are so acutely faced with the task of fulfilling to the utmost, and with maximum consistency, the directive of the party formulated by Comrade Stalin at the XVIth Congress:

'It is necessary to draw the attention of the broad masses to the resolutions of XVIth Congress on the national policy of the party, by struggling on two fronts, and by bearing in mind our international purpose: the fusion of nations, languages and cultures as a long-range aim, but until then—the achievement of national equality in the economic and cultural sphere, by helping the backward nations to catch up with the advanced ones.'

DOCUMENT NO. 17

EXCERPTS FROM: THE STRUGGLE AGAINST NATIONALISM AND THE LESSONS OF THE UKRAINE[1]

by S.D.

... The nationalistic outbursts in the Ukraine, which have assumed particularly acute forms lately, must be considered in the light of the international situation, and especially in connection with the coming to power in Germany of Hitler and his 'great policy' of severing the Ukraine from the USSR, and occupying it by German or German-Polish forces.

Let us outline, in brief, the manœuvres of the Ukrainian bourgeois counter-revolution during the period of the Revolution. For a number of years the Ukraine was the scene of a fierce civil war between the Soviet regime and the united Russian counter-revolution, in which the generals Krasnov, Denikin, and others, as well as the Ukrainian nationalist bourgeoisie personified by Petlura, Vinnichenko and many others, were active. The Soviet regime in the Ukraine, with substantial and fraternal help from the Russian Soviets under the leadership of the Central Committee of the party, succeeded in smashing the 'Central Rada', the 'Ukrainian Directorate', and winning over to the Soviets these Ukrainian masses which formerly followed the nationalist parties, and even the best elements of the Ukrainian nationalist parties.

... When the Ukrainian military organization was formed in Galicia in 1921 it selected from its ranks some people and instructed them to penetrate the Soviet institutions of the Ukraine and even the ranks of the party, in order to conduct sabotage there, preparing the intervention and inducing the Ukrainian [communist] politicians to adopt a nationalistic line. It was for this sort of work that people such as Grushevski, Chechel, Shrag, Khristyuk and others went to the Ukraine. Vinnichenko, too, at that time played an important part as a double-dealer, [by endeavouring] to assume a prominent Soviet post in the Ukraine. A manœuvre of the same kind was made by the petty-bourgeois Ukrainian parties of

[1] *Revolutsia i Natsionalnosti*, 1934, No. 1, pp. 17–22.

The Struggle for the Collectivization of Agriculture

Borotbists, Ukapists and others, which included a great many people with hostile aims.

The party is well aware of the great and stubborn struggle waged by the Central Committee of the CP of the Ukraine, under the leadership of Comrade Kaganovich, against deviations in the national question—against Great-Russian chauvinism and local nationalism and the individual chauvinistic deviations of some public figures in state and cultural construction in the Ukraine. During that period was revealed the so-called 'Shumskism', which was defined as a nationalistic counter-revolutionary deviation. Shumski was removed from the Ukraine. But he resorted to the method of double-dealing. He made an appropriate statement, confessed and hypocritically criticized his errors in public and, promising to mend his ways, succeeded in regaining once more the party's confidence.

At that very time Maksimovich (who is now known to be an agent of the Polish secret police) and Solodub were expelled from the Ukraine; Vasilkov and Turyanski, who were members of the Communist Party of the Western Ukraine, were also revealed as agents of Pilsudski.

In 1929 the Yavor movement and the counter-revolutionary 'Union for the Liberation of the Ukraine', in which the Ukrainian Social Revolutionaries took part, were discovered in the Ukraine. The trial of the members of that organization helped in many ways to reveal the activity and bourgeois ideology of the Ukrainian nationalists.

But since that trial the Ukrainian organization [of the party] has for the last two or three years relaxed its struggle against bourgeois nationalism and nationalistic deviations. This was expressed in a mechanical approach to Ukrainization, without taking account of the peculiarities of the individual districts. During that period, several aspects of the national regeneration of the Ukraine in Bolshevik ways[1] were allowed to fall into the hands of hostile elements. . . .

. . . In the People's Commissariat of Education, Skrypnik encouraged a 'theory' whereby children speaking a 'mixed dialect' must be ukrainized, which amounted, in effect, to compulsory Ukrainization. Moreover many officials in the People's Commissariat of Education thought that altogether no Russian was spoken in the Ukraine, and especially not by the children.

---

[1] *Bolshevistskaya Ukrainizatsia. Ukrainizatsia* means the transfer of the key positions in academic and industrial life which, for historical reasons, were in the hands of the Russian minority to Ukrainians, and also the development of Ukrainian culture amongst the skilled workers (most of them Russians by origin). The adjective *bolshevitski* warns against a confusion of the cultural change with a political one. See above, pp. 79–80.—R.S.

The Struggle against Nationalism, and the Ukraine

The Petlura elements worked out plans for artificially de-russifying the Russian workers and asserted the need for developing amongst them an [Ukrainian] national consciousness, while Skrypnik himself began to nurse a special theory of national-Bolshevism. His colleagues in the People's Commissariat of Education, Girchak, Kantselyarski and Karpenko, were most active accomplices and transmitters of all these extremely harmful 'theories'.

In order to reveal Skrypnik's errors in greater detail let us look back into the history of our party. Let us recall the common stand adopted in 1922 by Skrypnik and Rakovski—at present an outspoken supporter of counter-revolutionary Trotskyism—on the question of the organization of the USSR.

A rather acute struggle developed over the forms which the Soviet Union was to assume, revealing two basic opinions on the national question.

These two opinions were led on the one hand by Comrades Lenin and Stalin, and on the other by Rakovski and Skrypnik. . . .

Rakovski and Skrypnik posed the national question not as part of a general question subordinated to the problems of the class struggle, but as a self-contained question dominating our entire policy towards the nationalities.

From this starting point, Rakovski and Skrypnik deduced that ours is not a unified state but an alliance of separate and independent states none of which abandons any of its supreme prerogatives in favour of the Union.

. . . To show the extent of this decentralizing tendency, it is sufficient to refer to Rakovski's postulate on railways. Contrary to the fact that the party had laid down, as a matter of principle, the need for a unified centralized Commissariat of Railways, Rakovski wrote:

'The administration of an enormous network of 60,000 versts on a territory of 20 million square versts is beyond the strength of a single Commissariat. As an artery of economic life, the railways must be brought near the local economic organs, and obviously the time will come when the railways of the Union will be divided into two categories: railways of All-Union importance and railways of local importance. The former will be under the direct management of the All-Union People's Commissariat, the latter will be subordinated to the Councils of People's Commissars of the individual Republics. The same applies to the telegraph, the post and the telephone. There is already a strong tendency in favour of transferring the telephone network to the individual governments and provincial Executive Committees.'

There is no longer any particular need to analyse this nationalistic theory which is based on the postulate that the centre must not direct the local institutions, even in those branches which particularly require centralization.

In their tendency to shake off the influence of the centre, Rakovski and Skrypnik went so far as to deny, even though indirectly, the need for All-Union Commissariats of Foreign Trade and Foreign Affairs. According to them the work of these Commissariats includes 'a whole sphere in which the governments of the individual Republics must retain the initiative.'[1]

At root, this dishonest formulation of initiative aims at completely undermining the cohesion of the Soviet Union in the sphere of defence, communications and representation in foreign countries.

All these distortions of the national question emanate from Skrypnik's very article 'Against the Distortions of Party Policy in the National Question' in which he asserts: 'It is not true that, in our country, national problems are subordinated to the general theory of the class struggle.'

He who stands for the severance of the national problem from the class struggle stands for the decentralization of the USSR, the base of world revolution—for he admits the possibility of a contradiction between the interests of the working masses of the nationalities and the interests of the proletarian class struggle—which is contrary to the foundations of Bolshevism. . . .

. . . Skrypnik in his writings often directly slanders the party and its method of solving the national question. He has no hesitation in saying, for instance, that 'for most of the members of our party the Ukraine did not exist as a national unit. There was only Little Russia as part of a single and indivisible Russia, something not clearly defined either in relation to Russia or to its own territory or even in its language.' (Skrypnik's *Collected Works*, Part I, p. 291.)

This is an assertion that the majority of the party adhered to the Great-Russian view on the Ukraine, denying it any recognition. This is essentially just what such gentlemen as Vinnichenko, Shumski and others are saying. Time and again Skrypnik has expressed his distrust and censure of the party, and not only regarding the first period of the Soviet regime. . . .

. . . By indulging in direct nationalistic attacks, which in general did not differ from the postulates of the White Ukrainian émigrés, Skrypnik has provided them with a definite ideological basis. Unfortunately these manifestations, instead of being condemned by the party organization, were long ignored.

How can one reconcile oneself to Skrypnik's statements that all

[1] See above, pp. 75–6.

The Struggle against Nationalism, and the Ukraine

Ukrainians, without class distinction, distrust everything coming from Moscow, which is the centre of the capital of the world revolution?

The following words of Lenin's are very appropriate to Skrypnik: 'If a Ukrainian Marxist allows himself to be carried away . . . to such an extent (by hatred of the Great-Russian oppressors) that he even transfers some of that hatred . . . to the proletarian cause of the Great-Russian workers, then he sinks into the bog of bourgeois nationalism.'

In opposition to the directives of our party, Skrypnik emphasized with no lack of clarity that it is the task of the proletariat to develop more broadly the *national* consciousness of the masses. He laid down this sort of line when he said, at the All-Ukrainian Conference of national minority workers: 'It is our task to organize our activity in such a way as to enable the working masses of each nation to develop their national self-consciousness to the maximum.'

It is easy to imagine the distorting effect of such a line on the psychology of the mass of teachers, who include many backward and nationalistic elements.

In this connection it should be recalled that, according to the speech of Comrade Postyshev at the plenary session of the Central Committee and the Central Control Commission of the Ukrainian CP(B), Skrypnik has proposed to the political bureau of the Central Committee of the Ukrainian CP(B) that 1,500 teachers from Western Galicia should be recruited for the Ukraine.

. . . .

Owing to the disclosure of nationalistic counter-revolutionary tendencies which were in fact led by Skrypnik, the latter became the spokesman of all the elements wishing to sever the Ukraine from the USSR. [That is why], taking into account the international situation arising from the coming to power of the German fascists, the Central Committee of the Ukrainian CP(B), in its resolution on the report of Comrade Kossior to the plenary session of the CC of the Ukrainian CP(B), determined:

'Great-Russian chauvinism is still the principal danger in the whole Soviet Union and the entire CPSU(B). Nevertheless, in some Republics of the USSR, in particular in the Ukraine, the main danger, at this moment, is represented by the local Ukrainian nationalism, which merges with the [tendencies of the] imperialist interventionists. It is particularly necessary to bear in mind the new tactics of the Great-Russian chauvinists and Ukrainian nationalists, who are supported by the entire counter-revolution, including the Trotskyists, and who are now entering an alliance with one another on the common platform of severing the Ukraine from the USSR, for the purpose of weakening the positions of the USSR and strengthening the positions of capitalism'.

The CC of Belorussia has fully supported that resolution. . . .

The German fascists, striving to sever the Ukraine and Belorussia from the USSR, are trying to find a common language with the Polish fascists. At such a moment, local Ukrainian nationalism, which blends with [the plans of] Hitler and Pilsudski, assumes an entirely new role. From a theoretical deviation, it turns into *a militant weapon of world fascism*. It becomes, at this stage, the principal danger and makes it vital for the CC of the Communist Parties of the Ukraine and of Belorussia to wage a most irreconcilable struggle against the deviation towards local nationalism in the party and the nationalistic counter-revolution as a whole. This struggle must be crowned by a further expansion of socialist construction in all the sectors where concrete measures are taken for consolidating the Leninist national policy.

Apart from intensifying the struggle against local nationalism, it is necessary also to step up to the utmost the struggle against the Great-Russian nationalism, which remains the principal danger in the CPSU(B) and the USSR as a whole. The party as a whole must be vigilant lest the Great-Russian chauvinists should exploit the struggle against local nationalism for their own harmful purposes. . . .

PART IV

The Industrial and Cultural Revolution

DOCUMENT NO. 18

EXCERPTS FROM: THE FORMATION OF THE NATIONAL PROLETARIAT IN BASHKIRIA[1]

by V. BELITZER

... The year 1905 inaugurated the gradual growth in the numbers and revolutionary activity of the Bashkir workers.... But it was not until the October Revolution that the national proletariat of Bashkiria definitely came into being and continuous development.

After sixteen years of Bolshevik struggle for a consistent application of the Leninist national policy, and as the result of the First Five-Year Plan, the Autonomous Bashkir Republic is entering the ranks of the advanced industrial regions of the Union. Contributory factors were the inclusion of Bashkiria in the Ural-Kuznetsk combine, its close connection with the big industrial centres of the Urals—Magnitogorsk and Zlatoust—the restoration of the old industrial districts of Beloretsk and Baimak, the construction of very large motor and steam-turbine building plants, the exploitation of the extremely rich deposits of the Komarovo-Zigazin mines, the discovery of oil and so forth. The immense raw material resources of iron ore, non-ferrous metals, oil, building materials and shale provide a firm basis for the further industrialization of Bashkiria as a highly important district of ferrous and non-ferrous metallurgy, machine-building and chemistry.

Fifteen years of Soviet rule have changed Baskiria's appearance. Belonging to the old mining districts of the Urals, it represented until recently the survivals of the feudal method of production, with plants half destroyed by time and the civil war.

At present, Bashkiria with its new constructions, plants and geological prospecting work, attracts the attention of the party organizations, the public and the scholars of the entire Union.

The Chernikov combine merits particular attention. It derives its name from the station of Chernikovka on the Zlatoust railway line. The combine includes several industrial undertakings already in operation, such as the central power station, a brickworks and a match factory. In the summer of 1932 a timber and plywood mill and

[1] *Revolutsia i Natsionalnosti*, 1933, No. 7, pp. 44–48.

The Industrial and Cultural Revolution

a tanning extract plant were brought into production. Construction projects have been made for a steam turbine, an electrical engine, a metal scrap plant and a motor plant.

By resolution of the party and the government of July 27, 1931, the first state motor plant is to be built in the Ufa district, with an output of 100,000 engines of the 'International' and 'Continental' type, and 10,000 diesel engines in the first shops to be built. The construction of the industrial shop proceeded simultaneously with the building of the workers' club and theatre. The factory school for training the new cadres urgently required for construction jobs is to be completed by the autumn of 1932. Under the construction plan, workers' settlements have been erected north and south of the engine plant, with all the cultural, educational and business establishments required to serve each settlement: a co-operative store, a post office, bath-house, school, children's playground and so forth. The workers' barracks are beginning to be replaced by frame houses. . . . On the site of the plant, which covers a radius of approximately five kilometres, many subsidiary establishments, such as dispensaries, hospitals, fire brigade stations and so forth will be erected. At the north end of the plant an airport and a landing pier on the river Belaya are to be built. The motor plant is situated 12 kilometres from Ufa. In addition to the Ufa–Zlatoust railway, the plant will be connected later on with a railway from Ufa which will run past the metal scrap and steam-turbine plants and their workers' settlements as far as the electrical engine plant, the construction of which is under contemplation. Subsequently, Ufa will merge with the constructions of the Chernikov combine through the projected park for culture and rest.

The centre of the metallurgical industry of Bashkiria is the Beloretsk group of plants. The metallurgical industry is represented in Beloretsk by two big plants: the old metallurgical plant where the blast furnace was under reconstruction in the summer of 1932, and the steel-wire plant, the largest plant in the whole Soviet East. In this plant the best grades of steel wire are made from the high-grade Komarovo-Zigazin ores.

In the Second Five-Year Plan, Beloretsk, after the construction of the steel-wire plant *Gigant*, is to become the basis of the steel-wire industry of the entire Union, with an output up to 53,000 tons of high-quality articles.

The Beloretsk group includes the Tirlyansk plant and the Zigazin blast furnace. The raw material bases for the metallurgical industry are Inzer, with its timber-cutting enterprise and approximately 184 coking ovens, and the Zigazin-Komarovo mines.

The Formation of the National Proletariat in Bashkiria

The Beloretsk group of plants has made a great advance in output compared with 1913.[1]

The output of cast iron was 47·9 thousand tons in 1913.
„   „   „   26·4 thousand tons in 1927–28.
„   „   „   70·8 thousand tons in 1932.
The output of open-hearth steel was 32·5 thousand tons in 1913.
„   „   „   105·2 thousand tons in 1932.
The output of rolled metal was 24·2 thousand tons in 1913.
„   „   „   65·2 thousand tons in 1932.

In spite of the many achievements of the Bashkir Autonomous Soviet Socialist Republic, the third session of the All-Union Central Executive Committee noted that the Beloretsk plants have failed to reduce costs; and in accordance with the resolution of the joint plenary session of the Central Committee and the Central Control Commission of the CPSU(B) (in January)[2] it was decided to overcome the shortcomings in the work of the Bashkir enterprises by directing the main efforts to the completion of the constructions in hand and the assimilation of the new enterprises and the new technique, and by achieving better production indices.

The growing industry of Bashkiria raises in an entirely new way the question of forming, selecting and training national industrial cadres. The expansion of socialist construction and socialist planning require skilled workers (engineers, technicians, doctors), the promotion of the national elements to the work of economic organizations, and their participation in the economic planning of the Republic. The numbers of industrial cadres for the past years show a sustained increase, but the percentage of the national workers of the Bashkir Republic is still far from satisfactory.

Until 1931 even the computation of national cadres was badly organized; in many undertakings it was impossible to collect the elementary numerical data, to say nothing of differential statistics, on the national question. Even the more important organizations paid little attention to the problem of indigenization (*korenizatsiya*)[3] or the formation of cadres of national workers. Bashkirs were often lumped together with Tatars, which blurred the picture of the state of the national proletariat of Bashkiria. Only insufficient efforts were made to draw into industry the national element or even to estimate the labour force required. In most cases, things were allowed to

[1] *Pravda* January 18 [1933], Bulatov's Report.
[2] Which decided to replace the former emphasis on extremely quick expansion by a more moderate but more systematic and economical progress of investments (cf. Stalin, *Problems of Leninism*, Engl. ed. of 1940, pp. 415 and 418–9).—R.S.
[3] Cf. footnote above, p. 174.

The Industrial and Cultural Revolution

drift, and the desired results could not be attained. In the provincial industry, we had by October 1, 1926, 5·7 per cent Bashkirs and 1·8 per cent Tatars; by October 1, 1931, 8·4 per cent Bashkirs and 7·9 per cent Tatars. In heavy industry, by January 1, 1931, 10·5 per cent were Bashkirs.[1] In the Beloretsk metallurgical plant in 1931, 10·7 per cent of the entire staff were Bashkirs.

Nor is the proportion of Bashkirs great in the state apparatus. By October 1, 1948, the Bashkirs amounted to 4·7 per cent; by October 1, 1929, to 5·9 per cent; by October 1, 1930, to 6·3 per cent. As for individual enterprises, in 1931 the percentage of Bashkirs amongst the salaried employees of the motor plant was 2·37 per cent, in the steam-turbine plant 1·11 per cent, and in the office of the building trust 4·9 per cent. The question of extending the work with the national elements has been raised time and again in the columns of the Bashkir press and particularly in the journal *Khozyaistvo Bashkirii*.

In 1932 considerable improvements were achieved in this sector of work. Of the 37,000 workers and employees in the census[2] industry, the number of Bashkir workers was 5,300, i.e. 14 per cent.

In heavy industry, of the total of 17,471 workers, 20 per cent are Bashkirs.[3] In the wood-processing chemical industry by October 1, 1932, they amounted to 19·6 per cent. Although the questions of technical propaganda, improving skill and training national cadres have been fully raised, there is still a considerable shortage of skilled workers, even though hundreds of Bashkirs are already employed. At the Beloretsk metallurgical plant, of the 328 Bashkir workers, 25 are skilled, 109 semi-skilled and 194 unskilled. In the steel-wire plant, of the 133 Bashkir workers employed, 40 are skilled, 26 semi-skilled and 67 unskilled.

Some branches of industry and a great many subsidiary jobs are almost exclusively in the hands of the Bashkir population.

The greatest percentage of Bashkirs is to be found among the transport workers: in some districts it is two and a half times higher than the percentage of Russian workers. A considerable number of Bashkirs are engaged in timber cutting, where the percentage of Bashkir workers exceeds that of the Russian workers.

Such a preponderance of Bashkirs in some branches of industry, and the slow numerical increase in others, must be taken special note

[1] Materials added to the report of the government of the Bashkir Autonomous Soviet Socialist Republic to the IIIrd Session of the All-Russian Central Executive Committee, XVth Election Period.
[2] The census industry consisted of enterprises employing 16 or more workers where mechanical power was used, and 30 or more workers where no mechanical power was applied.—Tr. N.
[3] *Krasnaya Bashkiria*, 1933, No. 1.

The Formation of the National Proletariat in Bashkiria

of when studying the formation of cadres of the national proletariat. This process is largely conditioned by the way the metallurgical industry had developed in the past, and by environmental living conditions. The Bashkir people, as horse breeders from time immemorial, are familiar with carting; forestry, too, was a favourite occupation of the forest-dwelling Bashkirs. Moreover, these two types of occupation leave the Bashkirs almost entirely free during the summer when the population, in local parlance, used to go 'merry-making in the Urals'.

The tradition of nomadic camps, which assumed very interesting forms, was preserved right up to 1931–32. Thus, in the goldfields where Russians, Tatars and Bashkirs work, the latter have come to the mines since the Revolution and, at present, form up to 50 per cent of the workers there. In winter they live in wooden barracks, but in the spring their families, with their nomads' tents, move up to the gold-fields and settle about a mile away. The male workers live in the nomad camps and work in the gold-fields. A great number of Bashkirs, who have just come from the village, maintain their links with their household, which causes the fluctuation of labour to grow towards spring and the percentage of Bashkir workers to fall steeply.

The following is the picture of [labour] fluctuation in the enterprises in the summer months of 1932:

At the Steel Wire Plant
        February—133 [Bashkir] workers
        March—121 workers
        April—97 workers

At the Beloretsk Metallurgical Plant
        February—328 workers
        March—207 workers
        April—103 workers

[Bashkir] labour is enrolled through organized recruitment in certain districts by contracts with the national kolkhozy, since the mechanization of agriculture in the kolkhozy and sovkhozy releases surplus labour for the large-scale socialist factories and plants.

The industries of the Bashkir Autonomous Soviet Socialist Republic are rearing the best Bashkir shock-workers. In many factory shops, national brigades have been set up. The Factory and Workshop School at the motor plant is being built by a national brigade of members of the Centre of Engineers and Technicians. A national brigade has restored the No. 1 blast furnace; a national brigade was working in the open-hearth steel shop of the Beloretsk plant. The cost-accounting brigades[1] in the blast-furnace shop produced the best working indices for 1932.

From January 1 to July 1, 1932, 18 of the national workers at the Beloretsk metallurgical plant were promoted to more responsible work; they included several women.

The women in the Beloretsk metallurgical industry amount to 20 per cent. The national element among them is still scanty: of the 472 women working there, 24 are Bashkirs. Yet these workers' cadres, though numerically still weak, include Bashkir women who have worked in industry since childhood or have come to the factory from farm labour. This poorest section of the population is at the same time the most advanced and active one. At the present time an influx of young workers, and especially women, is noticeable in several branches of industry.

There are still too few party members among the national workers. In the factories they amount to scarcely 8 to 11 per cent of the whole party body. At the new construction sites in the summer of 1932 the efforts to draw young national cadres into the party and the trade unions were very weak. The mass and cultural-educational work among the national elements was somewhat better in the Beloretsk metallurgical industry. In the field of factory trade union committee activity, two workers have been specially released from industrial work for cultural and educational work among the Bashkir workers. Each factory shop has a Bashkir propagandist. Special work is done among the national women workers. Intensive efforts are made to overcome illiteracy and semi-illiteracy among the Bashkir workers (of whom there are 54 illiterates and 62 semi-illiterates in the Beloretsk plant). Courses for the Bashkir *aktiv* have been organized, and several persons have been sent to training courses for cell-secretaries, propagandists and so forth which were held out of town.

There is still no definite plan for mass work among the Bashkirs. In many fields the ground has but been sounded; there is an acute shortage of Bashkir cultural workers.

The shortage of Bashkir workers in the fields of culture and industry must soon be overcome, and is already being overcome, by young national cadres who have been extensively trained at the new construction site and in the centres of the metallurgical industry. By July 1932, 835 trainees of various specialities, including 114 Bashkirs and 116 Tatars, had attended the courses organized by the Centre of Engineers and Technicians at the motor plant. We have

---

[1] *Khozraschot* brigades are brigades in factory shops which keep a precise record of real costs of their work in relation to output and get premia according to results.—Tr. N.

The Formation of the National Proletariat in Bashkiria

already said that the members of that Centre are building the Factory and Workshop School. Some brigades have taken a hand in the construction of the club and the diesel-engine shop. The factory evening school under construction at the motor plant is designed for 2,000 people. Courses for electricians and motor men are run at the construction site. Every unskilled indigenous worker attends special courses: by May 1, 1932, 1,112 students had attended these courses for the 1931–32 session. The youth go from work to the Factory and Workshop School: in 1932 it was attended by up to 914 people, of whom more than 60 per cent were Bashkirs and Tatars (524 and 189 respectively). An industrial combine with a national section was set up in Beloretsk. Of the 140 students in the metallurgical technicum, 40 are Bashkirs and 30 Tatars.

Entire groups of Bashkir and Tatar workers have entered higher educational establishments, are taking correspondence courses, or have been sent to courses for red directors and rate-setters. Of the total of 86,209 new cadres trained since 1926, the Bashkirs amount to 31 per cent and the Tatars to 24·1 per cent.

National wall newspapers and factory newspapers are published in the factories (Beloretsk and Chernikovka). There are libraries with books in the vernacular. Special kindergartens and crèches for the children of Bashkir and Tatar workers, secondary factory schools and so forth have been set up. One of the shortcomings in trade union and cultural and educational work is the lack of organized alertness of the Bashkir and Tatar workers, and particularly of the women, in matters of daily life (for instance, in the matter of eliminating the flaws in the work of nurseries and kindergartens, the lack of hygiene, and disharmonies in domestic life).

The material position of the workers of Bashkiria improved considerably in 1932. The average daily wage rose from 2 rubles 20 kopeks in 1926–27 to 3 rubles 40 kopeks in 1932.[1] The housing

---

[1] The connection in which this statement is made may suggest an intention on the author's part to criticize the insufficient wages increase, notwithstanding the conventional introductory sentence. An increase in the proportion of skilled workers amongst the Bashkir workers, as claimed in the article, might easily explain most of the increase in average earnings; but even if the increase described were typical of the position of the individual worker it would hardly cover more than the increase in the cost of living from 1926–27 to 1932, even with allowance for the fact that the typical unskilled worker could hardly buy much more than his rations, the prices of which remained unchanged up to 1934. If we make allowance for the average being affected by a higher proportion of skilled workers (who, of course, would need a wages increase to pay for some improvement in housing standards etc.), it is clear that the real wages of an unskilled worker who did not acquire some new qualification considerably fell from 1926–27 to 1932. In view of conditions in the village, this does not exclude the probability that a poor peasant who became an unskilled industrial worker thereby improved his standard of life.—R.S.

problem requires a great deal of attention. A great proportion of the workers' barracks, especially at the new construction sites, are not suitable for living in; the barracks are unheated, very overcrowded and lack normal sanitation, the necessary furniture and elementary comforts. The housing problem is a cause of the flight of labour from the new construction sites.

Certain manifestations of Great-Russian chauvinism can still be observed in industrial work and daily life. Thus in the selection of labour, the administration gives preference to Russian workers. It has happened that Bashkir and Tatar workers were not paid in full. The more backward of the Russian workers occasionally show signs of scorn for their Bashkir or Tatar mates, use derisive and offensive nicknames and complain that the Bashkirs are crowding the Russian workers out of the plant. These Great-Russian outbursts are the result of kulak influence on the backward strata of the workers, and the struggle against them is in some places not yet sufficiently developed. . . . Such occurrences must be resolutely fought, making use of them for the purpose of educating the workers and consolidating through internationalist work the proletariat of the young industrializing Bashkir Republic.

DOCUMENT NO. 19

EXCERPTS FROM: THE BOOKS OF THE NATIONALITIES OF THE USSR DURING FIFTEEN YEARS[1]

by K. S. RYKHLEVSKI

The fifteenth anniversary of October is marked by immense achievements in the field of creating written and literary languages for the culturally backward nationalities. The workers, having set about developing their culture, which is national in form and socialist in content, started by creating a literature in their native tongue.

Our party and the Soviet Government have established all the conditions necessary for creating native printed languages for all the nationalities of the Soviet Union.

The territory of the RSFSR, according to incomplete data (for all the time new nationalities are being discovered of whom the bourgeois linguists and statisticians formerly had no notion), is inhabited by 131 nationalities. . . .

The broad masses were immensely assisted in assimilating culture by the introduction of the new latinized alphabet. During the last fifteen years the latinized alphabet has been introduced among the thirty million of the population of the USSR who speak the Turco-Tatar or Mongol languages.

The old Arabic multitonal alphabet, the synonym for the cultural enslavement of the Turco-Tatar peoples, being inaccessible and difficult to study, retarded the speed of overcoming illiteracy, and thereby also the rates of socialist construction among these peoples. It is not for nothing that the new latinized alphabet was and is being implanted in conditions of a bitter class struggle. At present the issue of books in the old Arabic alphabet has been completely suspended, and all publications (periodical and non-periodical) are issued exclusively in the new latinized alphabet.

. . . .

During the first period of sovietization, the party and the Soviet Government, apart from other most important tasks, faced also in

[1] *Revolutsia i Natsionalnosti*, 1932, Nos. 10–11, pp. 84–92.

The Industrial and Cultural Revolution

its full magnitude the task of raising the level of culture, of mass work in political education, of overcoming illiteracy and so forth. These tasks could only be solved by means of the printing press—books, journals, newspapers.

It was extremely difficult to create literature for the numerous nationalities. When a start was made with organizing publishing in the vernaculars, it appeared that many nationalities had absolutely no cultured people who could be drawn into this work. There was a complete absence of the polygraphic basis, of printing type, and in general of the technical equipment for publishing.

That is why, at the end of 1922, two special publishing enterprises were set up under the People's Commissariat for Nationalities which was directed by Comrade Stalin: the Eastern and Western Publishing Houses for the publication of literature in the languages of the nationalities.

One of their first publications in the vernacular was the Constitution of the USSR and the Declaration of the Rights of the Peoples of Russia, which had been issued under the signatures of Lenin and Stalin during the first week of the proletarian revolution.

The publishing houses issued literature in the following languages:

EASTERN		WESTERN
1. Tatar	6. Azerbaidjani	1. German
2. Uzbek	7. Kirghiz	2. Polish
3. Chuvash	8. Karachai	3. Latvian
4. Mordvin	9. Komi	4. Jewish
5. Mari	10. Adygei	5. Estonian

Both publishing houses issued approximately 58 books and pamphlets in a total of over 200,000 copies. The circulation of the papers and journals printed was about 30,000. The publishing house of the People's Commissariat for Nationalities devoted special attention to the culturally backward nationalities.

Apart from the Western and Eastern Publishing Houses, literature was published also by the new national publishing houses on the spot.

... At the beginning of 1924, the Eastern and Western Publishing Houses were merged in the unified 'Central Publishing House of the Peoples of the USSR attached to the Central Executive Committee of the USSR'.

With the organization of the CPH, the publication of national literature, especially for nationalities without political units of their own, assumed greater proportions, which helped the party to extend its influence to ever wider strata of workers and ever new national minorities.

The Books of the Nationalities of the USSR

During the first year of its existence, the CPH published literature in 25 languages and thereafter successively: in 34 languages in 1925, in 37 languages in 1926, in 44 languages in 1927, in 51 languages in 1928, in 56 languages in 1929, in 63 languages in 1930 and in 76 languages in 1931.

Future historians will find in the CPH a most interesting object of study. We shall dwell in somewhat greater detail with the activity of the CPH, since its output took up 60–70 per cent of the total printing output of the nationalities in the RSFSR. A distinguishing feature of the CPH was the universality of its publications, which included—side by side with small books for children of pre-school age or alphabets for illiterates—all types of literature, including scientific works.

The other distinguishing feature of the CPH was the multiplicity of its languages. It published literature in 76 languages.

During the period from 1923 to 1931, the CPH published the following:

Years	Number of Titles	Number of copies	Number of printed sheets
1923 г.	31	97·0	389·0
1924 г.	89	301·0	1,612·0
1925 г.	335	1,299·0	6,173·0
1926 г.	567	2,796·0	11,235·0
1927 г.	633	2,665·0	16,172·0
1928 г.	683	3,147·0	19,374·0
1929 г.	699	3,922·0	24,256·0
1930 г.	2,458	17,824·0	88,500·0
1931 г.	2,243	18,878·0	91,245·0
Total:	7,738	50,932·0	257,956·0[1]

[1] The figures for 1931 do not include the branches of CPH; its output together with that of its branches was approximately 20–30 per cent higher.

Thus the rates of development were colossal; in this respect 1930 was particularly characteristic, for the mass of printed matter published that year exceeded the total of all the preceding years taken together. Such rates of development in printing are possible only in the country of the proletarian dictatorship, in the country where socialism is being built.

The output of the CPH can be classified according to the types of literature shown in the table at the head of the next page.

The immense proportion of educational and social-political literature is noteworthy. The year 1930 showed a 30 per cent increase in the publication of educational literature compared to 1929. The

The Industrial and Cultural Revolution

Types of literature	Titles	Total size of publications (in printer's sheets)	No. of copies (in thousands)	Printed sheets (in thousands)
Social-political	1,689	6,106	9,767·7	35,624·5
Leninist	194	1,076	785·0	4,552·7
Educational	1,198	7,696	13,170·6	95,580·9
Popular-scientific	307	951	1,132·5	3,553·2
Agricultural	755	1,784	4,593·2	11,686·7
Artistic	638	2,373	2,258·6	7,460·5

decisive factor in this increase was the party resolution on universal [compulsory] education.

The Tsarist government, at a moment of leisure, somehow made the calculation that universal education in Russia would be possible of achievement only in the year 2001 (what exactness! precisely in 2001, neither sooner nor later). The Tsarist government, to its misfortune, failed to foresee such trifling occurrences as the October Revolution and the dictatorship of the proletariat which has mastered socialist rates of development, economy and culture, and roused the creative powers of millions of workers of all nationalities.

Parallel with the expansion of the CPH, local national publishing enterprise underwent an extensive development owing to the growth of socialist economy and culture. The development of local national publishing enterprise reduced the significance of the CPH. . . . The centre of gravity in the publication of national literature was shifted to the local national publishing houses.

The Central Committee of the CPSU(B) on August 15, 1931, adopted a resolution on the reorganization of the publication of national literature, whereby the CPH was wound up. The publication of literature for the nationalities with national publishing houses of their own was handed over wholly to the local publishing houses, whilst the publication for nationalities without national state publishing houses of their own was handed over to the system of OGIZ (State Publishing Organization of the USSR).

The resolution of the CC of the CPSU(B) gave still greater sweep to the development of local national printing. From the first years of Soviet government we had—already in the difficult years of the civil war—the rudiments of local national publishing houses, which later became such large enterprises as the *Ukrainian*, the *Central Asian*, the *Belorussian* and the *Tatar State Publishing Houses*, amongst others.

At present all National Republics, Union as well as Autonomous,

The Books of the Nationalities of the USSR

all National Provinces and some so-called 'non-territorial' nationalities (that is, those not in a state organization of their own), such as Latvians, Estonians, Jews and Greeks, have firmly established national publishing houses of their own.

On the territory of the RSFSR alone we have 12 republican and 15 national publishing houses. Apart from this, national literature is published by 14 central publishing houses, five territorial and five co-operative national publishing houses, so that national literature, in the RSFSR alone, is being published by 50 publishing centres.

All this has been created almost in a void, thanks to the Leninist leadership of the party and Bolshevik energy, persistency and faith in the rightness of the cause.

. . . .

... The total number of sheets of all the national printed matter in 1930 has increased[1] as against 1927 by 196·3 per cent. If we take, for the purpose of comparison, 100 per cent for 1927, we get, for the individual nationalities, the following percentages of increase over the preceding year:

Languages	1928			1929			1930		
	Number of printed units	Total circulation	Number of sheets printed	Number of printed units	Total circulation	Number of sheets printed	Number of printed units	Total circulation	Number of sheets printed
Azerbaidjani	114·0	128·7	147·2	140·0	160·7	164·0	204·9	321·8	258·0
Armenian	105·1	103·3	141·8	127·2	127·7	149·1	185·3	240·1	210·5
Bashkir	135·6	138·0	221·3	90·8	221·0	341·7	154·0	281·5	324·4
Buryat-Mongolian	41·0	34·1	70·9	153·8	302·3	511·2	92·3	215·9	325·4
Kazakh (including Kirghiz)	102·1	157·2	122·2	74·2	114·7	96·9	152·9	331·3	259·3
Chinese	131·7	97·3	113·8	328·3	323·2	393·9	105·0	450·0	1046·4
Komi (Zyrians and Permiaks)	105·7	112·8	185·8	134·0	176·1	274·4	203·8	389·9	513·2
Mari	139·1	102·1	95·7	250·0	216·7	223·3	315·2	439·6	373·3
Mordvin (Erzia and Moksha)	95·2	134·3	222·5	130·2	166·9	265·4	354·0	820·6	972·0
Ossetian	163·2	203·6	213·1	163·2	310·7	391·0	236·8	482·1	306·9
Tadjik	103·8	119·6	106·2	221·2	151·1	125·4	357·7	373·3	258·5
Chechen	214·3	188·3	183·7	219·0	115·0	79·5	390·5	483·3	439·1
Chuvash	138·6	166·3	200·3	203·6	272·4	284·9	297·6	617·9	746·7
Moldavian	66·7	35·3	17·2	575·0	454·7	780·5	341·7	382·4	464·8

Thus we get a well-proportioned system: on the one hand, the Russian press, which is more advanced, yields pride of place in the

[1] Translator's note: the Russian word *vopros* is obviously a printer's error; the meaning is *vyros*.

The Industrial and Cultural Revolution

dynamics of development to the culturally backward national publishing houses; on the other hand, we find also within vernacular printing a strong differentiation, whereby the more cultured nationalities yield pride of place in the dynamics of development to the culturally more backward nationalities.

... Between 1927 and 1931, the Union Republics issued 15,044 titles, 160,609,000 copies and 756,456,000 printed sheets. For the individual Union Republics the total amount issued every year can be classified in the following way:

Output	1927	1928	1929	1930	1931
Azerbaidjan SSR					
No. of printed units	673	858	997	1,426	1,513
Circulation in thousands	1,711	2,430	2,982	6,187	7,206
No. of printed sheets (in all editions) in thousands	7,219	11,349	13,108	20,152	27,485
Armenian SSR					
No. of printed units	353	372	457	613	630
Circulation in thousands	1,064	1,079	1,384	2,319	2,560
No. of sheets in thousands	5,388	7,292	8,282	11,681	11,740
Belorussian SSR					
No. of printed units	652	693	771	1,323	1,474
Circulation in thousands	1,785	2,246	4,346	8,458	10,716
No. of sheets in thousands	13,071	16,393	20,472	40,215	56,553
Georgian SSR					
No. of printed units	1,184	1,142	1,273	1,611	1,525
Circulation in thousands	3,157	2,950	3,323	6,240	6,147
No. of sheets in thousands	24,491	19,567	18,032	23,661	28,662
Turkmen SSR					
No. of printed units	146	165	166	189	192
Circulation in thousands	268	412	693	1,176	1,428
No. of sheets in thousands	1,198	1,652	4,190	5,792	9,912
Uzbek SSR					
No. of printed units	831	731	1,053	1,624	—[1]
Circulation in thousands	2,022	2,628	3,389	10,722	—
No. of sheets in thousands	10,620	12,455	15,698	36,219	—
Ukrainian SSR					
No. of printed units	4,687	5,695	6,680	8,079	8,086
Circulation in thousands	26,741	38,336	62,523	124,220	121,829
No. of sheets in thousands	170,265	219,067	309,221	535,252	586,885

[1] In the original, the figures for 1930 are repeated; it is not possible to state whether this was done in the absence of fresh ones, or because of a printer's mistake.—R.S.

A comparison of the rates of development of the printed output in the Union Republics between 1927 and 1931 with the rates of development of printing in the Soviet Union as a whole shows that

The Books of the Nationalities of the USSR

the rates of development in the Union Republics exceed those of the Union as a whole:

	According to printed units	According to circulation	According to total number of sheets
Percentage of increase for the Union as a whole between 1927 and 1931	63·7	276·1	187·0
Increase in the Union Republics	130·5	337·0	225·7

This average increase in the total output of the Union Republics differs as far as individual republics are concerned. The rates of increase between 1927 and 1931 in a republic such as the Azerbaidjan SSR, with its culturally more backward population, exceeded considerably the indices of development for all the National Republics taken together: the increase in the output of printed sheets in that Republic reached 280.7 per cent. . . .

DOCUMENT NO. 20

THE *KORENIZATSIYA*[1] OF THE NATIONAL SCHOOL[2]: RESULTS OF THE INVESTIGATION OF THE NATIONAL SCHOOL

by M. NADEZHDIN and M. SOLOMONOV

At the beginning of the Second Five-Year Plan, general education extended to all the National Republics and districts which used to be culturally the most backward ones, not to speak of such large Republics as the Ukraine, where as early as 1930–31 no more than 2 per cent of the children between eight and ten remained outside school. . . . In 1921–22, 1,430,000 children were taught in the schools of the Ukraine; in 1924–25, 1,844,000; in 1927–28, 2,383,000; in 1929–30, 2,873,000; in 1930–31, 3,758,000; in 1932–33, 4,208,000. No capitalist country has known such rates of making school education accessible to the children of the broad working masses. Let us quote a few more National Republics and Provinces:

Buryat-Mongolia, on the eve of the October Revolution, had only 48 schools, but in 1932–33 it had already 700, including 319 national schools. Before the Revolution, there were 1,000 pupils; in 1932–33 they numbered 67,000, including 27,000 Buryat-Mongols. 92 per cent of the children of the whole Republic had been admitted to the schools. Compared to the preceding year, the number of schools in the current school year increased by 8 per cent, and the number of national Buryat schools by 11 per cent. The number of pupils in the whole Republic has grown by 33 per cent, and for Buryat schools by 45 per cent. Thus, *the national school in the Republic developed faster than the Russian school*. Steps have been taken to admit 82 per cent of those completing the elementary (fourth group) national school into the fifth group, in the academic year 1932–33. In all national schools, the teaching is in the native tongue and in the Latin script.

The incorporation of *Bashkiria* in the Ural Kuzbas system makes for radical changes in her social and economic structure. Under the

[1] *Korenizatsiya*, in the context of this article, means the organization of the national school with a view to entrusting the teaching work to members of the indigenous population.—R.S.
[2] *Revolutsia i Natsionalnosti*, 1933, Nov. 1.

How the National School is made Indigenous

conditions of rapid industrialization and a consistent application of the Leninist national policy, immense successes have been achieved in Bashkiria also on the front of elementary education. Before the Revolution, the Bashkirs did not even have a written language of their own, nor were there any [Bashkir] children in the Russian schools. The proportion of the children of all nationalities who attended school in the territory of Bashkiria prior to the October Revolution hardly amounted to 30 per cent. The illiteracy among the Bashkirs reached 99·5 per cent, i.e. it was almost total. By 1929–30 58 per cent of the children had been admitted to the schools, and to-day 99·3 per cent of the children of school age are attending school in Bashkiria. At the present time preparations are in hand for the introduction of universal seven-year teaching, which must be in operation in the 1932–33 academic year. So far, only 69 per cent of the children who have completed the first stage are attending the seven-year school.

In *Uzbekistan*, under the Tsarist regime, the general literacy of the population amounted to hardly 2 per cent. But in 1932 *every third inhabitant of Uzbekistan was receiving education*. The increase in the number of children admitted to education was particularly noticeable during the last few years owing to the introduction of universal elementary education. The teaching in all the schools under the People's Commissariat of Education of the Uzbek SSR, including also the secondary schools, is in the native tongue. In the 1932–33 academic year, all the higher educational establishments are to go over to teaching in the native tongue.

In *Tataria*, the plan for universal education has been accomplished by more than 90 per cent. Education in all the schools is conducted in the native tongue, and all the illiterate adults up to the age of forty have been drawn into education. A pedagogical institute and a communist institute for higher education[1] have been opened. Before the Revolution the literacy in Tataria amounted to 19 per cent, at present it exceeds 90 per cent. Universal elementary education has already been introduced. Tataria is tackling the introduction of the seven-year [programme of] universal education.

A recent mass check on the national schools in the RSFSR has revealed that, among the overwhelming majority of the nationalities (except for the territory of the extreme north), universal education has, in fact, already been introduced, and that 80 per cent of the teaching in the first stage is in the native tongue. This means that universal school education has been introduced in 70 languages, and

[1] A higher party school with emphasis on general politico-economic teaching. —R.S.

The Industrial and Cultural Revolution

that it includes as many as 2,060,000 children, as against 1,506,000 children in the 1930-31 academic year.

The check-up has also shown that the plans for universal education and the *korenizatsiya* of the national schools have been accomplished in the main by the time fixed by the government. Several national autonomous units have reached, before the appointed time, the preliminary figures of the universal education plan allocated to them. They include *Daghestan, Bashkiria, Buryat-Mongolia* and others. In 1932-33 many national units are to pass from the four-year course of universal education to the seven-year course *in the villages* as well as *in the cities*. These include *Chuvashia, Tataria*, the *Crimea*, the *Western Province*. In other national units, in the 1932-33 academic year, the seven-year course of study is introduced only in the cities, at the new constructions, in the state farms and in the districts of complete collectivization.[1]

The achievements in school development are both quantitative and qualitative. It has been shown beyond doubt that *compared to pre-revolutionary times the content of the work of the national school has changed in matters of principle; many national schools are making exemplary efforts in reorganizing their work* by consistently conforming to the resolution of the CC of the CPSU(B) of September 5, 1931.

In various parts of the RSFSR (such as the Nenets and Vitimo-Olekmin counties, in Buryat-Mongolia, Kalmykia, Daghestan, in the Volga-German Republic, Tataria and others) many schools have been able to put the organization of teaching work into proper order. They have raised the quality of communist upbringing and education, and have mobilized the forces and resources of the local public for the cause of education. The work of the pioneer organizations and pupils' self-government in the national school have been developed.

Owing to the introduction of universal education and the ever-expanding *korenizatsiya* of the school, the national teaching cadres have considerably grown in numbers, and the teaching staff has much improved as a result of the influx of komsomol members, workers and collective farmers. In some districts the party and komsomol members among the teachers amounted to 20-30 and even 50 per cent.

The construction of school buildings has been accelerated. In Daghestan, apart from the schools provided for in the budget, 100 buildings are being constructed solely by the forces and resources of the local working population.

[1] It may be useful to compare these sanguine expectations with the fact that, in the USSR as a whole, the seven-year school has become general only during the current (1950-55) Five-Year Plan.—R.S.

How the National School is made Indigenous

In many distant and out-of-the-way districts of semi-nomadic regions, where 75 per cent of the schools are in buildings [for other purposes which have been] adapted to school needs, the necessary repairs are often neglected, and the population is not being sufficiently drawn into the work. Alongside the advanced national autonomous units (in the Central Black-Earth Region, North Caucasia, the Urals and Daghestan) there are many others where the school buildings have been left unfinished for several years.

But wherever the people know how to adopt local building materials, the plans for school construction are accomplished successfully (Eastern Siberia, Daghestan, the Leningrad Province, the Volga-German Republic).

The organs of National Education are not giving sufficient direction to school construction. The People's Commissariat of Education of the RSFSR has worked out a building project for the five-year school, but it has not yet reached many of the outlying national districts.

The following is a picture of the work in the national schools. With some difficulty the brigade inspecting national schools reached the Avar *aul* of Sugrat (Daghestan). The only means of getting there was on horseback over mountain paths. The inhabitants of the *aul* had built a good school: at present the school has eight forms. The teacher showed the brigade a thorough plan of study for 1932–33. By attending the current lessons, the brigade ascertained that the [teaching of] arithmetic, geography and social sciences was properly organized. The pupils from the mountain tribes showed good interest. In the opinion of the brigade leader, they knew more than is required of them (in the elementary school). A locksmith's shop, a joiner's shop and a smithy are attached to the school, but their equipment is equally primitive: there is not a single lathe. In the workshops the pupils are taught by an Avar instructor. The older pupils themselves make the school furniture, and also the tools required for their workshops—planes, benches, joining planes, drills, chisels, knives. They have replaced on their typewriter the Russian by the Latin script and are producing complicated things such as knives, razors and so forth. The fame of the school, from which well-trained master craftsmen are graduating, has spread throughout the whole of Daghestan.

. . . .

[But] apart from the considerable successes which have been achieved, the work of most of the national schools is still unsatisfactory. In some schools, distortions of the party line on universal education and the polytechnization of the school are reflected in the use of the pupils as a labour force, and in the overburdening of the teachers with technical office work. When that occurs, the level of knowledge among the pupils goes down, and in many national schools it is plainly unsatisfactory. It happened that the number of subjects has been reduced, so that the school education was whittled down to overcoming illiteracy.

Nor are the problems of anti-religious and international education given their due place in the national school. The ways and means of that work are outmoded: religious holidays are sporadically used as occasion for it instead of its being integrated with the whole of teaching.

The *korenizatsiya* of the national school is still far from complete. There are still cases of Russification of the national school, of chauvinism on the part of the predominant nationality and of a failure duly to rebuff it. Thus, the investigation has produced evidence of Tatarization of Bashkir schools in Tataria.

The *korenizatsiya* of the school meets with great difficulties, especially in districts where the national minorities are interspersed among the mass of the population of a different nationality. Generally the nationality which is more numerous is better provided with teachers and text-books. That is why more attention must be paid to the national minorities and to their cultural requirements. It has been observed, for instance, that in the Tatar Republic the Nenets schools have no text-books. In the Ukraine, too, the needs of the national minorities' schools in many places are taken too little account of.[1]

In those national minorities' schools of Magnitogorsk which have been inspected, the new school curricula are in the Russian language: this greatly impedes the work of the teachers who do not speak Russian. The Tatar-Bashkir schools have no text-books in the vernacular, and during the whole of the last academic year Russian text-books had to be used. The schools had also to make frequent use of the local Tatar newspaper in lieu of text-books. The Tatar-Bashkir Factory Workshop School has no text-books in physics and mathematics at all (not even in the Russian language), except for one or

---

[1] Presumably this refers to the Russian as well as to the Jewish etc. minorities. I had myself in 1931 the opportunity to notice fantastic cases of disregard for the right of the Russian workers to use their mother-tongue: these cases cannot even be described as merely local excesses, as the underlying theory of Ukrainization was stubbornly defended by one of the leaders of the Ukrainian party organization with whom I discussed it. On instances of export of this type of romantic nationalism even to Siberia see below, p. 209. See also above, Document 17, pp. 182–3.—R.S.

How the National School is made Indigenous

two copies used by the teachers. The investigating brigade has also noted that the curricula of these schools do not draw enough on the concrete local material—such as the construction of Magnitogorsk, and sovkhoz and kolkhoz development in the Magnitogorsk district. The subjects of natural science are not sufficiently related to the mineral resources of the Urals.

In many districts of the Urals, *korenizatsiya* has not been applied to more than 50 per cent of the national schools of the higher grade. Characteristically, the teachers in the local organizations are advancing the following unconvincing 'justifications' of the slow rates of *korenizatsiya*. If, they say, the secondary school teaches the children in their native tongue, they will not be able to enter the higher educational establishments or technicums; they will either not pass the entrance examination or find study difficult.

At the same time, cases of what might be called artificial *korenizatsiya* of the schools are evident. This applies, in particular, to the Ukrainian schools in Western Siberia and others. In those districts attempts at *korenizatsiya* of the schools are made against the wishes of the population, who have long forgotten their native tongue and for whose young generation, in particular, it has become alien and unfamiliar. Such attempts are a distortion and violation of the party's policy of switching the schools to the pupils' mother-tongue.

The lack or shortage of text-books, periodical text-books and teaching appliances is the sorest spot in the work of the national schools. It is, to a large extent, the root cause of the slowness with which the national schools are being based upon the indigenous civilization. When teaching mathematics, the teacher explains it in the native tongue, but when writing down the theorem on the blackboard, he uses the Russian language and quotes Russian scientific terms. This, of course, makes it very difficult for the children to understand the theorem. The Provincial State Publishing House must do everything possible to increase, both in the centre and locally, the publication of text-books for the national schools. It is necessary to give the collective of [text-book] authors the benefit of public attention and assistance.

The *korenizatsiya* of the schools depends in particular on the training of the teaching cadres. The qualifications of most of the national teachers are unsatisfactory: in some regions 50–70 per cent of the elementary school teachers have only had elementary education and short-term training. The efforts to improve the qualifications of the national teachers are not yet up to the required level.

Correspondence teaching in the national language is almost wholly

The Industrial and Cultural Revolution

lacking, and the teacher who has finished the elementary school, has attended [but] two or three months' courses, and knows no Russian, has often no means of improving his qualifications.

The instructors and the organs of National Education are not giving enough methodological direction to the work of the national teachers as a whole, nor do the schools serving the masses receive sufficient assistance from the model national schools. Most of the national regions suffer from an almost complete lack of methodological literature in the national languages on the teaching curricula and the polytechnization of the schools.

The People's Commissariat of Education of the RSFSR has raised the extremely important question of concentrating the training and retraining of cadres of teachers and instructors in methodology and the publication of text-books and methodological literature in the national languages for small groups of national minorities in those Autonomous Provinces, Territories and Republics where those particular nationalities predominate. But such a concentration does not in any way imply that the National Education Departments of those districts and the other educational and public organizations, Soviet bodies, assistance councils and so forth are released from the duty to assist in every way in the training of cadres and the provision of the national schools with text-books and teaching aids in the native tongue.

Consultation in aid of the young teacher must be organized at the model schools and pedagogical technicums and institutes in every district. It is necessary to hold regular conferences of young teachers, and in the schools to attach them to old and experienced teachers.

Due attention should be paid to the training of women teachers. In some national districts where environmental survivals are particularly strong, it is necessary at this stage to organize special schools for girls, since they are not allowed to go to schools where men are teaching. The local organizations and the local public do not always pay attention to this aspect of the matter.

A negative factor considerably affecting the work of the national schools is the extensive non-attendance by the pupils, particularly towards the end of the year: this occurs even in those national schools which are crowded at the beginning of the academic year. In some national districts, as many as 50–60 per cent of the pupils are falling off. In some schools of Kirghizia and Bashkiria, only 40 per cent of the pupils had remained in the schools by May 1932. In certain schools of Daghestan, Kalmykia and the northern territory, attendances fell to 15 per cent in the spring of 1932, and in the Komi province the lessons ceased officially by May 1. The shortcomings

How the National School is made Indigenous

in the provision and maintenance of the schools and boarding schools, salary arrears, or failure to supply hot meals—such are the reasons why the pupils are staying away from the schools. Their dropping out, therefore, is due to the lack of administrative abilities and initiative on the part of the local organizations, individual district officials and the schools themselves. Of course, the movement of groups of the population in the national regions to the pastures and to fishing and [other] seasonal work has also a serious effect on the school attendance by the end of the academic year. This is an additional proof that the local authorities have not yet learned to adapt themselves to the specific conditions in which semi-nomadic populations live.

Small-scale schools, travelling schools and separate schools for girls are often lacking in those districts where they are particularly required. There are also few schools for backward children. It happens that, in one and the same group, an eight-year-old pupil sits beside a fifteen-year-old one.[1]

In several republics and provinces (Kalmykia, Kazahkstan, Bashkiria) it has happened that the local organizations have failed to ensure that the teachers received their salaries in time and were provided with the stipulated food norms. The poor material position of the teachers cannot, of course, but affect the quality of the teaching. There is no need to prove that satisfactory material provision (school buildings, equipment, supplying the teachers with necessities) is a most important factor in improving the quality of the teaching in the difficult and peculiar conditions of the national schools.

The local means and resources for improving the provision of the schools are not sufficiently utilized. There is little information about the organization of school kitchen gardens, rabbit hutches and similar subsidiary economies.

It is necessary to devote more attention to the peculiarities of the national schools, the peculiarities of the national minority schools, the problems of universal education, the polytechnization of the national schools, the removal of the 'inherent shortage' of school buildings, the training of cadres, and the publication of text-books and literature in the native tongues. It is necessary to improve the guidance provided for the national school by the People's Commissariat of Education and the organs of National Education.

---

[1] Soviet educational standards, at least those aimed at, are illustrated by the fact that this phenomenon, only too familiar in village schools in Western countries, is specially complained of.—R.S.

DOCUMENT NO. 21

ON NATIONAL CADRES[1]

by K. TOBOLOV

... During the first years of the Revolution, the proletariat in the central industrial districts could and did employ in the economy and the state apparatus a certain number of bourgeois specialists, former subordinate officials, and so forth. The dictatorship of the proletariat was, of course, based on the old Bolshevik guard and the strong and comparatively numerous proletarian cadres in the central districts. The working-class masses, steeled in the struggle against Tsarism and in the civil war, were the richest reservoir supplying fresh cadres for leading work.

In this respect the National Republics were obviously less favourably placed. First of all, the backward national districts had no old and experienced Bolshevik guard. Secondly, it was next to impossible to employ in the state apparatus of the newly formed Autonomous Regions and National Republics the old cadres [of officials] who were unsuitable because of past social position and colonizing habits. But the most serious feature here was the total or almost complete absence of proletarian centres and the weakness or, in most cases, non-existence of the proletarian cadres which could have provided the apparatus of the new Soviet national units with leading cadres. That is why the state apparatus of many National Republics absorbed class-alien ex-Tsarist interpreters, the offspring of the national bourgeoisie, the clergy and other members of the bourgeois-nationalist intelligentsia.

In the first years of the Revolution, the civil war and economic construction these cadres, which were strongly infected with nationalism, went with the Soviet regime. The fellow-travellership of these national-democratic elements with the proletarian revolution was conditioned by the [common] struggle against the danger of the restoration of Tsarism and the attempts of the white armies to restore the colonial domination of the Russian landlords and bourgeoisie.

But with the transition to the reconstruction period, the expanding socialist offensive and the sharpening class struggle in the country, these fellow-travellers of the proletarian revolution began to waver.

[1] *Sovetskoye Stroitelstvo*, 1933, No. 7–8 (slightly abridged).

On National Cadres

The threatened restoration of the colonial rule of the Russian landlords and the bourgeoisie lapsed. The hopes of the national-democratic elements in the National Republics to set up national-bourgeois states, instead of the Soviet Republics, collapsed. So did their anticipation of the internal transformation of the proletarian dictatorship and its peaceful transition to capitalism. Hence the vacillations and occasional desertions to the camp of the enemies of the Soviet regime among individual and, at times, active officials of the Autonomous Regions and Republics. This was illustrated by the striking withdrawal of the Sultan-Galiyev group in Tataria, the Crimea and Bashkiria.

But the occasional desertions of single and, at times, even groups of leading officials in the Republics and Autonomous Regions do not, under any circumstances, justify defamations of the old national cadres of non-working-class origin. The thing to do is to wage a resolute struggle against the ideologically alien elements among the old national cadres and simultaneously to persist in the work of re-educating (under the fire of proletarian criticism) their more progressive and better section.

Apart from the policy of preserving the national cadres mainly by re-education, the present new stage makes it imperative to train, for the Republics and Autonomous Provinces, new leading proletarian cadres of party workers, engineers and technicians and economists from the workers, collective farmers and poor peasants of the formerly oppressed nationalities.

The history of the revolutionary struggle, and the socialist construction in the USSR, have shown many times that the abrupt turning points of the Revolution demand a certain retraining of the old cadres, causing a certain portion of the leading officials to fall off and new leading cadres to advance into the foreground. This is what happened during the October Revolution, the civil war and the transition to the reconstruction period. And it is happening, on a larger scale, in the present epoch of the expanding Socialist offensive and the Second Five-Year Plan leading to the classless socialist society. . . .

. . . The growing pains affecting the development of industrialization and collectivization emanate in the main from the cultural, technical and economic backwardness of our country and have, in this respect, historical class roots. But they are at the same time also due to defects of leadership in our planning system stemming from the problem of cadres. The question here is how to organize, distribute and lead people. In the struggle for the successful application of the Second Five-Year Plan and against the difficulties of our development, the subjective factor, i.e. the quality of leadership and of the leading cadres, is of immense importance.

The task of training new cadres was the focal topic of the party during the period of the XVIth Party Congress. According to its resolution,

'*the problem of the leading economic and technical cadres*, the whole magnitude of which has been brought out by the Central Committee, *is becoming the key problem of our socialist construction*, and [hence] one of decisive importance. Only if the forces of the whole party and the working class make further efforts to train cadres from working-class people, and only if there is a decisive improvement in this field, will it be possible to secure that Bolshevik rates in the socialist industrialization of the country continue to be achieved.' [1]

If the problem of training new leading cadres presents certain difficulties even in the central industrial districts, its solution in the backward National Provinces is made still harder by additional complications. The training of leading national cadres is hampered, above all, by the weakness of the national proletarian cadres. There are the day-to-day conditions of national life and the national languages of the masses which have to be taken into account, and finally the extreme lack of old cadres. Up to the present we have been very slow and made many mistakes in training national cadres. Some officials fail to take into account the whole complexity of, and the great responsibility inherent in, the training of national cadres. This question is closely connected with the position of the national intelligentsia.

The bulk of the old national intelligentsia, owing to its social past, is alien to the Soviet regime. Its members originate mostly from the commercial bourgeoisie, colonizing officials, the Moslem clergy and feudal strata; at best they are petty bourgeois by birth. In regard to ideology and education, the old cadres of the national intelligentsia are predominantly pupils of religious schools, office translators or employees of the bourgeois commercial and industrial apparatus. But their special characteristic is the vast preponderance, amongst them, of people with humanistic specialities (teachers, lawyers, men of letters) over those with technical qualifications (engineers, agronomists, technicians). This applies equally to the Tatar, Georgian or Uzbek intelligentsia and that of other nationalities. Owing to these peculiarities of the national intelligentsia, its social heterogeneity, lack of ideological steadfastness and humanistic education, a vast proportion of its members are clearly unfit to

[1] Stenographic Report of the XVIth Congress of the CPSU(B), p. 713.

On National Cadres

accomplish the tasks inherent in socialist reconstruction and in the intensified class struggle.

It is precisely at the time of socialist reconstruction and of sharpening class struggle that the lacking steadfastness of a great many national intellectuals, and hence the whole importance of creating a new Soviet national intelligentsia, becomes evident. It should be said that the successful establishment of a new national intelligentsia of industrial [experts] and technicians is instrumental in gradually eliminating the problem of the national intelligentsia in its old sense....

During the restoration period we were compelled to make use of the entire national intelligentsia, and this was feasible because, while we were setting up National Republics and Autonomous Provinces, implanting Soviet national culture, developing literacy in the vernacular, laying the foundations of economic centres and so forth, the groups of the national intelligentsia who are far from, and at times even hostile to, socialism could and did co-operate with us. But now that we have entered the period of socialism, it becomes obvious to us, and to them, that their social expectations have miscarried. And this is the reason why vacillations and unsteadiness have set in among the fellow-travellers of yesterday.

This could be proved by scores of examples. But it is sufficient for this purpose to adduce some facts, say, from the life of the Turkic intelligentsia in Azerbaidjan.

In Azerbaidjan, at the turn of 1929–30, the Turkic intelligentsia included a considerable proportion of active counter-revolutionaries; more than half were wavering, and hardly more than a third were loyal to the Soviet regime. In this state of affairs the anti-Soviet intelligentsia, as the element strongest in influence and activity, constituted the 'leading element'.

In one form or other nearly all the strata of the intelligentsia, from the humanistic to the technical, were infected with nationalism. The tendency in favour of severance from the Union was fairly widespread. The right wing of the national intelligentsia was closely connected with the Mussavat—the party of extreme anti-Soviet reaction. The apparatus of the cultural front was strongly infested with nationalists.

The basic aim of the right wing of the nationalist intelligentsia is to educate the youth in a nationalist spirit. The teachers in the technicums and other educational institutions in Azerbaidjan included many obvious nationalists. Few party members but many former beys and merchants were doing educational work. The nationalists made frequent use of geography to sow [the seeds of] nationalism; they spread illegal Turkish and Mussavat literature and organized

The Industrial and Cultural Revolution

underground circles. It is significant that during the last year, owing to the improvement in our relations with Turkey and the intensified attempts at anti-Soviet intervention in the West, a section of the Turkic intelligentsia has changed its orientation, on Western imperialism. In this connection a section of the Turkic intelligentsia is substituting anti-Armenian nationalism.

The new stage of socialist construction which is accompanied by an acute intensification of the class struggle and a differentiation within the intelligentsia has introduced certain correctives into the old party directives.

The resolution of the CC of the CPSU(B) of June 1929 on the report on the work of the CC of the Communist Party of Uzbekistan says:

'The socialist offensive against the feudal and capitalist elements of the town and village is provoking rabid resistance on the part of the merchants, beys and clergy *with the assistance of the nationalist intelligentsia*. In the struggle against the consolidating proletarian dictatorship, the bourgeoisie strives to inflame national chauvinism.' [1]

The ensuing events fully confirm the correctness of the instructions and warnings issued by the CC of the CPSU. The discovery of the counter-revolutionary nationalistic organization called 'The Party of National Independence'[2] in the apparatus of the People's Commissariat of Education and the cultural institutions of Uzbekistan, the revelation that seven out of the nine members of the collegium of the People's Commissariat of Education were found to belong to that organization, and the fact that the writers' organization of Uzbekistan, 'The Red Pen', the mouthpiece of the People's Commissariat of Education *Maarif Vi-Ukuntugi*, the Fergana pedagogical technicum, the newspaper *Yangi-Fergana* and others were in the hands of the counter-revolutionary nationalists, apart from everything else, revealed distinctly unhealthy tendencies in the ranks of the national intelligentsia.

The above shows that we cannot approach, without differentiation, the national intelligentsia in the various Republics and Autonomous Provinces. In the most backward national districts (*rayony*), among the Turkmens, Chechens, Adjarts, Kurds, etc., the formulation of the IVth Conference on the Nationalities[3] is still basically valid. In these districts every intelligent official who is more or less loyal is precious to us and almost irreplaceable. We still cannot do without these people when it is a matter of raising the backward national masses to the cultural level of the central regions.

[1] *Pravda*, June 4, 1929. [2] See above, p. 176.
[3] See above, pp. 65–6.

On National Cadres

But there are advanced Republics and Autonomous Provinces in the USSR where the class struggle has reached maximum intensity and where the formulation of 1923 is losing its validity. In Tataria, Georgia, Armenia, Uzbekistan and Belorussia, the possibility of making use of the entire national intelligentsia is now ruled out. The socialist offensive in these countries will develop against a certain nationalistic section of the national intelligentsia which has gone over, or is going over, to the class enemy. That is why it is absolutely essential to differentiate among [the various sections of] the national intelligentsia, especially in these Republics. Nevertheless it would be extremely harmful not to make patient and persistent efforts to discover if only temporary supporters even among the class-alien nationalist section of the intelligentsia, and not to make full use of the old national intelligentsia. At the same time, we must understand that not even the most insignificant ideological sector of [our] work can be left under the influence of the old national intelligentsia. The important thing to realize now is that the task of training new national cadres of workers and collective farmers is becoming more acute than ever.

We must wage a merciless struggle against individual party members ganging up with the class-alien nationalist intelligentsia and organizing behind the back of the party the bourgeois intelligentsia against the party line. There were many such cases in the party organizations and the Communist Party of the nationalities. Thus it was discovered some years ago that obviously nationalistic elements of the intelligentsia had their agents in the ranks and even in the CC of the Communist Party of Belorussia. In Tataria in 1927 a group of 82 bourgeois nationalist intellectuals sent to the provincial committee of the party a protest against the introduction of the latinized ABC among the Tatars. But it was only recently that the author and ideological inspirer of that protest, which had been qualified by the provincial committee of the CPSU as national bourgeois pressure on the party, was revealed as the former right-wing 'Communist' Moukhtarov who has now been expelled from the party as an active follower of Sultan Galiyev. And lastly, in 1928, Southern Ossetia was visited by an investigating commission of the CC of the Georgian Communist Party. The commission received from a group of the national Ossetian intelligentsia a declaration which was alleged to be directed against Georgian chauvinism. This is not to say that there is no Georgian chauvinism; of course there is, and we must fight it.[1] But it is important to note that the then director of the section for agitation and propaganda of the party

[1] See above, p. 179.

provincial committee had summoned one of the influential non-party cultural workers and suggested to him to submit that particular declaration. There were many more cases of this nature in the National Republics and Autonomous Provinces and they must be combated without mercy.

To create the new national proletarian intelligentsia is a most important part of the class struggle. What we have to do now is to train not an intelligentsia in general but, firstly, our own cadres of the proletarian intelligentsia from the various nationalities of the USSR, and, secondly, such cadres as would, above all, be the exponents of definite technical and industrial knowledge. The instructions contained in Comrade Stalin's speech about mastering technique and rearing the cadres of an intelligentsia of technicians are still more important for the Republics and Autonomous Provinces than they are for the central districts.

The National Republics and Autonomous Provinces must now train, above all, engineering and technical cadres for industry and agriculture, officials for the Soviet and the state economic apparatus and, finally, the leading cadres of the party apparatus.

... In several Autonomous Provinces and National Republics a considerable portion of the intelligentsia of technicians in industry and agriculture is already made up of indigenous working people. For example, in Chuvashia, in 1931, 253 out of 617 specialists, i.e. 41 per cent, were Chuvashs.

Yet a great many Republics and Autonomous Provinces are still very backward in the training of leading national cadres. The successes achieved in this field are insignificant compared to the magnitude of the task of training specialists from the various nationalities. Thus, in the local industry of the Tatar Republic, in 1929, only 8 per cent of the specialists were Tatars. In the same year, in the districts of Tataria, only 25 out of 262 doctors were Tatars. Until recently, the planning authorities of Tataria have failed to realize the immense importance of training Tatar specialists.

Even in the more advanced and cultured National Republics, the state of the national technical cadres is unsatisfactory. Thus, according to the data of the former Supreme Council for National Economy of Uzbekistan, in April 1931 only 13 of the 429 engineers and technicians employed in the industry of the Republic were Uzbeks, i.e. 3 per cent.

Apart from the (numerical) shortage of specialists from the various nationalities of the USSR, there is also the question of the quality of the cadres. Specialists from the formerly oppressed nationalities are often inferior in general knowledge and practical skill. For example,

On National Cadres

of the 6,445 engineers and technicians in the Central Asiatic Republics in 1929, 1,311, or 20·3 per cent, were graduates of higher educational establishments; 626, or 9·7 per cent, were former students who had failed to graduate; 3,119, or 48·3 per cent, had secondary education; and 1,401, or 21·7 per cent, were practical workers without special technical training.[1]

These figures illustrate the great shortcomings in whatever intelligentsia there is in the Republics and Autonomous Provinces. There can be no doubt that the big hitches which occurred in the accomplishment of the industrial financial plans, and especially in the construction of the big new undertakings and hydro-stations in the Republics and autonomous areas, are partly due to the lack of engineers and technicians, and even more so to their poor qualifications. This raises the urgent problem of how to improve the training of cadres of technical specialists from the various nationalities of the USSR. Yet the outlook for the training of cadres of technical specialists in the National Republics is still dim. The responsible planning, economic and party organs in several Republics are not paying enough attention to this question. For example, the agricultural economy of Central Asia needs cadres of 6,739 people with higher and 12,711 people with secondary education. But the present network of the higher schools in Central Asia can only turn out 1,730 specialists with higher qualifications (25·7 per cent of what is required) and the technicums only 2,472 workers with medium and lower qualifications (19·5 per cent of what is required). The same is true of industry. Central Asia needs engineering and technical cadres of 2,724 people with higher qualifications and 8,200 people with medium qualifications. But the existing network of higher and secondary educational establishments in the Central Asiatic Republics is only capable of turning out 1,190 workers with higher qualifications (42·9 per cent) and 1,035 workers with medium qualifications (12·6 per cent).[2]

This is also the position in many other National Republics. For example, although Kazakhstan requires 32,000 specialists, only 5,500 can be had from the local educational establishments.

In this connection it should be stated that in some Republics and Autonomous Provinces a certain number of officials have a wrong approach to the training of specialists' cadres from the indigenous nationalities. It is inevitable and, at times, even expedient to employ in some National Republics the engineering and technical cadres from the central industrial regions of the USSR. This will be

[1] *Revolutsia i Natsionalnosti*, 1930, No. 3, p. 76.
[2] *Narodnoye Khozyaistvo Srednei Azii*, Nos. 3–4, 1930, pp. 15–16.

The Industrial and Cultural Revolution

particularly valid during the next few years, especially in National Republics (such as Kazakhstan) where the industrialization is developing at spectacular rates.

But every effort must be made to concentrate the training of engineers and technicians within the National Republics themselves. This is the only way to solve the task of training engineering and technical staffs from the *basic nationalities*. The erroneous line of obtaining specialists from the educational establishments of the Union must be resolutely corrected.

Even in the reconstruction period, the leading cadres in some advanced National Republics were greatly infested with socially alien elements. Thus, in Uzbekistan in 1929, as many as 45 per cent of the responsible Uzbek officials in the central republican administration originated from merchants, mullahs and other alien elements. In such circumstances, the problem of training leading cadres for the Soviet apparatus from the ranks of the workers is of tremendous importance. . . .

However, despite the great shortcomings of the cadres of the leading state institutions and the economic apparatus, several Republics have been very successful in training leading economic officials. Thus, in April 1931, in the business organizations and enterprises of Uzbekistan, 33 of the 66 leading officials were Uzbeks; 38 had originally been workers and 16 employees; 54 were members of the CPSU(B).

One of the great defects in the training of new leading cadres for the economic, and especially the Soviet, apparatus in the Autonomous Republics and Provinces is that too few of the indigenous workers and collective farmers are promoted to leading work. Such promotions, which were insufficient in the central apparatus of the USSR during the last years, are even less frequent in some of the Republics. . . .

Although the training of cadres is somewhat better organized in the humanities, the numbers of available teaching cadres, especially in the primary and, to some extent, also in the secondary schools in most of the Republics and Autonomous Provinces, show an enormous shortage of national teachers. The national pedagogical cadres are not only weak numerically, but also socially infested with class-alien elements. Up to the present, a substantial number of teachers in primary and secondary schools in the Republics and Autonomous Provinces have been of clerical, commercial and kulak origin, or from other socially alien and hostile strata. This accounts for all sorts of religious, nationalistic and kulak tendencies among a section of the teachers.

On National Cadres

An even greater fact in the training of national teaching cadres is the weak grounding which they are receiving. The immense and rising demand for teaching cadres in the backward National Republics makes it impossible to give the teachers an all-round and more thorough training. Hence it has happened in Kirghizia and Turkmenia that almost illiterate people who had just finished the schools for illiterate adults [*likbez*] or attended short-term courses, were often teaching in primary schools. This means it is extremely urgent for us to train cadres of national teachers who are sufficiently literate and equipped with the theory of Marxism-Leninism. The cultivation of technical knowledge among the national teachers and, through them, among the national masses is also of immense importance.

However, apart from the above-mentioned defects, the National Republics have achieved very great successes in the training of national teachers and pedagogical cadres for secondary and higher education. Thus, in such backward Republics as Turkmenia, more than one-third of the teachers in the primary schools in 1930 were party and komsomol members. In some Republics a great many teachers are workers and even more are village poor or collective farmers by origin. The national teaching body, which has grown numerically and socially, represents in its mass an immense army faithfully supporting the party and the Soviet Government in the struggle for collectivization and the cultural revolution.

Lastly, the training of national cadres is of immense importance for the party apparatus. True, most of the Republics and Autonomous Provinces lacked both an old and experienced Bolshevik guard and leading party cadres steeled in the struggle against Tsarism. . . . But it is equally true that during the past years the immense successes achieved in the application of the national policy of the party and the expanding industrialization and collectivization have produced in the national districts new leading cadres of party officials who are workers and toilers by origin. Moreover, a portion of the old cadres has been tested, consolidated, ideologically re-educated and steeled as Bolsheviks. A glance at the leading cadres of party officials in any Republic and Autonomous Province shows how much they have grown in the last few years.

The youthfulness of the national Communist Parties and national party organizations and the absence or weakness of national proletarian cadres have affected the state of the leading party cadres. In some national districts all these impediments hampering the development of cadres of party officials have been revealed in a concentrated and acute form. In the Tatar party organization, for example, a group of former party officials, at the time when the class struggle was unfolding and sharpening, landed in the camp of the counter-revolutionary Sultan-Galiyev movement.

But the isolated cases of failure in the education and further consolidation of party cadres do not justify the unhealthy tendency shown in some national party organizations to defame and belittle wholesale the old party cadres of the National Republics. Such tendencies manifested themselves most sharply in the Communist Party of Uzbekistan during the IVth Kurultai (Congress). Another striking case of underestimating the value of the tested cadres of national officials who had arisen during the period of revolution, civil war and the first years of socialist construction occurred in Azerbaidjan in 1929 in connection with the replacement of the so-called leadership. Even in the advanced proletarian party organization of Baku there were (isolated) attempts to defame the Turkic cadres of party officials. The CC of the CPSU has resolutely repudiated these unhealthy inclinations. . . .

The inter-group struggle which occurred in many national party organizations during the NEP and even the reconstruction period, particularly inside the leading body of the national organizations, and which is still not infrequent even now, continues to have a negative effect on the formation and ideological development of the national party cadres. There were many fairly clear cases of such group struggles expressing, and aiming to protect, the interests of kulak and bey elements. This happened in Kazakhstan, Tataria, Uzbekistan and the party organizations of many [other] National Republics. . . . To bolshevize the national party organizations, it is necessary above all to produce cadres of leading party officials who are steadfast Bolsheviks, educated in the spirit of internationalism. Such Bolshevik cadres are also needed to wage a most resolute struggle against national seclusion [and] a decisive two-front fight against Great-Russian chauvinism and local nationalism. . . .

The decisive condition and the basic source of producing leading national officials is the formation of national proletarian cadres. The party and the government have paid serious attention to this matter ever since the beginning of the Revolution. Owing to the successful fulfilment of the First Five-Year Plan, considerable industrial establishments have already been set up in most of the National Republics and Provinces. They will be the basis for the many thousands of new cadres of the national proletariat to be formed. This will make it possible to accelerate greatly the *korenizatsia* and the formation of cadres of national officials for all the branches of state, economic, cultural and social development.

DOCUMENT NO. 22

ON NATIONAL CADRES OF SPECIALISTS[1]

by B. R.

'Of all the valuable capital available in the world, the most valuable and decisive capital is people, cadres. One must understand that, in our present conditions, "cadres decide everything".' (From the speech of Comrade Stalin at the graduation of the Military Academy, May 5, 1935.)

... The old regime has left to the National Republics and Provinces, which were born in the proletarian revolution, no or almost no cadres of national intelligentsia capable of working honestly for the building of socialism. It is well known that under Tsarism only few individuals from the formerly oppressed nationalities were able to attain higher education, and these were mainly from privileged kulak and well-to-do families.

The leadership by and assistance from the proletariat of the USSR and its party which consistently applies the Leninist-Stalinist national policy, have secured unprecedented rates of economic and cultural construction in the Soviet national districts. The huge scale and high rates of socialist construction in the National Republics and Provinces, which drew into production the broadest masses of the multi-national working population, have immensely increased the need for national cadres of specialists in all branches [of development].

The combination of these two factors has brought about a most acute shortage of cadres in the National Republics and Provinces, and in the first place of *national* cadres of specialists. All available information on how and to what extent in most of the National Republics and Provinces the diverse departmental organs have succeeded in their tasks shows that specialists are definitely lagging behind in this respect, compared to groups of leading workers on the one hand and junior staff on the other. . . . The training of national cadres capable of making the fullest possible use of technique and assimilating thoroughly and effectively the immense help given to the nationalities by the workers' and peasants' governments—this is the

[1] *Revolutsia i Natsionalnosti*, 1935, No. 10.

The Industrial and Cultural Revolution

most basic and decisive task in the development of the National Republics and Provinces at the present time.

... How is this problem solved in practice? At the present time[1] the Soviet National Republics and Provinces have dozens and hundreds of higher educational establishments, set up in the period of national economy restoration, and chiefly in the years of the First and Second Five-Year Plan.

Uzbekistan which, prior to the October Revolution, had not a single higher educational establishment, now *has sixteen educational establishments and higher technical educational establishments* (three industrial, one transport, three agricultural, four economic, four educational and one medical). Turkmenia, whose peoples before the Revolution could not even dream of higher education, has now already three higher educational establishments (one agricultural, educational and medical each). Tadjikistan, culturally one of the most backward districts before the Revolution, has four higher educational establishments. Tataria has twelve. Kazakhstan has ten higher educational establishments, all of which have been set up under the Soviet regime (the university, the higher technical educational establishment [VTUZ] for mining and metallurgy, two agricultural, one economic, four educational and one medical higher educational establishments [VUZ]). Bashkiria has five higher educational establishments, Daghestan three, Buryat-Mongolia three, Chuvashia three, Kirghizia two, Udmurtia two, the Mari Autonomous Province three. Thirty higher educational establishments have been set up in the National Republics and Provinces of the Transcaucasian Federation, and fifteen in the Belorussian Republic. An immense network of 131 higher educational and technical educational establishments has been developed in the Soviet Ukraine.

Regarding the organization of higher education, the most backward Republics are Karelia and Yakutia, which have so far only one VUZ each, and the Karakalpak Autonomous Republic, which still has none.

All these figures provide another irrefutable proof of the exceptional attention and care which the party and the government have devoted, and are devoting, to the cause of training national cadres of specialists for every branch of economy and culture.

However, despite the great achievements in setting up the basic network of higher educational establishments for the nationalities, the organizing of teaching is still far from consolidated.

A considerable proportion of the higher educational establish-

[1] Information for the academic year 1934–35.

On National Cadres of Specialists

ments in the Republics and Provinces are still very young and more or less short of cadres of professors and teachers, teaching equipment and appropriate accommodation. The number of students is comparatively low. Whereas in the USSR [as a whole], in the academic year 1934–35, each higher educational establishment averaged 857 students, the average was 377 in Turkmenia, 308 in Kazakhstan, 376 in Daghestan, 250 in Chuvashia, 250 in Karelia, 195 in Tadjikistan, 151 in Kirghizia, 119 in Buryat-Mongolia, and in Yakutia only 59 students. [On the other hand,] the 'saturation' of higher educational and higher technical educational establishments in Georgia (1,361 students) and Azerbaidjan (1,117 students) is much above the average.

In the 1934–35 academic year, for the *first time* in the USSR, a detailed computation was made of all those newly admitted to the higher educational establishments and those [already] studying in them, according to the indices for January 1, 1935.

The results of this calculation demonstrate one of the greatest achievements in the application of the Leninist-Stalinist nationalities policy. Of the students admitted to the higher educational establishments of the USSR in the autumn of 1934, 50·99 per cent were from non-Russian nationalities; and by January 1, 1935, of all the students of the higher educational and higher technical educational establishments of the USSR—industrial, social-economic, educational and for public health—45·61 per cent were from the non-Russian nationalities.

These figures illustrate clearly *the immense rise in the cultural level of all the formerly backward nationalities of the Soviet Union who have achieved equality on such levels of culture as higher education.*

On the other hand, the analysis of the results of the computation of students in higher educational establishments reveals a considerable unevenness in the development of education among the individual nationalities of the Soviet Union, a fact deserving the greatest attention.

All nationalities of the Soviet Union can, in this respect, be divided into three basic groups: *the first group* consists of those nationalities whose share in VUZ and VTUZ students is higher than the percentage of the nationality among the population of the USSR; *the second group* consists of those nationalities amongst whom these two percentages are approximately equal; *the third group* consists of those nationalities whose percentage of VUZ and VTUZ students is lower than the share of the nationality in the total population of the USSR. Though such a comparison is rather relative and

The Industrial and Cultural Revolution

formal, it enables nevertheless a comparative estimate of the rates of development of higher education among the individual nationalities of the Soviet Union. Here are the numerical data:

First Group

Name of the nationality	Percentage of the nationality—		
	of the population of the USSR	of the students of the autumn intake of 1934	of all students by January 1, 1935
Armenians	1·07	2·38	2·30
Georgians	1·24	3·16	3·53
Jews	1·82	12·5	13·27
Ossetians	0·185	0·51	0·35
Poles	0·53	1·05	0·75
Latvians	0·09	0·13	0·18

These nationalities are advanced also in many other respects, and the development of higher education among them is undoubtedly on a high level.

Second Group

Name of the nationality	Percentage of the nationality—		
	of the population of the USSR	of the students of the autumn intake of 1934	of all students by January 1, 1935
Belorussians	3·23	3·94	2·97
Buryats	0·16	0·11	0·09
Komis	0·15	0·14	0·13
Karelians	0·17	0·16	0·13
Germans	0·84	0·87	0·68
Tatars	1·99	1·44	1·34
[Azerbaidjan] Turkis	1·16	1·36	1·31
Ukrainians	21·2	17·58	14·3
Chuvashs	0·76	0·59	0·46

It may be said that the development of higher education among these nationalities proceeds at a normal rate.

On National Cadres of Specialists

Third Group

Name of the nationality	Percentage of the nationality—		
	of the population of the USSR	of the students of the autumn intake of 1934	of all students by January 1, 1935
The mountain tribes of Daghestan	0·464	0·16	0·12
Nigushs	0·05	0·03	0·02
Kabardins and Balkars	0·118	0·07	0·03
Kazakhs	2·70	0·61	0·40
Kalmyks	0·09	0·06	0·04
Kirghiz	0·52	0·08	0·03
Karakalpaks	0·1	0·002	0·0004
Maris	0·29	0·14	0·11
Mordvins	0·91	0·28	0·27
Oirots	0·027	0·003	0·002
Tadjiks	0·67	0·17	0·10
Turkmens	0·46	0·12	0·07
Udmurts	0·34	0·16	0·09
Uzbeks	2·66	0·57	0·55
Cherkesi	0·044	0·020	0·020
Chechentsy	0·217	0·010	0·010
Khakassy	0·031	0·010	0·001
Yakuts	0·16	0·02	0·04

This group shows the considerable backwardness of several nationalities in the training of national cadres, especially in Republics with particularly high rates of industrial development (for instance Kazakhstan).

The figures quoted must be seriously taken into account, and the necessary conclusions must be drawn, in the first place, by the management of every higher educational establishment whose duty it is to show the utmost concern for the students from nationalities which used to be culturally backward. These figures, in the second place, must attract the most serious attention of the party organization and governments of the Republics and Provinces concerned, on whom depends the successful training of contingents of young national workers who are to be directed to higher educational establishments.

The backwardness of some nationalities in the development of higher education must be overcome in the shortest possible time.

DOCUMENT NO. 23

ON NATIONAL SOVIET CADRES[1]

by A. TELIKHANOV

Comrade Stalin's speech to the graduates of the Red Army Academy obliges the organs of the Soviets to raise, in all urgency, the question of training Soviet cadres. . . . Under present conditions, our successes in administration depend on there being enough people capable of carrying out without deviation the general line of the party and of consolidating the Soviet state, by organizing and training for Soviet work the broadest masses of the workers and kolkhoz members—people familiar with Soviet work and the technique of administration, and knowing how to promote its advance.

This applies, to a large extent, to the National Republics and Provinces, whose need for trained cadres [of administrators] especially from the indigenous population is still greater. In spite of the general improvement in the cultural and political level of the Soviet national cadres, there is still a lack of trained leading officials of the city soviets, district executive committees and village soviets of the National Republics and Provinces.

One of the indications of the qualifications of the Soviet officials is the level of their education. Of the present chairmen of the district executive committees in the Belorussian Soviet Socialist Republic only 9·6 per cent have higher education, 24·7 per cent have secondary education[2], and 65·81 per cent have elementary education; among the chairmen of city soviets there are none with higher education, 1·2 per cent[3] with secondary education, and 58·8 per cent with elementary education. In the Transcaucasian SFSR, the position is somewhat better: the district executive committee chairmen with higher education amount to 23·37 per cent, those with secondary education to 45·8 per cent, and those with elementary education to 30·1 per cent; among the chairmen of city soviets 15·6 per cent, have higher education, 35·9 per cent secondary education and 48·5 per cent elementary education. In the Uzbek SSR, only 3·3 per cent of the city soviet chairmen have higher education, 3·3 per cent have secondary education, but 93·4 per cent have

[1] *Revolutsia i Natsionalnosti*, 1935, No. 12.
[2] At that time, the seven-year school was qualified as (incomplete) secondary education.—R.S.
[3] 51·2 per cent in the original appears to be a mistake.—R.S.

elementary education. In the Turkmen SSR, of a total of 72 chairmen, deputy chairmen and secretaries of district executive committees, only one has higher education, 15 have secondary education, while 56 have elementary education. Among the 20 holders of the same posts in the city soviets of Turkmenia, there is not one with higher education, only three have secondary education, while 17 have elementary education.

These figures show that the training of the leading cadres in the local links of the soviet system is particularly weak in *the Central Asiatic Republics*. This is confirmed by the following information. In the Uzbek SSR, of the 1,232 chairmen of *aul* soviets, 227 (i.e. 19·1 per cent) are almost illiterate (*malogramotniye*). In the Turkmen SSR, of the 343 *aul* soviet chairmen, 115 (34·6 per cent) are uneducated; in the Tadjik SSR, the percentage of almost illiterate chairmen of village soviets is 38.

The fact that there are so many almost illiterates among the leading cadres of the local soviets obliges the soviets and executive committees to expand the training and retraining of these cadres.

In several National Republics and Provinces, the part played by the indigenous population in the soviet apparatus (its *korenizatsiya*) is little developed. Among the 398 leading and responsible officials of the district executive committees and village soviets in Kabardino-Balkaria, only 206 are indigenous; yet 25 of the above posts are vacant. Of the 1,122 village soviet chairmen in the Bashkir Republic, only 340 are Bashkirs; of the 51 chairmen of district executive committees, only 20; only 24 district executive committees have Bashkir secretaries, the rest have Russians. Yet 15 posts of district executive committee chairmen and deputy chairmen and 55 posts of district executive committee instructors have hitherto remained vacant. In the Chuvash Republic, of 2,232 officials of district executive committees and village soviets, 1,746 are indigenous. In the Adygei provincial executive committee, of the 40 Adygeis only 16 can write in their native language. In the provincial executive committee and party provincial committee, only Russian is spoken, and even in some district organizations the Adygei language is avoided. In the apparatus of the Chechen-Ingush provincial executive committee there are officials who know neither the Chechen nor the Ingush language. The secretary of the Balkar village soviet in the Chechen-Ingush province accepts applications from the local population only in the Russian language.

Nor do all territorial institutions and organizations pay sufficient attention to recruiting supplementary staff of the [soviet] apparatus from the national cadres. For example, in the multi-national North

The Industrial and Cultural Revolution

Caucasian territory, the territorial land administration has, among its staff of 300, not a single indigenous member. Nor are there any in the territorial administrations for communications, internal trade, finance, communal economy, the State Bank and the Agricultural Bank. The officials of the Public Attorney's Office of the territory, when receiving indigenous callers, were compelled to search the whole city for a casual interpreter.

The limited extent of *korenizatsiya* of the soviet apparatus in several National Republics, Provinces and Territories *shows that these latter have failed sufficiently to grasp the foundations of the Leninist-Stalinist nationalities policy*, and that they have not followed the most important directives of the party aimed at bringing the state apparatus close to the masses and drawing the broad masses into the administration of the state.

In spite of the shortage of cadres, and especially national ones, some local government organs of the National Republics and Provinces, instead of taking care of these cadres, treat them with scant regard. This is proved by the fluctuation in the soviet cadres of the National Republics and Provinces, which, according to data for the first half of 1935, is considerably higher than in the central districts of the RSFSR. Whereas in the territories and provinces with the worst fluctuations in the soviet cadres (the Kirov and Saratav territories, and the Chelyabinsk and Chernigov provinces), about 10 per cent of the village soviet chairmen were removed in 1935, the dismissals from these posts in the Adygei province in the first half of 1935 reached 39 per cent, in the Karachai province 28 per cent, in the Kabardin-Balkar province 23 per cent, in the Cherkess province 21 per cent, and in the Volga-German Republic 22·5 per cent.

The same disregard for the indigenous officials prevails also in some territorial organizations. For example, in the Azov-Black Sea territory, during 1935, six senior indigenous instructors and the head of the Nationalities Department were dismissed from the apparatus of the territorial executive committee.... In the Nationalities Department three directors, five instructors and six secretaries have been replaced in the course of last year. Most of the officials are being removed from their work because of *insufficient training*. But few of the leading organizations in the National Republics, Provinces and Territories deduce from this [fact] that it is necessary to pay more attention to train and retrain them and to assist them more in their work.

Lately, some Republics have intensified the training and retraining of the soviet cadres. Thus, in the Ukraine in the first half of 1935, 470 chairmen and 500 secretaries of village soviets have attended

On National Soviet Cadres

courses; and approximately as many will be trained in the second half of the year. In the Azerbaidjan SSR, in 1935, 700 village soviet chairmen and 400 secretaries will have attended monthly courses. Courses on local government are already being held in Baku and in Nagorny Karabakh. The following Autonomous Republics and Provinces of the RSFSR have developed the training and retraining of soviet cadres: the Volga-German Republic (185 persons under training), the Crimea (268), Tataria (196), Bashkiria (117), Chuvashia (236), Mordovia (141) and Udmurtia (83).

But these courses do not solve the problem of cadres. The courses are designed for periods from one to three months (the latter are very rare). The broad soviet *aktiv* is being 'trained' mainly in five-day seminars.

These courses, of course, do not give enough knowledge to the chairmen and secretaries of the village soviets and the soviet *aktiv*. In order to do their job properly, the village soviet chairmen and secretaries now require knowledge not only of local government, but also of agricultural technique, the handling of machines and so forth. In the National Republics and Provinces, the officials of the soviet and the soviet *aktiv* are still greater, for the work of the soviets here is far more complex, while the cultural and political level of the masses is as yet comparatively low.

In order to secure trained cadres for the state apparatus of the National Republics and Provinces, *it is necessary in the first place to expand the training of national cadres in the higher special educational institutions.* The existing network of institutes for local government (*sovetskoe stroitelstvo*, verbally 'Soviet construction') cannot cope with the task of training soviet cadres for the National Republics and Provinces. Nor are there as yet such institutes in every Union Republic. There are none in the Belorussian SSR, the Turkmen SSR, the Tadjik SSR. By January 1, 1935, the six institutes for local government in the RSFSR were attended by 465 students from 45 indigenous nationalities. The RSFSR consists of 14 Autonomous Republics, 12 Autonomous Provinces and 9 National Counties, which include more than 600 districts and about 11,000 rural soviets. It follows that an average of less than one indigenous student per district graduates from the institutes for local government per year. It is absolutely essential to increase the capacity of the 'dwarf' institutes for local government in the RSFSR to at least 400 vacancies each (at present 250 to 300 people are studying in each institute). It is [also] necessary to expand the Samarkand institute of local government by transforming it into a territorial institute training cadres for all the Central Asiatic Republics.

The Industrial and Cultural Revolution

Several National Republics and Provinces have *agricultural high schools and courses in Marxism-Leninism*. These educational institutions are mainly for leading district officials of the party, directors and officials of the political departments of the sovkhozy, party organizers and so forth. Only a few individual graduates of the agricultural schools and the courses on Marxism-Leninism are employed in the soviets. That is why it would be opportune to raise before the appropriate organs the question of attaching to the agricultural high schools and courses in Marxism-Leninism special sections for local government, if only for single groups of 30–40 people. Formerly there used to be such sections in the soviet party schools.

A considerable number of officials enter the soviet apparatus of the National Republics and Provinces straight from the secondary schools or technicums. They are employed as financial inspectors, instructors, secretaries of soviets and executive committees, statisticians and so forth. [But] most of them cannot cope with their duties, since they know neither the theory nor the practice of soviet work. Therefore it would be expedient to introduce a special subject, 'local government', into the higher schools and technicums.

The insufficient standard of the training provided by the permanent courses of local government is borne out, above all, by the proportion of those graduating from the courses who have quickly to be sifted out of the soviet apparatus. During the last five years, no less than 100,000 people have attended the special courses on local government: this equals the total number of leading local officials of the soviets and executive committees. In fact, however, not more than 10 per cent of these officials have actually finished the courses for local government.

In some Republics and Autonomous Provinces one can count on one's fingers the people working in the soviets who have finished the courses for local government. For example, in the Cherkess province, among the 114 leading district and rural officials there are none; in the Karachai province only one of 140 officials has finished the courses; in the Adygei province there are 9 out of 160; in the Kabardin-Balkar province 17 out of 398; in the Khakas province 19 out of 136; in the Komi province 33 out of 437; in Daghestan 72 out of 1,325; in Udmurtia 82 out of 1,245; in the Volga-German Republic 38 out of 830; in the Bashkir Republic 210 out of 4,085; and so forth.

These data confirm how important it is to take careful stock and make good use of the cadres of graduates from special courses; and they also show that nothing is done to attach the trained cadres firmly to consolidate the apparatus of soviets.

On National Soviet Cadres

The basic drawbacks of the courses in local government in the National Republics and Provinces are that they are too short (most of these courses last from 10 to 15 days, or a month), that the students are not well prepared, that not enough of them are indigenous elements or party members, and that they do not assimilate properly the subjects of the courses.

Experience has shown that the courses in local government must be convened for not less than two months. It must be seen to that they are attended by people whose level of pre-training is the same; and the majority of the students must be recruited from indigenous soviet activists whose class-conscious attitude has been tested and who have proved their worth in practical work. So far, for example, the courses have been attended in Karakalpakia only by 13 indigenous students out of a total of 30, in Karelia by 17 out of 40, in Bashkiria by 21 out of 72, in Oirotia by 37 out of 71, in the Mari province by 18 out of 40, in Mordovia by 38 out of 93, in the Crimean Republic by 98 out of 185, and so forth.

If the students have the same standards of literacy and general preliminary training, this will facilitate the assimilation of the subjects; a certain amount of preparation will help them, in particular, to go deeper into the problem of how to instil, in practice, the native tongue into the work of the soviet apparatus, failing which it is unthinkable to base administration upon the indigenous population.

The experience gained in organizing the courses in local government has shown that most serious attention must be paid to such organizational problems as the preparation of suitable premises for the studies and for hostels, the provision of food, the supply of textbooks for the students, the selection of teachers, and so forth. Such preparation will prevent [the tendency] among the students to drift away, which is very high in some Republics and Provinces. . . .

Another means of training and retraining the soviet cadres is by *correspondence courses in local government*, which, however, are unknown in most of the Republics. This is due to the irresponsible approach of the leading officials to the training of cadres and their lack of confidence in the utility of such courses. A resolute struggle must be waged against this opportunist attitude, and the persons who are wrecking the training of cadres must be severely punished.

In conclusion, a few words about *the training of the cadres in the day-to-day practical work in the soviets and executive committees*. The system of training and educating the soviet cadres by means of drawing the broad soviet *aktiv* into the practical work of the soviets is still far from being generally applied. In order to expand this kind of training of the soviet cadres, it is necessary to organize the work of the sections [and] deputies' groups around a real and vital issue, drawing extensively on the initiative and creative possibilities of all the members of the soviet and its sections who are capable of making a contribution to the job; to expand the practice of combining assignments,[1] by giving every holder of more than one office permanent assistance in his work; if necessary to appoint supernumerary instructors of soviets and executive committees and supernumerary inspectors of finance and land agencies, the militia and so forth, entrusting these non-staff officials with concrete and useful work, and helping them to carry it out.

The training and retraining of cadres, the [proper] care of cadres, the promotion and proper employment of people—these are matters of such importance that they cannot be delegated to minor officials. They must always receive personal attention from the chairmen of district executive committees and city soviets, and the heads of the organizational sections of the Central Executive Committees of the National Republics and of the provincial executive committees.

[1] The term applied, *sotssovmestitelstvo*, suggests an interpretation of the practice (which since has been rejected for obvious practical reasons) as a social service rendered by the holder of a plurality of administrative posts (for one salary) as distinct from the ordinary *sovmestitelstvo*: i.e., for example, the habit of doctors to make up for the insufficiency of their salaries by holding more hospital appointments than was good for the patients.—R.S.

DOCUMENT NO. 24

LOOK AFTER THE FULFILMENT OF THE MANDATES FROM THE ELECTORS[1]

by L. RABINKOV

The account-rendering and election campaign of the soviets will start shortly among the millions of working people of the Soviet Union and will sum up the results of the glorious road traversed by the soviets since the last elections. The successful completion of the great undertakings of the First Five-Year-Plan and the fulfilment of the tasks of the Second Five-Year-Plan is the best proof of the work done by the soviets under the leadership of the Communist Party. The successes of the soviets and the successes of the country as a whole have been secured by drawing the broadest masses of the urban and rural workers into the work of the soviets and every sector of socialist construction.

The conditions under the proletarian dictatorship have opened up limitless possibilities for making use of the creative activity of the masses. Vladimir Ilyich has pointed out that 'we have a wonderful means of increasing our state apparatus tenfold, at once and with one stroke, a means which no capitalist state ever had nor could have at its disposal. It is a wonderful thing to draw the workers, to draw the village poor into the day-to-day work of running the state. . . .'

The bourgeois constitutions, as a rule, forbid the electors to give the deputies mandates and instructions of any kind, nor are the deputies allowed to receive them. This is being justified on the grounds that parliamentary deputies are 'the representatives of the nation as a whole', and not of their constituency. But the real purpose is to sever the deputies from the masses, and to turn them into loyal servants of the dominant groups of the bourgeoisie.

The position is quite different under the dictatorship of the proletariat.

The mandates from the Soviet electors (*nakazy*) establish the closest link between the Soviet deputies and the electors. By receiving the electors' mandate the soviets, in the person of the deputies, undertake definite obligations about the fulfilment of which they report

[1] *Revolutsia i Natsionalnosti*, 1934, No. 9 (slightly abridged).

periodically to the electors. The electors, on the other hand, by supervising the fulfilment of their mandates, direct the fire of proletarian self-criticism on the entire work of the soviets, thereby helping to overcome whatever shortcomings are revealed, and to improve the work of the soviets. . . .

During the elections of the soviets in 1931 and their subsequent report-making campaigns, the electors were very active in issuing and amending mandates in various fields of soviet and economic construction.

It is sufficient to mention that in a mere 170 towns and workers' settlements (out of a total of 643) situated in 17 territories, provinces and national autonomous units, approximately 30,000 amendments to the mandate[1] were adopted. Nor were the electors in most cases content with issuing mandates to the deputies. They pledged themselves for their part to fulfil the production tasks, and to improve the work in enterprises and institutions, sovkhozy, kolkhozy and so forth, mobilizing themselves to carry out the tasks set by the party and the government. . . .

A recent check by the All-Union Central Executive Committee on the fulfilment of the electors' mandates has shown that the overwhelming majority of the soviets have ensured the timely fulfilment of the electors' mandates.

Moscow and Leningrad soviets have taken the lead in the fulfilment of mandates and in working with their electors.

The political mandate from the Moscow committee of the party, together with the electors' amendments, became the programme of action of the Moscow soviet and its praesidium. The mandate included every branch of economic and cultural construction and the development of the amenities of Moscow, overlooking none of the problems either great or small. Apart from the mandate to build the Moscow underground railway, to complete the construction of the giants of industry at the appointed time, to organize the building materials industry, to build the Palace of Soviets[2] and so forth, the electors are also issuing mandates to complete temporary con-

---

[1] During the period before the 1936 constitution the party issued at the eve of every election campaign a draft mandate outlining its policies, with some adaptation to local conditions. The adoption of this basic mandate in the election meetings in the factories etc. was a matter of course, corresponding to the unanimous vote for the official candidates which since has become current. In addition, however, amendments concerning local needs and municipal policies were moved: if adopted, they served as directives for the deputies elected in the meetings (cf. S. and B. Webb, *Soviet Communism*, 3rd. ed. pp. 18 and 31.).—R.S.

[2] The repeated inclusion of this project, a final decision on which, in fact, has not been taken up to now, illustrates the propaganda element contained in the *nakazy*, aside with actual tasks of local government.—R.S.

The Fulfilment of the Mandates of the Electors

struction in the shortest possible time, to prohibit the washing of parquet floors, to plant trees in streets and squares, to extend the squares, to pave the streets with asphalt-concrete, to speed up the building of four-axle tramcars, to lay out new tramlines, to install hydrants, to build factory food kitchens, to extend the network of canteens and kiosks, and so on and so forth.

The Moscow soviet, to which the best shock-workers of the city's enterprises were elected, proved to be at the height of its calling.

For instance, the city roads section, in 1932–33, has paved an area of 396 square metres. Of the 100 hydrant geysers installed by the trust *Mosvodoprovod*, 41 geysers have been put up by mandates from the electors. Ninety per cent of the alterations and extensions in the tram routes were carried out by the *Mostramvaitrest* according to the electors' mandates. A number of new tramlines envisaged in the mandates have been opened. . . .[1]

In Leningrad, too, the other large proletarian centre, the work of carrying out the electors' mandates is in very good force. After the Leningrad soviet had been re-elected the 300,000 amendments received from the electors[2] were grouped in 14,616 summary mandates, which included 39,968 points, before they became the basis of the practical work of the soviet. During all these years, the Leningrad soviet has paid the most serious attention to these mandates, ensuring that their fulfilment was continuously checked by deputies' groups and sections of the soviet, and that the latter reported regularly to the electors on the fulfilment of the mandates. The Leningrad soviet has ensured throughout that the electors' mandates are extensively carried out. Thus, in every establishment of the soviet, certain persons were made responsible for the carrying out of the mandates; the members of the deputies' groups for checking and supervising the fulfilment of the mandates had to maintain connections with the electors; several conferences were attended by the managers of departments and trusts of the Leningrad soviet, the persons responsible for carrying out the mandates and the chairman of deputies' groups and sections of the soviet; the work of the institutions, deputies' groups and sections

[1] Rabinkov here enumerates five lines serving villages near Moscow. After, he mentions even the Moscow Underground (the building of which, of course, was in fact a major policy decision on the national level).—R.S.

[2] This enormous figure—one amendment per less than three electors—can hardly express more than notes taken during the discussion meetings. Some obvious demands—such as for better housing—occur in nearly every speech, others—say for the construction of a tramway urgently needed by the workers of some factories—in nearly every speech made in the meetings of the district concerned. 14,600 may roughly correspond to the number of electioning units (many of them smaller enterprises) in a town such as Leningrad.—R.S.

in fulfilling the electors' mandates was inspected for the whole of the city. . . .

Nevertheless the work of the Moscow and Leningrad soviets had several shortcomings. These included insufficient checks by deputies' groups and sections over the fulfilment of mandates, delays, on the part of the deputies' groups, in informing the electors on the results of fulfilling their mandates, and frequently a formal approach by individual organs of the soviets to the fulfilment of electors' mandates. . . .

All these shortcomings were also reflected in the work of several other soviets of the Union. Thus, the Kazan city soviet, when grouping the incoming mandates according to separate fields of work and summarizing the mandates in a pamphlet, has failed to ensure that their fulfilment should be regularly reported. At the same time, a study of the work of the soviet in its various sectors shows that it has done much in carrying out the electors' mandates. By mandate of the electors, 95,950 square metres of new housing sites have been built; a water main with a total length of 6,000 metres and 29 water hydrants have been installed; 12 kilometres of sewers have been laid and put into operation; 2 bath-houses capable of serving 700 people per hour have been built; 3 public laundries have been opened; the rolling stock of the tramlines has been increased (from 69 units in 1931 to 123 units by the beginning of 1934); the motor transport of the city has been increased from 8 units to 33. During the same period, a total area of 8 hectares of gardens and squares have been laid out; the building of a park of culture and rest has been started; a fruit-tree nursery has been established, and the city has been planted with trees. In 1933 alone, as many as 20,000 young seedlings have been planted, and so forth.

By mandate from the electors, the Kazan city soviet has [also] done much in the sphere of cultural development: the number of pupils in the schools of the I and II grades has increased from 20,000 to 36,000 in 1933 and to 44,882 in 1934; the number of children in nurseries and playgrounds has risen from 4,500 to 11,000. Illiteracy has been almost eliminated. The new polyclinic No. 2 with 11 consulting rooms, an out-patients' clinic for venereal diseases, and an institution for addicts to alcohol have been built. Twenty-eight medical centres have been inaugurated in [various] enterprises, and seven nurseries and babies' sanatoria.

Despite [these] great achievements, a check on the work of Kazan city soviet reveals also several defects in the fulfilment of the mandates—superficiality, carelessness and a formal approach. For example: the electors' mandate to repair the bridge on Novo-Gorshechnaya Street is counted as having been carried out, since

The Fulfilment of the Mandates of the Electors

the repair was done twice—yet the bridge is unsuitable for traffic. Although the city soviet has fulfilled the mandate to extend the network of bath-houses, it has failed to ensure the supply of fuel, so that the bath-houses are working irregularly: and there are long queues, uncleanliness and disorder. Although the city soviet has considerably extended the network of public canteens (118,000 lunches per day in a town with 270,000 inhabitants), it has failed to ensure high-quality food or to pay attention to cleanliness in the canteens. While making great efforts to plant trees [in the city], the city soviet has taken no measures to protect them; although extending the housing area, the city soviet has not seen to its maintenance, nor to a minimum check on cleanliness (in the very centre of the city, a certain Batrakov kept a cow in his flat).

Nor has sufficient attention been paid to the fulfilment of the mandates in the Northern Caucasus and the Azov-Black Sea territory. Thus, owing to bad accountancy and weak supervision, the city soviet and the district soviet in Rostov-on-Don have failed to carry out many workers' proposals regarding communal economy, cultural services, amenities of daily life and supplies for the workers. In the Derbent city soviet, in Daghestan, all the amendments to the electors' mandates were simply lost. They were not summarized in a single document, nor did the sections of soviets and the deputies check up on the fulfilment of the mandates.

In Novosibirsk, no systematic efforts are made to fulfil the mandates: the work is done in spurts and left incomplete. In 1932, the city soviet fixed a month for supervising the fulfilment of the mandates, and drew up to 15,000 people into the work. But the results of that supervision month were neither discussed by the city soviet nor reflected in its work. This illustrates a purely formal and bureaucratic approach to such a highly important field of activity of the organs of the proletarian dictatorship.

A check on the fulfilment of the mandates, undertaken by the All-Union Central Executive Committee, makes it possible to illustrate this work of the soviets by means of the figures in the table at the top of the next page.

The figures below show that, in spite of poor accountancy,[1] fulfilment of mandates in almost all the national autonomous units has been on a high level, and that basically most of the soviets are waging an active struggle for the fulfilment of the electors' mandates.

---

[1] Rabinkov fails to define proper accounting, and even to discuss the basic problem of statistics in which a major municipal undertaking (possibly not fulfilled) may appear as a unit alongside with the demand for the repair of a definite house, and the likely consequences of insisting on high 'fulfilment figures'.—R.S.

The Industrial and Cultural Revolution

Data for the Second Half of 1932

Autonomous Soviet Socialist Republics and Autonomous Provinces	Village soviets			City soviets		
	No. of village soviets	Mdts. given	Mdts. carried out	No. of city soviets	Mdts. given	Mdts. carried out
Bashkir ASSR	80	270	256	2	99	6
Buryat-Mongolian ASSR	86	159	97	2	no information	79
Karelian ASSR	178	91	79	4	131	80
Kirghiz ASSR	58	151	85	9	88	63
Volga-German ASSR	204	209	170	2	76	47
Tatar ASSR	1,426	2,756	1,993	17	1,183	733
Chuvash ASSR	618	680	623	4	20	15
Komi Autonomous Prov.	101	88	64	1	169	70
Kabardino-Balkar A.P.	96	66	48	1	31	17
Udmurt A.P.	255	128	85	3	131	51

The fulfilment of the electors' mandates is closely connected with the accountability of the soviet deputies before the electors. . . .

. . . The activity of the electors at account-rendering meetings of the soviets can be illustrated by the following example: in 101 city soviets of the RSFSR, in the first half of 1933, the account-rendering meetings were attended by 422,000 people out of a total of 647,000 electors, i.e. 65·3 per cent, and in some territories the attendance of the electors rose to 75·3 per cent.

Nevertheless it happened in several territories and provinces that certain soviets for a considerable time failed to render account to the electors. Such soviets are marked by the presence of many passive deputies and a careless attitude to the electors' mandates.

In the current year, the soviets are to be re-elected. This requires a great deal of preparatory work. The entire work of the soviets before the elections must be based on 100 per cent fulfilment of the electors' mandates and a tightening of the soviets' links with the electors.

Prior to the elections, it is necessary to make serious efforts in preparing the electors' mandates by drawing on the experience gained in the account-rendering campaign.

The practical experience of preceding elections revealed several shortcomings in the preparation of the electors' mandates. Obviously unrealizable amendments to the basic mandate were often accepted, without taking account of the material possibilities, the dates of

The Fulfilment of the Mandates of the Electors

fulfilment and so forth. The result, in the very first period of the work of the soviets, was a whole category of unfulfilled mandates.

Another very serious omission was not to systematize the mandates received, leaving them on separate sheets of paper, i.e. in the form in which they had come in from the electors. This made for an irresponsible attitude in carrying out the mandates, a considerable proportion of which were lost, and the electors were unable to supervise their fulfilment.

Yet another grave feature is the irresponsibility noticeable in some soviets on the occasion of the distribution of the incoming mandates among the departments and institutions, and the simultaneous selection of the people responsible for carrying out the mandates. In these soviets, the mandates were not being tackled until the eve of the account-rendering campaigns, and it is evident that most of them remained unfulfilled.

All these errors must be removed from the present account-rendering and election campaign, and it should be seen to that the electors' mandates are prepared and checked in an exemplary manner.

DOCUMENT NO. 25

COMPLAINTS FROM THE WORKING PEOPLE WARN US OF WEAKNESSES IN THE WORK OF THE SOVIETS[1]

by T. KRUGLOV

(Based on materials from the Secretariat of the Chairman of the All-Russian CEC and the CEC of the USSR)

M. I. Kalinin's 'Reception Room' (Secretariat) has existed for fifteen years.

During these fifteen years it has earned for itself unlimited authority and the affection of millions of workers. One might say with certainty that there is no corner in the Soviet Union where people do not know of 'Kalinin's Reception Room' and do not approach it with every kind of sore problem. Apart from receiving tens of thousands of applications in the course of a year, it is visited by tens of thousands of visitors from every part of the Soviet Union who wish to call personally on the Head of the Union, Mikhail Ivanovich Kalinin. Only a few days ago a group of nationals arrived from the Northern Caucasus, in order to report personally to Mikhail Ivanovich on their achievements in kolkhoz construction in the National Provinces.

The least numerous of the visitors are those reporting victories, for such reports can be easily sent by post. The personal approach to [Kalinin] amounts mostly to complaints about shortcomings in the work of the local soviet apparatus, about excesses in certain economic and political campaigns, and about administrative arbitrariness of individual zealous administrators and so forth.

The tens of thousands of applications, appeals and complaints which passed through the Reception Room last year and the almost identical number of applications in the current year provide most valuable evidence of our achievements and shortcomings. By means of these human documents it is possible to reveal almost without fail the weak sectors of our soviet work, and to ascertain where the soviet apparatus is working well and where it is working badly,

[1] *Revolutsia i Nationalnosti*, 1934, No. 11 (slightly abridged).

Complaints from the Working People

where the staff of leading officials is good and where it is not. They are also documents reflecting, like a peculiar mirror, the practical work of socialist construction in the most diverse sectors. That is why it is a highly important business for the soviets and executive committees to study attentively, and to deal quickly with, the applications and complaints coming in from the population.

A particularly characteristic feature of the present period of socialist construction is the abundance of complaints about expulsion from the kolkhozy. This shows how great is the people's preference for the kolkhoz system. Those wrongly expelled (which unfortunately is not an infrequent occurrence) urgently seek the protection of every grade of authority; they often write to the Reception Room that, unless they *are restored to the kolkhoz where they had worked conscientiously for many years, they will be faced with a complete catastrophe.*

When dealing with complaints, every one of them without exception requires a critical approach; not to observe this [rule] means to commit a serious mistake. At the same time, however, every complaint must be handled with special care.

Unfortunately, the complaints do not always and everywhere receive such attention. There are many shortcomings in the work of some soviet organs, for example, in the Voronezh and Udmurt provinces, the Bashkir Republic, the Mordvin and Mari provinces and several districts of the Crimea. During the last six or seven months of 1934 the influx of complaints from the Autonomous Republics and Provinces has much increased. A thorough study of these complaints shows that the local soviet apparatus in several National Republics has cadres whose political training is very weak. The result is that the examination of complaints is affected by intolerable red tape. Complaints remain without attention for a year or a year and a half, during which time the aggrieved person is subjected (sometimes quite wrongfully) to repressive measures.

At the present time, the basic defect in the work of the district executive committees of the national autonomous units, when dealing with complaints, lies in their utterly uncritical approach to the materials drawn up by the village soviets, which often write their documents from oral statements of individual citizens; classifications of persons according to their economic status are deliberately misleading. As a result of such an inhuman and formal attitude, repression falls on households of working peasants or of meritorious partisans and Red Army men—veterans of the civil war and so forth.

Here are several characteristic cases.

The Industrial and Cultural Revolution

M. E. Komlev (Zhai-Gurta village of the Seltin district in Udmurt province) was expelled from the kolkhoz and dispossessed in 1933 because his father had a small handicraft brickworks. But the plaintiff himself had served as a volunteer in the Red Army and actively taken part in the civil war. The district public attorney protested against the illegal repressions to which the man was subjected; the district executive committee did not uphold the protest. M. I. Kalinin proposed that the plaintiff should be restored to the kolkhoz and that all repressive measures against him should be cancelled.

V. N. Potapov (of the Lower-Mukhtan village soviet in the same district) was also expelled from the kolkhoz on the basis of the classification of his father's household, although he and his father had divided their property back in 1925. The plaintiff had fought in the civil war and worked for several years in elective posts in his village. The Secretariat proposed that Potapov should be restored to the kolkhoz.

D. L. Zagrebin (Debess district in the same province) was also expelled on the basis of the classification of his father's household, but he himself is a former Red Army man. Owing to the red tape prevailing among the local soviet and in the public attorney's office, the case dragged on for one year and a half, and it was only owing to the intervention of the Secretariat that Zagrebin was restored to the kolkhoz.

Hundreds of complaints about wrongful dispossession and expulsion from the kolkhozy are coming from the Udmurt province. The greatest sinners in this matter are the Seltin, Yukamen, Alnash, Yakshir-Bodyin and Vavozh districts. In the course of six months in 1934, the Reception Room received more than 500 complaints from Udmurtia, compared to 700 complaints from the entire Gorki territory (of which Udmurtia is a part). This abundance of complaints from Udmurtia reveals the bad state of its soviet apparatus and its intolerable attitude to the complaints from the workers.

In some districts of Bashkiria, too, such as the Sterlitamak, Bizhbuliak and Yanaul districts the state of affairs is bad. This year the kolkhoz section of the Reception Room received about 200 complaints (which is considerably less than last year). The brigade of the *Krestyanskaya Gazeta* (peasant newspaper) which investigated on the spot the expulsions from kolkhozy in Bashkiria has established the fact of mass infringements. [There follows an enumeration of characteristic examples of wrongful expulsion from the kolkhozy.]

It is the intention of M. I. Kalinin's Reception Room in the near

Complaints from the Working People

future to send several officials to the localities, in order to bring order into the work of dealing with complaints. . . .

. . . There are also a great many districts in the Mari province where not enough importance is attached to a proper analysis of the complaints. According to materials from the Secretariat, the Gorno-Mari district is considered as one of the worst, for the complaints lodged here come up against red tape and a careless and bureaucratic attitude to the needs of the working people.

Compared to the other Republics and Provinces, few complaints came from Kirghizia this year. This is, of course, no reason to assert that the work of its soviet apparatus is ideal and that the examination of complaints on the spot is perfect. The 100 complaints which arrived at the Reception Room from Kirghizia show that some links of the apparatus are dealing with complaints in a formal way.

The small number of complaints from Kirghizia and the Kalmyk province is due to a certain dispersal of the population and to incomplete postal communications in some places. The central authorities are receiving many complaints from the Crimea and Tataria. In the course of seven months in 1934, the Reception Room had about 600 complaints from the Crimea and approximately 500 from Tataria. . . . The Karasubazar district alone sent 20 per cent of the complaints which M. I. Kalinin's Reception Room received from the Crimea. This proves that the soviet apparatus of that district is obviously in a bad state, and that not only the village soviets are utterly indifferent to the complaints, but also the District Executive Committee itself. Again and again the soviets in that district were giving the peasant plaintiffs fictitious, utterly unjustifiable and even fantastic classifications (such as ownership of 400 hectares of land, or of 200–300 head of cattle, employment of 20 farm labourers and so forth). [But] the check-ups revealed that the households were always those of working peasants, and that not even the grandfathers and great-grandfathers of the plaintiffs had ever owned such an amount of land or cattle.

Only the most irresponsible administrator can permit himself such an absurd licence in giving the higher-ranking organs completely nonsensical information about the plaintiff.

It should be pointed out that the Crimean Central Executive Committee does not struggle hard enough against this kind of irresponsibility on the part of the local soviet officials. In spite of many letters from the Secretariat of the Chairman of the All-Russian Central Executive Committee, nothing decisive was done in the Karasubazar and other districts in order to regularize the handling of the complaints. . . .

The Industrial and Cultural Revolution

In the Shugar district (Tataria), both in 1933 and 1934, there were cases of administrative over-zeal in the confiscation of property and sowings affecting masses of people. These repressive measures were a violation of the direct instructions from the government and the party. The work of mass enlightenment was often replaced here by the bare rule of administrative orders. . . .

PART V

Later Developments in Soviet Nationalities Policies

DOCUMENT NO. 26

EXCERPTS FROM: ADMINISTRATIVE REGIONALIZATION OF THE USSR COMPLETED[1]

by A. KURSKI

... In accordance with the articles 13 and 22 of the Stalin Constitution, the Azerbaidjan, Georgian, Armenian, Kazakh and Kirghiz Republics are transformed into Union Republics, and the Kabardino-Balkar, the North Ossetian, the Chechen-Ingush, Mari and Komi provinces into Autonomous Republics. At the same time the Constitution established a stable system dividing the USSR into territories and provinces.

These changes in the territorial demarcation of the Soviet Union, which complete the gigantic transformation of the country inaugurated by the great Socialist Revolution in the USSR, are the result of the consistent application of the Leninist-Stalinist national policy, the tremendous growth of our national economy, and the new socialist distribution of productive forces. They are the guarantee of a further increase in the prosperity of the National Republics and Provinces of the Soviet Union.

Planned economy makes it possible to demarcate the country in accordance with the general tasks of the development of national economy and the natural resources and peculiar development of the individual districts, whilst the territorial division of administration in bourgeois countries serves primarily the purpose of police regulation. This was the reason why the division of pre-revolutionary Russia into provinces (*Gubernii*) and districts (*uyezdy*), as introduced by Catherine II, had continued without change for over 140 years. The stability of the administrative-territorial division of Tsarist Russia was at the same time the consequence of the general economic backwardness of the country and its extremely slow economic development.

By dividing and estranging the nationalities, the administrative division of Tsarist Russia was an instrument of national oppression. Thus before the Revolution the territory of the Ukrainian SSR was divided into 13 provinces, that of the Kazakh SSR into 11, of the Georgian SSR into 5, and so forth.

[1] *Planovoye Khozyaistvo*, 1936, No. 11.

Later Developments in Soviet Nationalities Policies

The regional demarcation (*raionirovaniye*) of the USSR represents a division at one and the same time on economic and on administrative territorial lines. This follows wholly from the nature of the socialist state which accomplishes the unity of political and economic leadership. The theses of the report of the All-Russian Central Executive Committee to the Ninth All-Russian Congress of Soviets (1921) defined the basic principles of the regional demarcation in the following way: 'Regional demarcation must be based on the economic principle. A region is a particular territory of the country, which is economically as coherent as possible, and which—by a combination of natural peculiarities, cultural heritage and the preparedness of the population for productive work—is one of the links in the common chain of the national economy.'

By contrast to the bourgeois method of regional demarcation, which arose from a spontaneous specialization of the territories, the method of socialist demarcation is based on the guiding role of planning, in accordance with which new economic regions are set up. The demarcation of economic regions on the basis of specialization is determined not only by their present economic geography, but first and foremost by their potential capacities in relation to the general tasks of developing the national economy of the USSR.

The setting up of economic regions of the USSR is part of the national policy of the party and the government.

'Already at the very inception of the idea of regional demarcation of the Union, it was clear that the national principle (the principle of the self-determination of the nationalities in the USSR) and the principle of regional demarcation on economic lines are mutually complementary: the division of big national units such as the RSFSR into economic regions, and the inclusion of smaller national autonomous units retaining all their prerogatives and peculiarities, are a complete safeguard both of national self-determination and of the requirements of planning.'[1]

... The elimination of obsolete links in the administrative division, the breaking up of territories and provinces into smaller units, and the formation of new districts, bring closer contact between the socialist state apparatus and the workers, and develop democracy. At the same time, the demarcation of the country is one of the most important premises for economic planning. The XVth Party Congress, in its instructions on drafting the First Five-Year Plan, pointed out the necessity of completing the demarcation of the country 'for the purpose of placing the country's economic life, to the largest possible extent, under the planning authority.' The

[1] *The First Five-Year Plan* [Russian edition], Vol. III, p. 11.

Administrative Regionalization of the USSR Completed

demarcation of territorial units (republics, territories and provinces), each of which represents a single administrative and economic entity and fulfils a definite function in the all-Union division of labour, makes it possible to co-ordinate the tasks allocated to the branches of the all-Union economy, and to establish the closest links between the industries and enterprises of a Union scale with the local economy. The formation of economic regions as supporting bases of planning was necessary for devising a single economic plan at the regional level. This made it possible to plan more completely and thoroughly the economy of the Soviet Union as a whole and of each region in particular, and to draw the broad working masses into the planning process. . . .

. . . .

The starting point of the new demarcation of the country was the formation of National Republics and Provinces inaugurated soon after the October Revolution. 'The Declaration of the Rights of the Peoples of Russia', signed by Lenin and Stalin in November 1917, proclaimed 'the right of the peoples of Russia to free self-determination, including [the right of] secession and independent statehood.' The setting up of Union and Autonomous Republics and Provinces began during the civil war. The Belorussian and Ukrainian Soviet Republics were formed in 1919. Hand in hand with the liberation of territories of Soviet Russia from the White Guards and interventionists went the establishment of the Soviet Republics of Central Asia and Transcaucasia.

In his letters 'To the Workers and Peasants of the Ukraine on the Occasion of the Victories over Denikin', 'To the Communist Comrades of Turkestan', 'To the Communist Comrades of Azerbaidjan, Georgia, Armenia, Daghestan and the Gorskaya Republic', and several other documents, Lenin demanded maximum care for the young National Republics and the exercise of the greatest patience and caution in creating a Union of nations.

On the initiative of Lenin and Stalin, the federation of Transcaucasian Republics came into being in March 1922, displaying 'a model of peace among nations never experienced under capitalism and impossible under the bourgeois regime' (Lenin).

The process of the self-determination and unification of the peoples of Soviet Russia led to the establishment, at the end of 1922, of the Union of Soviet Socialist Republics, representing 'the concluding stage in the development of forms of co-operation which, in this case, assumed the character of a military, economic and political unification of the peoples into a single multi-national Soviet state.'[1]

The national structure of our country, as it emerged at the beginning of the restoration period, was confirmed in the Constitution of the RSFSR adopted by the Fifth All-Russian Congress of Soviets and thereafter in the Constitution of the USSR as confirmed by the Second All-Union Congress of Soviets, which established the voluntary unification of four Soviet Republics, the Russian Socialist Federated Republic, the Ukrainian Soviet Socialist Republic, the Belorussian Soviet Socialist Republic and the Transcaucasian Socialist Federation of Soviet Republics. The national demarcation in Central Asia took place at the end of 1924 when two new Union Republics were organized, the Uzbek and Turkmenian Soviet Socialist Republics. They were admitted to the Soviet Union at the Third All-Union Congress of Soviets in 1925.

This demarcation, as Comrade Stalin has stated, manifested

'the deepest aspirations of the masses of the people of Turkmenia and Uzbekistan for their own organs of power which are close and intelligible to them. In the pre-revolutionary period, these two countries were torn to shreds by their division into various khanates and states, which provided a convenient field for exploiting machinations of the 'powers that were'. Now the moment has come to reunite these tattered shreds into independent states, in order to bring the working masses of Uzbekistan and Turkmenia close to, and knit them together with, the organs of power. To demarcate Turkmenia means, above all, to reunite the tattered parts of these countries into independent states. That these states later desired to join the Soviet Union as equal members goes to prove that the Bolsheviks have found the key to the deepest aspirations of the popular masses in the East, and that the Soviet Union is the only voluntary union of the working masses of various nationalities in the world. In order to reunite Poland, the bourgeoisie required a number of wars. In order to reunite Turkmenia and Uzbekistan the communists required but a few months of explanatory propaganda.'[2]

In 1929, the Tadjik Republic was detached from the Uzbek Republic. Its entry into the Soviet Union as the seventh Union Republic completed the national demarcation of the peoples of Central Asia. These were the basic stages in the process of forming the national structure of the USSR.

The formation of the National Republics and Provinces of the Soviet Union was paralleled by the simultaneous process of delimitating the economic districts of the country.

[1] Resolution of the XIIth Party Congress on the report by Comrade Stalin.
[2] Stalin, 'On the Political Tasks of the University of the Peoples of the East', *Problems of Leninism*, 9th [Russian edition], p. 136.

Administrative Regionalization of the USSR Completed

The Seventh Congress of Soviets, convened in December 1919, instructed the All-Russian Central Executive Committee 'to work out in practice the question of a new administrative division of the RSFSR.' The elaboration of the principles of regional demarcation and the delimitation of the units of economic administration started in February 1920 with the organization of the administrative commission attached to the Praesidium of the All-Russian Central Executive Committee.

The State Electrification Plan (GOELRO) marks a most important stage in the development of economic demarcation. This first tentative plan for restoring and reconstructing the national economy on the most up-to-date technical basis laid the foundations for the future regional demarcation of the country. 'The re-appraisal of the interrelations of the basic branches of production', says the introduction to the GOELRO plan, 'is closely linked with the geographical redistribution of the industrial areas themselves. It is in accordance with the natural resources of those areas and with the incipient regime of a planned socialist economy that the RSFSR must be subdivided into new economic regions, which will be the forerunners of the future flourishing communes of the fully developed system of liberated labour.'

The GOELRO plan envisaged eight economic regions (the Northern, Central Industrial, Southern, Volga, Urals, West Siberian, Caucasian and Turkestan). It thereby advanced for the first time the idea of a genuine demarcation on economic lines taking for a starting point the planned specialization of the districts of the country in conformity with the new distribution of industry as the leading side of the national economy. The GOELRO plan was the first to draw the new regional outlines, making rational use of the immense natural resources of the country.

The Eighth Congress of Soviets [1920], which approved the elaboration of the State Electrification Plan 'as the first step in the great economic undertaking', emphasized the need 'to speed up the new delimitation of the RSFSR into units of economic administration primarily on the basis of economic connection.'

The principles of district demarcation on economic lines drafted by the administrative commission of the All-Russian Central Executive Committee were confirmed at the second session of the VIIIth Convention of the All-Russian Central Executive Committee (March 1921). According to these principles, the introduction of the new administrative and economic demarcation must not be deferred, as the existing administrative division no longer corresponded to the new political and economic requirements. It was proposed to adjust the new demarcation to the conditions of the transition period in conformity with the newly emerging economic regions which had not yet taken definite shape.

Thereafter the Gosplan [State Planning Commission] of the RSFSR, established in 1921, became the centre for working out the problems of demarcation. Gosplan, linking work on the principles of demarcation with planning, proposed that the delimitation of an economic region be governed by the plan of its economic development.

Gosplan envisaged the formation of twelve regions in European Russia: the North-Western, North-Eastern, Eastern, Central-Industrial, Vyatka-Vetluga, Ural, Central Black Earth, Central Volga, Lower Volga, South-Western, Southern Mining and the Caucasian.

In Asiatic Russia the formation of nine regions was envisaged: the Western Siberian, Kuznetsk-Altai, Yenissei, Lena-Angara, Yakutian, Far Eastern, West Kirghizian, East Kirghizian and Central Asiatic.[1]

In making these suggestions, Gosplan acted upon the principle that, given correct demarcation, the national autonomous units and National Republics would not only not lose the rights granted to them, but would acquire a firm basis for their development.

The principles of economic demarcation elaborated by GOELRO and carried further in the draft of Gosplan were submitted for confirmation to the XIIth Party Congress [1923]. The Congress, in its resolution, 'recognizes the former administrative economic division of the Republic as no longer conforming to the new political and economic requirements of the country, but considers at the same time that the introduction of a new division on lines of economic administration requires a careful approach and much time for its final accomplishment.' The Congress instructed the Central Committee of the party to see to the introduction of more planning into the work of changing the administrative and economic division of the Republic, and to consider the project of a division of the economic administration, submitted by Gosplan and the administrative commission of the Praesidium of the All-Russian Central Executive Committee, only as the preliminary working draft requiring additional checks and amplification on the basis of practical experience. The Congress desired to introduce the new plan of economic administrative division by way of experiment in the Urals and the North Caucasus.

The demarcation of the Ural region was completed by the end of

[1] I. G. Alexandrov, *The Foundations of the Economic Demarcation of the Regions of the USSR* [in Russian], Moscow, 1924.

Administrative Regionalization of the USSR Completed

1923. The first North Caucasian Territorial Congress was held in January 1925. The district demarcation of Siberia was accomplished at the end of 1925 and of the Far Eastern territory at the beginning of 1926. District demarcation was carried out simultaneously also in the Ukraine, the Belorussian Soviet Socialist Republic, the Northern Province and Central Asia.

The original scheme of demarcation underwent several changes in the process of application. These changes were, in the first place, in the direction of combining agricultural and industrial regions. Thus, the agricultural areas of the West Siberian territory (the Ishim and Tobolsk counties) were attached to the industrial Urals, while the industrial Kuznetsk-Altai region and a part of the Lena-Angar region as well as the agricultural areas of the West Siberian and Yenissei regions were included in the Siberian territory. A part of the southern mining district and the northern part of the Caucasian district were included in the North Caucasian territory.

In the second place, changes were made for the purpose of better co-ordination between the economic regions and the national structure of the country. For example, the Karelian Autonomous Soviet Socalist Republic, which had come into being in July 1923, was excluded from the North-Western Province originally envisaged by Gosplan and organized as a separate economic region; the Bashkir Autonomous Soviet Socialist Republic, previously included in the Ural province, was also made into an independent region. In place of the Caucasian region, the North Caucasian territory was set up at the beginning of 1924, and so forth.

Economic demarcation was a most important factor in accelerating the economic restoration of the country. An appraisal of the experience of demarcation, which was carried out by the Workers' and Peasants' Inspectorate in 1926, showed that the economic and cultural development of the demarcated provinces had in some cases overtaken the average rate of development in the RSFSR and USSR. The organization of planning, too, improved in the demarcated regions.[1]

Basically the new system of the administrative-territorial arrangement of the country was completed by the beginning of the First Five-Year Plan.

The establishment of economic regions had an immense influence on the development of economic planning by making it possible to plan the national economy at the regional level. 'It became possible

[1] Resolution of the Council of People's Commissars of the RSFSR on the Report of the Workers' and Peasants' Inspectorate on the Investigations into the Results of Regional Demarcation in the Urals and the North Caucasus.

for Soviet planning to operate at the regional level, and this coincided in time with the completion of the basic features of the division of the Union into economic regions.'[1]

The development of national economy, the consolidation of districts on the level of local government,[2] the new tasks facing the districts—all this made it necessary to replace the triple system of administrative-territorial division by a dual system, and to eliminate one of the links of the administrative-territorial division, i.e. the counties.

'The expansion of the volosts and their transformation into districts, the abolition of the gubernias and their transformation into smaller units (counties), and finally the creation of provinces (*oblasti*) as direct points of support for the Central Committee,' said Comrade Stalin at the XVIth Party Congress, 'such is the general picture of demarcation. The purpose of demarcation is to bring the party and soviet apparatus and the economic and co-operative apparatus close to the district and the village, in order to be able to solve in good time the urgent problems of agriculture, of reconstructing and raising the level of agriculture. In this sense, I repeat, demarcation has given an immense advantage to our entire construction.

'But, has everything been done to bring the apparatus really and genuinely close to the districts and villages? No, not everything.... In order to achieve this, two things at least must be done: (1) it is necessary to abolish the counties, which are becoming an unnecessary intermediate link between the province and the district, and to strengthen with the county officials thus released the district organization; (2) to link the district organizations directly with the provincial or territorial Communist Party Committee or the Central Committee of a national Communist Party. This would complete the business of demarcation and the task of bringing the apparatus close to the districts and villages.'[3]

In summing up the outcome of the organizational reconstruction of the organs of the proletarian dictatorship in conformity with the new tasks of the reconstruction period, the XVIIth Party Congress [1934] noted the importance of 'the further development of regional demarcation—the abolition of the counties, the establishment of

---

[1] *The First Five-Year Plan*, Vol. III, p. 11.
[2] Literally 'low-level districts'. The terminology of this article, as of others dealing with the subject, is confused by the application of the word *Raion*, which at this place and in current administrative practice denotes the small unit between province and locality (usually below the size of a British county) for the description of large economic regions, comprising a plurality of provinces and of, or above, the size of a major European country. Historically, the confusion originated from the fact that large-scale regionalization, as described in this article, coincided with the replacement of the small administrative districts of the Tsarist time (*uyezdy*) by large ones (*raiony*).—R.S.
[3] Stalin, 'Political Report of the Central Committee to the XVIth Congress', *Problems of Leninism*, 10th [Russian] edition, pp. 406–7.

new districts and the organization of the political sections of the MTS and state farms which brought the leaders close to the village and kolkhoz and has corrected the worst defects of the work in the village; the organization of provinces in the Ukraine, the division of some provinces and territories into smaller units, and so forth.'

The improved distribution of the productive forces, achieved by the beginning of the Second Five-Year Plan, brought about radical changes in the character of the provinces of the USSR, so that 'the old division of our provinces into industrial and agricultural ones has already been outlived' (Stalin). The immense new complexity of the regions as economic organisms, the establishment of links within and between regions, and the very substantial tasks set before the economics regions by the Second Five-Year Plan have led to the formation of new administrative-territorial units by further economic demarcation. In 1932, provinces were set up in the Ukraine, Kazakhstan and in several territories. At the beginning of 1934 many economic regions were broken up into smaller units.

The growth of the second metallurgical base,[1] the construction of very great enterprises in the Sverdlovsk, Chelyabinsk and adjacent areas made it necessary to divide the Ural province into the Sverdlovsk and Chelyabinsk provinces. The division of the North Caucasian territory into the North Caucasian and Azov-Black Sea territories was necessitated by the development of the industry of the territory, and by the need to bring about a further improvement of its agriculture and an intensive development of the economy and culture of its national units.

The creation of large industrial centres in Saratov, Stalingrad and Astrakhan, accompanied by the general economic development of the Lower Volga territory [which included these towns], led to its division into two independent territories. The expansion of many new branches of heavy industry, the development of the food industry and of large-scale mechanized agriculture in the Central Black Earth region led to the establishment there of the Voronezh and Kursk provinces. The centres of the new territories and provinces are the industrial key-points which have emerged as the result of the more even distribution of industry in the USSR.

The continued development of the Uzbek, Turkmenian and Tadjik Republics, and the new tasks allocated to them under the Second Five-Year Plan, required that the Central Committee of the CPSU(B) and the Union Government should exercise direct leadership over the Central Asiatic Republics. The Central Asian Bureau

[1] I.e. of the Ural-Kuznetsk combine, as distinct from Russia's traditional metallurgical base in the Southern Ukraine.—R.S.

of the CC of the CPSU(B), the Central Asiatic Economic Council and other economic organizations common to the Central Asiatic Republics were abolished in 1934.

The division of economic regions into smaller units was an integral part of the general reconstruction of the organs of Soviet and economic administration and was, at the same time, a result of the broad process of dividing the local districts on the basis of the MTS.

'The successes achieved in the socialist reconstruction of agriculture, the consolidation of the kolkhozy, the emergence of the kolkhoz *aktiv* and of a firm foundation for the party organization in the village, the improvement in the work of the district committees of the party, made it necessary to complete the district demarcation which was started with the abolition of the counties, and to close the gap between the organs of administration and the village.'[1]

The general results of demarcation in the USSR can be seen from the following table:

Number of Units of Territorial Administration

State formations and administrative units	In the Russian Empire as contained in the present frontiers of the USSR	1/I 1923	1/I 1930	1/I 1933	1/VII 1936	Under the [Dec.1936] constitution
Union Republics	—	4	7	7	7	11
Basic Republics of Transcaucasia	—	3	3	3	3	—
Autonomous Republics	—	10	15	16	19	22
Autonomous Provinces	—	16	17	17	14	9
Territories (*kraya*) and provinces (*oblasti*)	—	—	13	21	31	37
Provinces of the Far Eastern territory and Kazakhstan	—	—	—	10	14	8
Counties (*okruga*)	—	—	228	15	38	38
Districts (*raiony*)	—	—	2,917	2,451	3,279	3,279
Gubernias	74	75	—	—	—	—
Uyezdy	705	766	26	—	—	—
Volosts	13,919	13,659	245	—	—	—

[1] 'On the Political Sections in Agriculture', Resolution of the CC of the CPSU(B) of November 28, 1934.

Administrative Regionalization of the USSR Completed

The new Stalin constitution of the USSR completes and confirms by legislation the new system of administrative territorial division of the Soviet Union, providing for further prosperity of the socialist economy. 'There are people in the USSR', said Comrade Stalin at the Eighteenth All-Union Congress of Soviets [1936], 'whose untiring eagerness to refashion territories and provinces introduces confusion and uncertainty into the work. The draft Constitution puts a bridle on them. And this is all to the good because, in this respect as in many others, we need an atmosphere of certainty, stability and clarity.'[1]

. . . .

... An integral part of the process of demarcation is the formation of national territorial units which make it possible for the nationalities of the USSR to overcome their economic and cultural backwardness.

The new prosperity of the National Republics is strikingly illustrated by the data shown on page 260 on the development of industry in the Union Republics.

The high rates of industrial development in the Republics of the formerly oppressed nationalities which have outstripped the rates of development in the old industrial districts, have produced radical changes in the economic and industrial structure of the National Republics. These have now become complex economic aggregates. Side by side with the cultivation of valuable technical crops and cattle-breeding, coal, metals, chemicals and electric power are acquiring increasing importance in the economy of these Republics. The construction of enterprises processing agricultural raw materials is expanding. Engineering industries, which under capitalism are the privilege of the metropolitan centres, are coming into being.

The peculiarity of the industrial development in the national areas lies in the fact that the creation of large-scale and technically up-to-date industry there has by-passed the intermediate stages of development. The process of building up the industries and assimilating the new enterprises has had an immense influence on the entire economy of the national areas. The greater evenness in the distribution of industry in the USSR has provided the premise for eliminating the economic inequality among its nationalities. . . .

---

[1] Notwithstanding this intention, which was expressed in the enumeration of the major territorial units in the 1936 constitution, redivision of territories and provinces (which *post factum* is legalized by appropriate amendments to the constitution) has continued up to the present day.—R.S.

Later Developments in Soviet Nationalities Policies

Large-scale Industry in the Union Republics
(in million rubles at 1926–27 prices)[1]

Union Republics	1913	1924	1935	1935 as a % of 1913	The proportion of the output of large-scale industry[2] in the output of industry as a whole in 1935 (in %)
USSR	10,251	4,660	59,345	578·9	93·1
RSFSR	750·0	3,309·0	42,904·9	572·0	93·7
Ukrainian SSR	2,125·3	803·9	11,287·4	531·0	92·3
Belorussian SSR	89·0	38·0	1,084·8	12·2 times	86·7
Azerbaidjan SSR	378·0	No inf.	1,667·1	441·0	96·9
Georgian SSR	43·0	26·0	640·9	14·9 times	86·9
Armenian SSR	14·4	No inf.	142·9	992·3	80·2
Turkmenian SSR	20·9	16·3	171·1	818·6	88·5
Uzbek SSR	268·8	106·8	837·5	311·5	90·5
Tadjik SSR	No inf.	No inf.	76·3	—	81·5
Kazakh SSR	50·9	19·5	432·4	849·5	80·9
Kirghiz SSR	1·2	1·7	99·8	83·2 times	80·1

[1] According to the data of the Central Statistical Administration (author's note).

In a critical evaluation of this and similar tables published by Soviet authors, readers should not pay undue attention to the pretended precision, including the use of decimals in output proportions calculated on a basis in itself problematic. First, enormous percentages of increase follow even from moderate investments if the starting point was nearly zero; the most that can be concluded from increases such as noted for Belorussia, Georgia and Kirghizia is the fact that attention was devoted to territories the industrial development of which was formerly neglected. Secondly, the calculation of output in so-called 1926–27 prices, which was used all the time (it was abolished only in 1951, after repeated criticism of that index inside and outside the USSR), suffers from an over-weighting of products introduced after that standard year. As branches of production new to the USSR were unlikely to be started in backward regions with a little skilled working-class, this source of error rather affects the RSFSR and possibly the Ukraine, and leads to an underestimate of the proportional development of National Republics with old-established industries. The output of Uzbekistan textiles or of Azerbaidjan oil may, indeed, have increased to an extent as indicated in the tables; it does in no way follow that the progress of these Republics was below the Union average, if the latter were calculated according to a standard less exposed to fallacies than the '1926–27 prices'. The use of the latter at an occasion like the present one, where it results in minimizing the desired propagandist effect, illustrates the error of those Western critics who have explained the use of that index by propagandist interests (there are other and nearer explanations, in particular: the interest of Soviet managers in claiming fulfilment and over fulfilment of their plans, and of Soviet planners in not provoking a reluctance of managers to start new branches of production).

Yet Kurski's and similar authors' bona fides renders their statistics not more reliable a picture of the relative progress of the diverse Union Republics. The most that can be said is that progress in all the territories with fairly developed industries was fairly proportional, but that particular efforts were made to start new industries in territories where, before, there had been none.—R.S.

[2] I.e. enterprises employing over 30 workers without power or over 16 with power.—R.S.

DOCUMENT NO. 27

LAND NATIONALIZATION IN THE NEW WESTERN REPUBLICS AND PROVINCES[1]

(Survey)

by PROFESSOR P. TOLSTOI

I

The first legislative acts laying the foundations of the new regime in the territory of Western Ukraine and Western Belorussia, Bessarabia, Northern Bukovina, Estonia, Latvia and Lithuania comprised the *Laws on Land Nationalization*.

In Western Ukraine and Western Belorussia land nationalization was proclaimed in Lvov and Belostok by the National Assemblies freely elected on the basis of the universal, equal, direct and secret ballot, immediately after the military defeat and the disintegration of the Polish state. The declarations 'on the confiscation of the landlords' land'[2] were adopted by the National Assembly of the Western Ukraine on October 28, 1929, and the National Assembly of Western Belorussia on October 30, 1939. In the Baltic republics, the declarations 'on the proclamation of the land as national property, i.e. state property',[3] were adopted by the National Diets of Lithuania and Latvia on July 22, and by the State Duma of Estonia on July 23, 1940. . . .

The basis of the new land regime of Bessarabia and Northern Bukovina was established by the decrees of the Praesidium of the Supreme Soviet of the USSR of August 15, 1940.[4] Since Bessarabia formerly had been an integral part of Soviet Russia, occupied in the spring of 1918 by landlord-bourgeois Rumania, its forcible severance had never been recognized by the Soviet Government; hence the decree 'on the restoration of the Soviet land laws' was promulgated on the territory of Bessarabia, 'in accordance with the decree on the land adopted by the second All-Russian Congress of

[1] *Sovetskoye Gosudarstvo i Pravo*, 1940, No. 11 (slightly abridged).
[2] See *Pravda*, October 29 and 31, 1939, and *Izvestia*, October 29 and November 1, 1939.
[3] See *Pravda* and *Izvestia*, July 23 and 24, 1940.
[4] See *Pravda* and *Izvestia*, August 16, 1940, and *Vedomosty Verkhovnovo Sovieta SSSR*, September 4, 1940, No. 29.

Land Nationalization in the New Western Republics

Soviets on October 26 (November 8), 1917'. Since Bukovina had formed an integral part of Austro-Hungary until the end of the first imperialist war and, after the disintegration of the Hapsburg Empire, had been annexed by Rumania, a special decree was issued 'on the land nationalization on the territory of Northern Bukovina'.

All these legislative acts followed the path blazed by the world-historic first decree of the Soviet Government 'On the Land' of October 26 (November 8), 1917: they incorporated the following basic principles:

(a) proclamation of the land with its mineral resources, forests and waters as national property, and establishment of exclusive state property rights in their regard;

(b) liquidation without any compensation (confiscation) of all landlord, church and altogether the whole of large-scale unearned landed property, including live and dead stock, and farm buildings;

(c) transfer of the confiscated land to the tenure of the working peasantry;

(d) liquidation of the former debt obligations and the numerous taxes and payments which placed an intolerable burden on the working peasantry.[1]

In accordance with the declarations made by the National Diets of Latvia and Lithuania and the State Duma of Estonia, 'the maximum size of the land allotted for tenure to the working peasants is established at 30 hectares'; [but] there was no such limit in the legislative acts on land nationalization in the other republics.

These decrees, while eliminating the parasitic private capitalist ownership in land, at the same time guarantee the complete inviolability of the working peasants' land tenure and private property. In satisfying the primordial craving of the peasantry for land in the form of the familiar individual households, these decrees inaugurated, like the land decree of October 26, 1917, the first stage of the radical transformation of the land relationships in the village—the stage of distributing the basic mass of the confiscated land among the landless peasants and those short of arable land.

[1] The release of the working peasant from the old debt obligations, taxes and dues was formalized by the resolutions of the Council of Peoples' Commissars of the USSR of December 28, 1940, 'On the Taxes and Dues from Peasant Households in the Lithuanian, Latvian and Estonian Soviet Republics' (*Svod Postanovleni SSSR*, 1941, No. 1, p. 12). The different strata of the peasantry were treated in different ways. For households which used to possess more than 30 hectares of land, as well as those with 10-30 hectares and regularly hiring agricultural labour, the rate of the land tax in the Lithuanian SSR and of the tax on immovable property in the Latvian and Estonian SSR was increased (for 1940).

'Every attempt to infringe on personal peasant property, or to force on the working peasants the organization of kolkhozy, will be sternly punished[1] as harmful to the interests of the people and the state'—such was the announcement made in the declaration of the Latvian and Lithuanian Diets and the State Duma of Estonia.

. . . .

The foundations of the land system on the basis of land nationalization, as stated in the above declarations, were consolidated in the Constitutions of the Estonian, Latvian and Lithuanian Soviet Socialist Republics, which were confirmed by the Provisional Supreme Soviets of these Republics on August 23–24, 1940.

These constitutions are taking account of the fact that Estonia, Latvia and Lithuania are still in the initial stage of socialist construction. That is why the formulation of these constitutions (in Chapter I, 'The Social Order') regarding the land regime (as well as industry and trade) contains certain peculiarities that differ from the wording of the 1937 constitutions of the old Soviet republics.

The Baltic constitutions make no mention of kolkhozy—neither of the property of individual kolkhozy (article 5), nor of kolkhozy side by side with public organizations (first paragraph, article 7), nor of the land tenure of kolkhozy (article 8), nor of subsidiary personal households and personal land tenure by kolkhoz households (second paragraph, article 7).

Owing to this, the constitutions of the Baltic Soviet republics stipulate not only, like the other constitutions, that 'side by side with the socialist system of economy . . . private households of individual farmers are admitted . . .' (article 8) but, unlike the constitution of the old Soviet republics, they also lay down that the working peasant households are guaranteed gratuitous and termless land tenure: 'peasant households are confirmed in the gratuitous and termless tenure of the land held by them within the limits fixed by law' (article 9).

II

The history of each of the new Soviet territories has many characteristic peculiarities which have left their mark on the land system and the position of the peasantry.

Before the political map of Eastern Europe was redrawn, as a result of the imperialist war of 1914–18, Estonia, Latvia, Lithuania, Western Belorussia, a portion of the Western Ukraine and Bessarabia

[1] In the declaration of the State Duma of Estonia: 'will resolutely be counteracted'.

formed part of Tsarist Russia, while others like Eastern Galicia (and a portion of the Western Ukraine) and the northern part of Bukovina were under the rule of Austria-Hungary.

Their political fate differed also after 1918 until the establishment of Soviet power in 1939–40. Estonia, Latvia and Lithuania became new and formally independent states—bourgeois republics. Western Belorussia and (both parts of the) Western Ukraine were forcibly incorporated in the new Polish state. And Bessarabia and the northern part of Bukovina were seized by Rumania.

After the great Socialist October Revolution, nearly all these territories had short periods of Soviet rule, between 1917 and 1920, but the political situation in which it was established (in some territories several times) differed in accordance with local peculiarities.

None the less, the land system and the position of the peasantry in these territories, prior to their reunion with the Soviet Union in 1939 and 1940, had several features that were more or less common to them all.

The agrarian policy of the bourgeois governments in these territories, between 1918 and 1939 (1940), was sharply nationalistic. They cultivated emphatically bourgeois land ownership of the new dominant nationality. The Belorussian and Ukrainian village in Western Belorussia and the Western Ukraine was being strongly Polonized by means of Polish colonization; the Ukrainian village in Northern Bukovina and the Moldavian and Ukrainian village in Bessarabia were Rumanified.

Nevertheless, because of the proximity of the Soviet frontier, the agrarian policy of these countries was bound to be much more affected by the impact of the new Soviet agrarian order than that of more distant countries. Under pressure from the peasant masses, in a situation marked by a growing revolutionary movement in the village, all these territories between 1919 and 1922 solemnly proclaimed and inaugurated 'agrarian reforms' which, it was declared, were to benefit the landless peasantry and those short of arable land, and to satisfy to a certain extent their land hunger at the expense of larger landed property. But later on, very little was done in the promised sense. The reforms remained either almost wholly on paper (in Poland—in the territory of Western Ukraine and Western Belorussia) or they were used mainly in the interests of a reactionary nationalistic agrarian policy—to set up and consolidate kulak households of the dominant nationality (in Estonia, Latvia, Lithuania, Northern Bukovina and Bessarabia).

All these 'agrarian reforms' of the bourgeois governments after the first imperialist war only aggravated the position of the poorest peasantry: having remained without land, it was compelled to seek employment as farm labour; yet farm labour wages were falling owing to a drop in demand arising from the curtailment of the large estates.[1]

Nor did the 'agrarian reforms' raise the prosperity of the peasant smallholders with insufficient stock who had been allotted land. They were unable to recuperate from the weight of the large land-redemption payments, from the bondage imposed on them by the credit terms, the growing taxation and so forth. The number of peasant households auctioned off because of non-payment of obligations due grew from year to year (in Lithuania, for instance, during the last year 13,000 households).[2]

All these western republics and provinces had also common forms of peasant land ownership which were distinct from peasant land ownership in Central Russia. They had not a trace left of communal land-holding based on levelling-out through redistribution. Peasant land ownership was based on farmsteads, without periodic levelling-out through redistributions, and with a great deal of settling separately in detached farms (especially in Estonia, Latvia and Lithuania).

. . . .

Western Belorussia and the Western Ukraine, already backward under Russian and Austro-Hungarian rule, had a still more miserable existence under Polish overlordship. They were in the position of cruelly exploited colonies with an industry which was not only stagnating but actually shrinking. In view of the immense proportion of large-scale Polish private land ownership, and owing to the harsh policy of Polonization pursued by Poland (that sickly offspring of Versailles, inflated beyond measure by incorporating numerous national minorities), the Ukrainian and Belorussian peasantry in the eastern peripheries of Poland (the so-called *kresy*) in the last twenty years suffered from the sharp hostility of the Polish ruling circles, headed by the Polish magnates and gentry.

The 'agrarian reform' proclaimed by the Polish Seym in July 1919

[1] For greater detail on the bourgeois 'agrarian reforms' in these countries after the first imperialist war (from 1919 onwards) see *The Agrarian Revolution in Europe*, a collection of articles edited by Sehring (translated from the German), 1926, pp. 41–56, 193–242, 243–72, 273–92: 'Agrarian Reforms in the Bourgeois Countries after the Imperialist War', *Great Soviet Encyclopedia*, Volume 1, 1926, pp. 492–4, 498–506; 'The Agrarian Problem in the West in the Epoch of the World War', *Encyclopedic Dictionary Granat*, seventh edition, Volume 46, pp. 562–71, 584–8, 593–7, 598–9.

[2] Cf. the report on the session of the Lithuanian Diet of July 22, 1940 (speech of the rapporteur, the deputy Mitskis), *Izvestia*, July 23, 1940.

Land Nationalization in the New Western Republics

and passed by it in July 1920, envisaged the allocation of land to the peasantry at the expense of large landed property (over 400 hectares, exclusive of forests). In practice, however, the reform was extremely slow in materializing; it was sabotaged outright by the ruling classes, and as soon as the alarm caused by the defeat in the Polish-Soviet war had passed, there was but an utterly insignificant reduction in the huge privately owned Polish latifundia which predominated precisely in Western Belorussia and Western Ukraine. Moreover, it was the worst land that was thus severed. The redemption payments were an extremely heavy burden for the households to which land was allotted.

But there was quite a different approach to the law on 'settlement' (1920 and 1932) concerning peasant households on the eastern borders of Poland owned exclusively by settlers of Polish nationality: Polish legionaries, soldiers, gendarmes and civilian officials. The purpose of this law, which was tackled energetically and quickly, was to establish a strong body of Polish kulaks in the Ukrainian and Belorussian village. Plots were allotted to the 'settlers' even at the expense of land owned by the Ukrainian and Belorussian peasant majority.

At the same time, under the slogan of regulating land relationships, the peasantry, although it had almost no forests of its own, was deprived of its ancient rights of wood-cutting for household needs, pasture and so forth in forests of the landlords, and became even more dependent on the latter. The obligations for road maintenance and road building (the so-called *sharvarki*) were exceptionally heavy. The continuously rising taxation placed a particular burden on the poor peasant households.

The position of the Moldavian and Ukrainian peasantry in Bessarabia under Rumanian rule (1918–40) was analogous.

Bessarabia is an agrarian country almost without industry, with a well-developed horticulture, fruit- and wine-growing and a high proportion of large estates.

The peasantry of Bessarabia, which had formed part of Russia from 1812 but was occupied by Rumania in the spring of 1918, hated the Rumanian regime all the more since it had not only stopped the distribution of the landlords' land inaugurated by the Soviet Government, but also restored most of the private landowners, above all the medium holders, in their rights to land ownership.

Later on, however, to mitigate the sharp peasant discontent, Rumania and Poland had to adopt agrarian reforms (1919) by compulsory alienation with compensation of landed property exceeding the established norm of 100 hectares. The agrarian policy of the ruling Rumanian boyars in Bessarabia was at the same time a policy of colonization, for both the Ukrainian minority and the Moldavian majority of the peasantry gravitated far more to the Ukrainian and Moldavian culture east of the Dniester (in the Ukrainian Soviet Socialist Republic and the Moldavian Autonomous Soviet Socialist Republic) than to the Rumanian culture west of the Pruth. In selecting the households that were to receive land, special attention was paid to the political complexion of each beneficiary—his 'reliability' and his 'merits' gained on behalf of the Rumanian authorities in the struggle against Bolshevism.

The land allocation under that 'reform' failed to improve conditions in the Bessarabian village owing to the onerous redemption terms (forty years), the peasantry's shortage of live and dead stock and lack of means for acquiring it, the bondage of credit terms, the exorbitant taxation, the forcible severance of the historical economic links with the Ukraine and the RSFSR, and the general conditions imposed by the unrestricted and arbitrary rule of the Rumanian bureaucracy and *Sigurantsa* [political police].

The incessant peasant risings in Bessarabia (notably in Khotin in 1919 and in Tatarbunar in 1924; according to the official statistics of the Rumanian government, there were more than 150 risings between 1919 and 1924) indicated the exceptional hardships of the peasantry under the yoke of the Rumanian regime, and especially its agrarian system. The increased peasant mortality tells the same tale.

The social structure of Northern Bukovina under Rumanian rule was very similar to the social structure of Eastern Galicia in the former Polish state. The majority of the rural population was Ukrainian, whilst the largest landowners were predominantly Polish. Economically Bukovina is rich in pastures and forests (the country of beeches) and has well-developed cattle-breeding.

Since its forcible incorporation in Rumania (after the imperialist war) Bukovina, too, experienced a policy of resolute Rumanification, especially by means of Rumanian colonization which the agrarian reform (of 1921) was designed to serve. Not only the public and crown lands of the former Austro-Hungarian monarchy but also the old fund of peasant lands were used for this purpose.

The *status of the peasantry of the two Baltic countries, Estonia and Latvia*, had many common features—both in the past when they formed part of Russia (from the eighteenth century until 1918) and during the twenty years when they were 'independent' bourgeois republics, i.e. before they joined the Soviet Union.

In both countries, the peasant reform which, over a hundred years ago, liquidated serfdom without allotting land to the peasantry (the reform of 1816-19) retained considerable significance. Until 1918, the land ownership here was concentrated mostly in the hands of the German barons, the descendants of the [Teutonic] knights (hence the predominant type of landed property—the so-called 'knightly estates'). The kulak stratum of Latvian and Estonian nationality was basically represented by farmers owning detached properties. The working masses of the peasantry served as farm labourers on the landlords' estates and kulak farms. No other part of Russia had so many landless peasants compelled to seek employment as farm labourers as the former provinces of Livonia and Kurland (i.e. the territory of Latvia): in Livonia the farm labourers amounted to 60 per cent and in Kurland to as much as 72 per cent of the entire population engaged in agriculture (in Russia they totalled an average of 17-18 per cent).

The Estonian and Latvian bourgeoisie, which came to power in the middle of 1918, marked the establishment of the new Estonian and Latvian bourgeois republics by the most ferocious chastisement of the urban and rural workers who had supported, and struggled for, the Soviet regime in the first half of 1918, when the red flag was unfurled in these countries. The subsequent bourgeois agrarian reforms of 1919 and 1920 by the Estonian and Latvian governments allotted land to those commissioned and non-commissioned officers of the young Estonian and Latvian armies who had particularly 'distinguished themselves' in the suppression of the revolutionary movement. The reforms transformed Estonia and Latvia into countries of large-scale peasant kulak households (the 'grey barons' of Estonian and Latvian nationality). The worst position was that of the village poor in Latgalia (the eastern part of Latvia bordering on the USSR), whom land shortage compelled to serve as the main source of cheap hired labour in agriculture.

The territory on which the bourgeois Lithuanian state was set up as a result of the revolutions in Russia and Germany after the imperialist war, and after the short period of Soviet rule, had been part of Russia for over a hundred years (from the time of the partitions of Poland at the end of the eighteenth century). It was an agrarian country with a low level of agriculture, in which large-scale and medium landed property, predominantly Polish and partly Russian, played the leading part, whereas most of the peasantry, mainly of Lithuanian nationality, were either landless or short of land. The characteristic features of class differentiation in the Lithuanian village were, on the one hand, a growing pauperization parallel with a continuous rise in the number of farm labourers (of whom the basic group were the so-called *ordinarniki* farm workers, hired for annual labour, together with their families) and, arising from this, the mounting emigration of the poorest strata of the Lithuanian peasantry to North America; and, on the other hand, an increase and consolidation of kulak holdings and separate kulak farms before and especially after Stolypin's agrarian legislation of 1906–10.

The agrarian reforms of the Lithuanian government during the first years of the republic (the reforms of 1920 and 1922) were directed in particular against Russian and Polish land ownership. The young Lithuanian bourgeoisie hastened to wind up the legacy of Tsarism—the land ownership by the Orthodox Church (the dominant religion was Catholicism) and the large-scale land ownership by Russian dignitaries and officials who had established themselves, after the suppression of the Polish rising of 1863, in the estates confiscated by the Tsarist government from the Polish insurgents and attached to the new landlords in the form of inalienable 'entailed' estates. A sharp anti-Polish note was given to the reform of 1922 after the occupation and severance of the city and district of Vilna by the forces of the Polish general Zeligovski. All those who participated in his campaign had their land confiscated.

Privately owned land above the limits of 80–150 hectares was subject to compulsory alienation with compensation. Land parcels were also transferred on the basis of compensation predominantly to the kulak stratum of the Lithuanian peasantry—in the first place to those who had taken part in military operations against the Polish troops of General Zeligovski and, to some extent, to veterans of the imperialist war. Separate settlement in detached farms was particularly encouraged. More than half of the land (2·2 million hectares out of 4·1 million) belonged to less than one-tenth of the total number of households (27,500 households out of 295,000).

III

The peculiar nature of agrarian relationships prior to the establishment of the Soviet regime has to a certain extent affected the way in which the new agrarian order was introduced into each of the new western Soviet republics and provinces.

Nevertheless the identity of purpose underlying the agrarian policy of the communist parties, the identical principles of land nationalization and abolition of the basic forms of unearned land ownership, the identical forms of collectivization and the identical method of Soviet democracy, brought about considerable similarities *in the way the fundamental reorganization of agrarian relationships* was applied in the new western borderlands of the USSR.

Land Nationalization in the New Western Republics

It was necessary, above all, to take account of the mistakes which had been committed by the Soviet regime between 1918 and 1920, during the initial stages of establishing new agrarian relationships in these territories as well as in some other [Soviet] republics (for example, in Hungary and partly in the Ukraine), which had caused the peasant masses, who were unprepared for immediate socialist reconstruction of agriculture, to sever themselves from the Soviet regime. It was particularly important to respond to the age-old longing of the working peasant masses by boldly tackling the *division of the mass of the landlords' estates for the benefit of the small peasant households, without yielding to the temptation to preserve the greatest possible number of large-scale farms as a basis for state farms or collective farms.* When the very first steps towards agrarian reorganization in the new western borderlands were made in 1939-40, they followed V. I. Lenin's instructions (1919):

'This is how the peasant thinks: "If there is a large-scale farm, that means that I am again a farm labourer." This is, of course, incorrect. But the peasant mind connects the conception of a large-scale farm with hatred, with his recollections of how the landlords had oppressed the people. This feeling is still there. It has not died out yet.'[1]

The land was reorganized on *the broad initiative of the rural working masses* in the Ukraine, Belorussia, Moldavia, Lithuania, Latvia and Estonia.

Everywhere, in the larger and smaller rural districts, after the establishment of the people's government, an *aktiv* was formed of people who under the bourgeois regime had already proved their devotion to the cause of the people. Special local committees, guided by the corresponding republican or provincial committees, were organized for the land [reform], the organization of land exploitation and so forth. In the Western Ukraine and Western Belorussia some of these local committees were set up even before the national assembly had adopted the declaration on the confiscation of the landlords' lands. They played an important part in the first days after the liberation from the Polish yoke, maintaining iron revolutionary discipline, protecting from loot the abandoned landlords' estates, buildings and stock, and seeing to the proper care of the property which had become the sacred and inviolable possession of the whole people.

The redistribution of the former unearned landed property had to be accomplished as a matter of urgency. It was necessary at once to wind up the exploiters' regime and allot land to the landless peasantry and those short of it, so as to make it obvious to the whole people that a

[1] *Lenin*, Vol. XXIV 3rd [Russian] edition, pp. 167-8.

fundamental revolution in the agrarian policy had taken place, and that the partition of the former unearned landed property was to be accomplished by the beginning of the new agricultural year. Accordingly, rigid time limits were fixed for the entire redistribution of the land (1½–2 months) and were more or less observed.[1]

In conformity with the legislature's directives on the new agrarian order, *norms were worked out and issued specifying the land subject and not subject to confiscation, the order of distributing the land fund among the landless peasants and those short of land and so forth. These norms were laid down in great detail for Latvia and Estonia*[2]. It was specified that the redistribution did not extend to lands within the administrative boundaries of the cities, [but] that the entire land belonging to churches, parishes, religious societies and monasteries was subject to confiscation and inclusion in the state land funds, the so-called Reserve Fund, as was also large-scale private landed property (in the Baltic republics land exceeding 30 hectares) and all land owned by the enemies of the people and by those who speculated in land (in the Latvian SSR).

Except for a small number of plots reserved for various state and public requirements, the bulk of the former unearned landed property which was confiscated, and the former treasury lands suitable for agriculture, were to be allocated to landless peasants and those short of land. The establishment of model state agricultural enterprises (state farms) was provided only for the largest and best organized privately owned estates, or for some adjoining properties which were drawn together into a single whole.

The maximum size of the new plots and of plots augmented for peasants short of land was fixed in Estonia, Latvia and Lithuania at from 8 to 15 hectares. It was suggested that the land should be allocated in the following order: to annual and seasonal agricultural workers, to peasants short of land, to migrants, to metayers and tenants (the Estonian SSR). Preference was given to families with many children. All those desiring to obtain land had to submit to the local land committees appropriate questionnaires (in Latvia

---

[1] In Latvia it was possible to complete the entire redistribution of the land by the date fixed by the Council of People's Commissars of the Latvian SSR, i.e. September 25, 1940. Cf. the report-meeting on the land distribution held by the People's Commissariat for Agriculture of the Latvian SSR in Riga, September 25, 1949, in the *Trudovaya Gazeta* (Riga), September 26, 1940.

[2] Cf. 'Law on the Land', by the government of the Latvian SSR, July 29, 1940 (*Trudovaya Gazeta*, August 2, 1940, supplement—*Trudovaya Derevniya*, No. 1), as well as the decree of the Council of People's Commissars and the CC of the CP(B) of the Estonian SSR, October 2 1940, 'On the Order of Allotting Land to the Landless Peasants and Those Short of Land', October 3, 1940 (*Trudovoi Putj*', Tallin, October 3 and 4, 1940).

there were even prepared questionnaires in four different colours according to the categories of priority of the population). In allotting land to landless peasants, the agrarian order to which the local population was used was taken into account, and various forms of settlement were allowed. In the Baltic republics, for example, even detached settlement was permitted, as far as possible in the form of 'households' groups'.

As was the case when the first laws on the land were applied in the RSFSR and the other Soviet Republics, the confiscation and distribution of unearned landed property and the entire reorganization of land relationships on the new Soviet territories was and is still taking place under the conditions marked by the *acute class struggle over the land.*

There was genuine happiness among the economically weak landless peasants and those short of land. 'Our cherished dream is coming true, the dream of the village poor and of the farm labourer, the dream of one's own plot of land sufficient to feed the family' —this was the unanimous opinion of those working in the village as reported by numerous correspondents from Western Belorussia and the Western Ukraine in the autumn of 1939 and from Estonia, Latvia and Lithuania, Northern Bukovina and Bessarabia in the autumn of 1940.

On the other hand, the capitalist elements in the village resorted, and are still resorting, to every means likely to hold up the distribution of land, so as to be able to retain the maximum. The periodicals of the new Soviet republics are quoting many concrete illustrations of the ways in which these elements resist the radical reorganization of the land. To incite the medium peasants against the Soviet regime, the class enemy spreads the provocative rumour that they, too, will be deprived of land, that agricultural stock will be removed from peasants *en masse*, that the harvest will be requisitioned, that forcible collectivization is imminent. The class enemy recruits his agents to act among the less conscious strata of the peasantry as servants of the kulaks, resorting to threats and, in some places, actual acts of incendiarism and murder. He excels in evading the activity of the land reform committees by fictitious divisions of the larger properties, concealing and camouflaging his ownership of several landed properties in more than one place, and endeavouring to set up fictitious 'protective' kulak collective farms (the collective farms of the 'grey barons').[1]

---

[1] Cf. for particulars the detailed article by the Secretary of the CC of the CP(B) of Estonia, N. Karotam, 'How the Landless Peasants and Those Short of Land were Allotted Land', *Trudovoi Putj*, October 28, 1940.

Later Developments in Soviet Nationalities Policies

The division of the former unearned landed property has radically changed *the physiognomy of the village* in all the new Soviet territories. The large estates of the exploiters (landlords and so forth) have been swept out without trace. Kulak land ownership has been substantially curtailed. The number of landless peasants and those short of land has been greatly reduced. The numerical strength of the medium peasantry has considerably risen.

In the individual republics and provinces, the following unearned landed property was included in the state land fund and transferred to the working peasantry for gratis and termless use: in the Western Ukraine (in the six provinces belonging to the Ukrainian SSR), more than one million hectares were divided among 400,000 households without or with insufficient land; in Western Belorussia (in the five provinces belonging to the Belorussian SSR), over 430,000 hectares; in the Lithuanian SSR, over 600,000 hectares, of which as many as 400,000 hectares were distributed among 72,000 households without or with insufficient land; in the Latvian SSR, approximately 550,000 hectares were distributed among 70,000 peasant households (these include 47,000 new households of formerly landless peasants or farm labourers who received 475,000 hectares, while 23,000 peasant households short of land received an additional 75,000 hectares); in the Estonian SSR, more than 300,000 hectares were distributed among 55,000 households (these include 23,000 newly established households of formerly landless farm labourers, while 32,000 peasant households short of land received additional land); in Northern Bukovina (in the Chernovits province which forms part of the Ukrainian SSR), 200,000 hectares; in Central Bessarabia, which forms part of the Moldavian SSR (according to preliminary data), approximately 250,000 hectares were transferred to the landless peasantry; in the Izmail (formerly Akerman) province in the territory of Bessarabia which is a part of the Ukrainian SSR, 65,000 hectares were distributed among 6,000 new households of landless peasants and farm labourers and 18,000 peasant households short of land.[1]

Altogether, according to preliminary, incomplete and still unprecise data, as many as 3·5 million hectares of cultivable land taken from unearned landed property were distributed among 0·75 million small peasant holdings which used to be either landless or short of land.

---

[1] The figures quoted have been taken from the following sources: M. Bril, 'The Liberated Western Ukraine', *Politizdat*, 1940, p. 16; *Pravda*, September 17 and October 14, 1940, and February 7 and 8, 1941; *Izvestia*, September 17, November 13, 19, 22 and 26, December 5 and 29, 1940, January 15, 1941; *Truzhenik* (Kaunas), November 3, 1940; *Trudovaya Gazeta*, September 26, 1940; *Sovetskaya Estonia* (Tallin), November 2, 1940. Corresponding data on Bessarabia for the Khotin province forming part of the Ukrainian SSR are lacking.

Land Nationalization in the New Western Republics

While allotting land to tens and hundreds of thousands of landless peasants and poor peasant households short of land, a whole set of measures were taken simultaneously to help them to become self-supporting, to acquire dwellings and farm buildings, and to organize their households which in most cases lacked the required agricultural equipment.

The live and dead stock confiscated from the landlords' estates is being extensively distributed among the new households of the poorest peasantry. Building material is being supplied from state timber funds (all the forests have been nationalized), and from the quarries producing building stones (the mineral resources have also been nationalized). The new households are offered special long-term credits for construction and the acquisition of the required agricultural equipment. Appropriate sums for this purpose have been assigned in the state budget (for example, 20 million lits in Lithuania, and 7·2 million lats in Latvia). A special preference credit is available to the poor peasant households without cows to enable them to acquire the animals (a credit total of 8·4 million rubles in Western Belorussia).[1] Encouragement is given to the organization of *Supriagi* (groups of peasants who combine for particular jobs such as ploughing, harrowing and threshing), which are particularly widespread in Western Belorussia. A network of state machine tractor stations is being rapidly set up in the former private estates to serve the peasant households with agricultural machines on a contractual basis. The best of the former large private estates, which provide the basis for state farms, fulfil an important function as socialist model households for the whole county, and lend practical assistance to the adjacent villages (with seeds, pedigree cattle and so forth).

IV

The first collective farms on the land freed from the exploiters were set up on the initiative of the farm labourers, village poor and medium farmers, and under the leadership of the working class during the first months of the genuine people's government.

It is obvious that the working people in the western republics and provinces are now far more favourably placed for the transition from the individual household to the communal kolkhoz household,

---

[1] Cf. the resolution of the Council of People's Commissars of the USSR and the CC of the CPSU(B) of January 20, 1941, on 'How to Overcome the Lack of Cows in Kolkhoz Households and the Households of Village Poor in the Western Provinces of the Belorussian SSR' (*Svod Postanovlenii SSSR*, 1941, No .4, p. 58).

and for developing and consolidating the kolkhoz structure in the village, than were the peasants of the old Soviet republics. . . . They can benefit from the enormous experience and immense achievements of the socialist economy of over 200,000 collective farms covering with a dense network the territory of the old Soviet republics.

The popularization of the collective farm system is immensely enhanced by the periodical press, the personal impressions which numerous delegates from the new Soviet republics and provinces have gained from the All-Union Agricultural Exhibition—a real people's university for socialist agriculture—by personal observations made by individual peasant delegates visiting certain advanced collective farms on the territory east of the former state frontier, and letters to the local press with colourful descriptions of the prosperity of kolkhoz life from collective farmers who used to live in the village in question but had since settled elsewhere.[1]

The peasantry in the new Soviet territories has no longer to grope its way from the traditional individual petty households to the large-scale socialist households. It need no longer look for the most practicable rules for producers' co-operatives in agriculture. The only statutory form of kolkhoz development that fits the present stage is already clearly defined—the agricultural artel, whose model statute has stood every test as 'the basic law regulating the organization of the new society in the countryside.'

The transition to the socialist artel economy on the part of the working peasantry which has been newly assimilated to the Soviet regime has been substantially eased by the powerful material and technical aid which the state gives to the collective farms, above all through the widely ramified network of state machine-tractor stations which are bringing into the village the most advanced and hitherto unknown technique of mechanized agricultural production. In the western provinces of the Ukraine over 170 machine-tractor stations have already been organized and more than 100 in the western provinces of Belorussia. In 1941, 115 machine-tractor stations were under construction in the three Baltic republics (40 in Lithuania, 50 in Latvia, and 25 in Estonia), 27 in the Izmail province, and 13 in the Chernovits province (Northern Bukovina).

The degree of initiative evinced by the working peasantry in the transition to the socialist kolkhoz economy in the various western republics and provinces, of course, differs. It is undoubtedly affected by certain traditional forms of economy and peasant settlement,

[1] Cf. the letter from the Caucasus (near Sukhumi) from settlers from Estonia, *Trudovoi Putj*, October 2, 1940.

Land Nationalization in the New Western Republics

and by the extent to which the local population is in contact with the population of the old Soviet republics.

Applications for collective farms to be set up are coming in from the peasants of entire villages, and often from nearly everyone in every household.[1] Collective farms are coming into being continuously. Thus, the Rovno province in the Western Ukraine had 14 collective farms in the winter of 1940, 37 at the time of the spring sowing, and 76 by the end of the agricultural year.[2]

At the first anniversary of the liberation from the Polish yoke, on September 17, 1940, Western Belorussia had about 600 collective farms comprising 30,000 households, and the Western Ukraine more than 400 collective farms.[3] By January 1, 1941, the total number of collective farms in the Western Ukraine (exclusive of the Izmail and Chernovits provinces) had risen to 571, comprising 34,000 households, in addition to 535 groups which had initiated the establishment of collective farms comprising collectivization of 14,000 households.[4] Collectivization has started in Northern Bukovina, where the first seven collective farms drew together over 1,000 village poor and medium farm households and socialized as many as 3,000 hectares of land.[5] In Estonia, the first collective farms (*Krasnaya Niva*, *Obshcheye Dielo* and others)[6] were set up three to four months after the establishment of the Soviet regime, i.e. as early as October 1940.

The collective farms are being established on the basis of the Stalin Rules of the Agricultural Artel.

In organizing collective farms in the large and small villages of the new Soviet territories, where only yesterday the landlord, the kulak and policeman were omnipotent, the farm labourers, village poor and medium farmers are displaying revolutionary class vigilance. As the well-known writer Vanda Vasilevskaya testifies in her article 'The First Kolkhoz', the working peasantry in Western Belorussia

[1] Cf. the article by the secretary of the CC of the CP(B) of Belorussia, P. K. Ponomarenko, 'The Triumph of the Liberated Belorussian People', *Pravda*, March 24, 1940.
[2] Cf. the article by the secretary of the Rovno Provincial Committee of the CP(B) (of the Ukraine), V. Begma, 'The Autumn Balance', *Izvestia*, October 27, 1940.
[3] Cf. the article by the chairman of the Council of People's Commissars of the Ukraine SSR, L. Korniets, 'On the Liberated Land', and the article by the chairman of the Council of People's Commissars of the Belorussia SSR, I. Brylinski, 'Sum Totals of Victory', *Izvestia*, September 17, 1940.
[4] Cf. the report of the vice-chairman of the Council of People's Commissars of the Ukraine SSR, Comrade Starchenko, to the plenary session of the Central Committee of the CP(B) of the Ukraine, *Pravda*, February 6, 1941.
[5] Cf. *Pravda*, February 14, 1941.
[6] Cf. *Sovetskaya Estonia*, November 7, and *Pravda*, October 10, 1940.

does not admit to kolkhoz membership anyone who at one time or other has been connected with the police, has failed to show his solidarity with the villagers, committed certain sins against the workers and the cause of the peasants, and thought only of himself, without sharing in the common life of blood and toil. . . .[1]

The public economy is getting well under way in the new collective farms: brigades and links are in the process of organization; livestock farms are being set up. From the thick of the peasantry which has been liberated from the yoke of the landlord and kulak, enthusiastic devotees of collectivization are beginning to emerge; they are the architects of the new free peasant life. New trades are appearing in the village—combine operators, tractor drivers, brigade leaders, appointed from local peasants, are given training at short-term courses. The buildings of the former landlords' estates, which have been taken over by collective farms and are carefully preserved, are used as schools, kindergartens, collective farm clubs, hostels, [accommodation] for tractor drivers and so forth.

In the Western Ukraine, in less than a year, 233 cattle farms, 185 sheep farms and 112 pig farms have been set up. By January 1, 1941, there were 742 livestock farms.

Many collective farms have obtained excellent results for the first agricultural year, and such earnings for artel members as the peasants could never have imagined before. For example, in the artel named after Stalin, in the Rovno province, the family of the former farm labourer N. Patii received for the labour-days it had put in: 300[2] pood of grain, 180 pood of potatoes and 5,000 rubles. In the artel named after Kirov in the same province, the woman link-leader M. Mazur and her family received for their labour-days as many as 250 pood of grain, 270 pood of potatoes and more than 4,000 rubles. Some collective farms, such as the kolkhoz named after Lenin in the village of Davidovichi in the Lvov province, were able to sell already in the first agricultural year 20 wagons of market grain, whereas the landlord's household, where this particular collective farm has been established, used to produce a maximum of 12 wagons of grain. The average grain harvest in the collective farms was considerably higher than that of the individual farmers; for example, in the Volynia province the proportion was 12·1 to 10·6 hundredweights [per hectare], and in the Rovno province 13·6 to 9 hundredweights.

. . . .

Comrade Stalin said: 'What we need is not just *some kind* of

---

[1] *Sotsialisticheskoye Zemlediliye*, September 17, 1940.
[2] I.e. *ca.* 5 tons.—R.S.

Land Nationalization in the New Western Republics

alliance with the peasantry, but only an alliance based on the struggle against the capitalist elements of the peasantry.'[1] Thanks to the wise agrarian policy of the Soviet Government, the working class has concluded just such an alliance with the peasantry of the new western republics and provinces, an alliance which guarantees the consolidation of the Soviet regime and the continued success of socialist construction in all spheres of national economy as a whole, and of the socialist reconstruction of agriculture in particular.

Only the Soviet regime, which has destroyed the private ownership of land, put an end to the hated landed property and proclaimed the land to be the property of the whole people, could open to the working peasant masses of the western territories from the Baltic to the Black Sea the road to prosperity and culture, and create the conditions required to overcome 'the idiocy of village life'.[2]

---

[1] J. Stalin, *Problems of Leninism*, 11th [Russian] edition, p. 233.
[2] Cf. K. Marx and F. Engels, Vol. V (Russian edition), p. 487.

DOCUMENT NO. 28

EXCERPTS FROM: EVERYDAY LIFE IN A
KARAKALPAK KOLKHOZ *AUL*[1]

by T. A. ZHDANKO

(Results of an Ethnographic Study on the Akhunbabayev
Kolkhoz in the Chimbai District of the Karakalpak
Autonomous SSR)

The Akhunbabayev kolkhoz covers an extensive territory of 4,170 hectares, of which approximately 2,000 hectares are well-watered arable lands, 208 hectares are pastures, 233 hectares form the irrigation system and approximately 450 hectares are sands. The livestock farms of the kolkhoz have 430 head of cattle, over 500 sheep and goats and 440 horses. The kolkhoz includes 214 households with a total population of 1,574. By nationality, all the kolkhoz members are Karakalpaks, except for the Uzbek agronomist-gardener recently invited from Samarkand, where he had graduated from the Agricultural Technicum, to superintend the big orchard and vineyard, the pride of the Akhunbabayev kolkhoz.

According to the kolkhoz members, the lands of the present two kolkhoz brigades used to belong, before the Revolution, to the rich kulak, Guleck-bey, of the Arelbai clan. He also owned about 1,000 head of cattle, flocks of thousands of sheep and goats, and 400 horses. As many as 100 dekhan[2] farm-hands were working on his fields and keeping his herds. Two of them—the sixty-four-year-old Yusupbek and the fifty-year-old Kanyaz—are now members of the Akhunbabayev kolkhoz. They tell us that Guleck-bey paid nothing to his farm-hands, beyond pledging himself to feed them and provide them with wives. Considering the ancient Karakalpak custom whereby matrimony had to be paid for in the form of the bride's ransom (*kalym*) so that, at times, the village poor, unable to save up for the *kalym*, had to remain single, such a commitment on the part of the bey was of great importance for the farm labourer. The

---

[1] *Sovetskaya Etnografia*, 1949, No. 2. The omissions concern mainly the description of the kolkhoz economy, so far as it is not conditioned by the specific Karakalpak setting. In the introduction (also omitted) the investigated kolkhoz is described as one of the best existing in the Karakalpak Republic.—R.S.

[2] Indigenous peasants (translator's note).

Everyday Life in a Karakalpak Kolkhoz Aul

bey, on the other hand, when it came to marrying off his dekhans, did not, of course, ever spend his own money on the *kalym* but compelled the village poor, who were dependent on him, to give their daughters away in marriage. The food which the bey allotted to his dekhans was very scrappy. For a whole year, a married man would get for his work not more than 20 batmens of grain [a batmen equalled 22 kg.], and a bachelor even less. Apart from the farm labourers, Guleck-bey had also tenant farmers (*zharymshi*), who worked on his land for a portion [usually half] of the harvest.

After the Revolution, the land and the herds of Guleck-bey were confiscated in 1924 and transferred, during collectivization, to three kolkhozy in the Chimbai district.

No less colourful a figure, typifying the exploiters' upper strata of the Arelbai clan (which lived on what is now the territory of the kolkhoz), was Kalila-Kadi, a judge, who also used to own land which is now the property of two brigades of the kolkhoz. He was a specialist in family and divorce cases and notorious for bribery, whereby he had made a great fortune. But the greatest source of his wealth was not land or cattle, but money and grain. He would give out grain, in return for a 50 per cent share of the harvest, to village poor short of grain for winter sustenance and for sowing. His money, however, went into commerce. Kalila-Kadi's sons, who used to travel to Orenburg and Perovsk, were well known as big traders. The kadi directed the education in the *aul*. He founded two schools (*mekteb*) and appointed two of his close relatives as mullahs (teachers).

Another notorious money-bag and exploiter was Sharip-Ishan, who was in charge of a big medress (mosque), the ruins of which are still preserved in the kolkhoz. His economic power and influence were very great. Dominating most of the mullahs of the surrounding villages, he collected through them the taxes for the benefit of the clergy. . . . Moreover he was in *de facto* charge of the waters of the Arelbai-Zhaba canal which fed all the lands of the Arelbai *aul*. His *aspekshi*, who were supervising the use of water, would not give a drop of water to the population without the Ishan's permission. The cleaning of the canal, too, was carried out by orders of the Ishan. He had so much taken possession of the Arelbai-Zhaba canal that it was latterly called by his name. Owing to lack of water, usurped by the Ishan, a portion of the Arelbai clan had to move to the Kuibyshev district.

. . . .

. . . The past history of the Akhunbabayev kolkhoz brings out clearly the basic features of the social and economic structure of

Later Developments in Soviet Nationalities Policies

Karakalpak society in the colonial period. The traditions of clan community are still firmly preserved in the minds of the population: the lands and irrigation canals were considered the property of the clans Arelbai, Kangly and others. In fact, however, the social structure of the Karakalpaks was dominated by a class division— which developed during the centuries but became most acute and deep on the eve of the great Socialist October Revolution. Inside the land and water community, particularly in the Chimbai district, hereditary land tenure by households was prevalent.[1] The land and water belonged to the beys and the clergy. The feudal system of exploitation (metayage *zharymshi*, dues and taxes and obligations in kind for the benefit of the beys, ishans and mullahs) blended with elements of capitalist relationships (commercial and industrial enterprises) which penetrated ever more deeply the Karakalpak colonial *aul*. Moreover, patriarchal clan survivals played an important part in the system of exploitation. The numerous indigenous farm-hands who were working for the beys and ishans were their kinsmen, and the serf-life exploitation of these dependent peasants retained the forms of 'intra-clan aid' illustrated by such facts as the 'remuneration' of labour by entering into an obligation to find a wife for the indigenous peasant (i.e. to pay the *kalym* for the poor kinsman) and feed his family. There were also other forms of 'intra-clan aid', such as the *kumiok*, a widespread custom of communal help in house-building or urgent field work, which took the form of mass service by the villagers in the bey's household. The feudal, patriarchal forms of exploitation, as is well known, were not peculiar to the Karakalpaks. They were inherent in the social structure of many peoples enslaved by Tsarist Russia, 'most of whom retained their cattle-breeding economy and patriarchal clan life . . . or had failed to advance beyond the primitive forms of the semi-patriarchal semi-feudal life'.[2]

The year 1929 can be regarded as marking the beginning of collectivization in the Chimbai district, for it was then that the first association for joint land tillage of the whole Keness *aul* soviet came into being here. The association lasted but one year. The kolkhoz *Leninshi* was organized in the former Khalmurat *aul* in 1930. The kolkhozy *Kzyl-Kala* and *Kzyl-Tu* were formed in 1932; the kolkhoz *Kohamshi*, which included the population and the land of the Shanshpai *aul* and the Sambet *aul*, in 1933; and the kolkhoz *Raiatkom* in Akkala in 1934.

[1] See *Materials on the Investigation of the Nomadic and Non-Nomadic Native Economy and Land Utilization in the Amu-Daryan Section*, Ed. 1, Tashkent, 1915, p. 175 [in Russian].
[2] J Stalin, [Russian] *Works*, Vol. V, p. 25.

Everyday Life in a Karakalpak Kolkhoz Aul

In 1936 the kolkhoz *Kzyl-Kala* was named after Akhunbabayev, and during 1937–38 the other four kolkhozy were merged with it, thus forming the Akhunbabayev kolkhoz with its present territory and population. . . .

. . . .

A highly important factor in the economic life of the Akhunbabayev kolkhoz was the reconstruction of the irrigation network. Before the Revolution, each of the clan *auls* had its lands along a canal cut by the respective clan straight from the Kegeili. As they were located on the lower reaches of the Kegeili, these canals received little water. The weak water pressure and its low level made it necessary to use *chigirs*—bulky water-raising contraptions with earthenware jugs for drawing the water tied to a wooden wheel. There were altogether 66 *chigirs* on that territory. Being of very small productivity, these *chigirs* required a great expenditure of labour and strength of the draught animals who were continuously turning the wheel. In view of the general water shortage the big beys and the clergy had completely arrogated to themselves the distribution of water inside the *aul*, so that lack of water became a customary calamity in agriculture. Moreover, the log structures of the canals were continuously silting up. The frequent duty of cleaning the irrigation network, imposed by the beys and the administration on the population, was a heavy burden for the village poor. The rich and medium peasants bought themselves off from doing this heavy work by bribery.

In 1936, a new large-scale distributing canal of the mechanical type was built for the purpose of regulating the water supply of the kolkhozy of the Keness and the Toza-Dzhola village soviets in the Chimbai district (including the Akhunbabayev kolkhoz). It is called October-Abad and, running parallel to the Kegeili, touches the heads of the kolkhoz distributor canals. The construction of the October-Abad canal was an important event in the life of the kolkhozy, for it solved the more than one hundred-years-old problem of watering their arable land. Irrigation by *chigirs* vanished. The old canals Arelbai-Zhab and Kangly-Zhab have been reconstructed; at present the Baganaly-Zhaba canal is under reconstruction; and the next tasks will be the reconstruction of the remaining kolkhoz canals, the construction, at the kolkhoz distributors, of concrete water dischargers, and the improvement of the small-scale irrigation network serving the land of the brigades and teams.

The collective farm no longer suffers from shortage of water. The release of water to the sectors of the brigades is carefully regulated by the experienced *mirab* Sagy Fattulayev. The kolkhoz fields, gardens, melon fields and the private plots of the collective farmers are covered with rich green. The broad streets of the central settlement, although not yet everywhere built up with houses, have been planted beforehand with Lombardy poplars, shady willows . . . and mulberry trees.

. . . .

The population and the territory of the kolkhoz are divided into production brigades. The brigades, scattered at considerable distances from each other, are organized on territorial lines, and situated in the localities of the former *auls* along the main irrigation canals. . . . The traditions of separate settlements of the old type are reflected in the composition of the brigades: in most cases, each represents a small subdivision of the clan which used to live in the same *aul*.[1]

The 214 households of the kolkhoz are divided into 14 working brigades (from 9 to 23 households per brigade) working on the crops on the irrigated lands. Each brigade consists of several teams. The cotton fields are distributed in such a way that each brigade is allotted 25–35 hectares, while 6–12 hectares are covered by the remaining crops. Each brigade has 20–30 workers, and in addition the kolkhoz has a grain brigade of 30, a vegetable brigade of 3, while 25 kolkhoz members are engaged on the cattle farms. About half of the total of over 400 working kolkhoz members are women.

. . . .

The reorganization of the villages forming part of the Akhunbabayev kolkhoz was started as far back as 1939. The public, business and cultural institutions and the farmsteads and private plots of the kolkhoz members are rationally arranged along streets fringed with irrigation ditches and planted with trees. The new layout will put an end to the survivals of the old scattered settlements by clan groups, which made for the seclusion and isolation of the population, enabling at the same time some families to satisfy their strivings for private property by arbitrary extensions of their individual plots at the expense of unappropriated lands adjacent to the kolkhoz fields. The project of the socialist reconstruction of the kolkhoz village has already been applied in practice. . . . In the centre of the village . . . the big new building of the kolkhoz administration is under construction. Its seven rooms include the chairman's reception room, the

[1] In the article, this is illustrated by a comparative table: of the 14 brigades, only two are mixed as regards their clan-structure, and even these only as regards the smallest sub-unit (*koshe*).—R.S.

Everyday Life in a Karakalpak Kolkhoz Aul

accountant's office, the general office, the room for the party and komsomol organization, and others. . . . The business buildings of the kolkhoz—the storehouses (for grain, vegetables and fruit), the garage, the village store, the carpenter's shop and the smithy—are nearby. Here, too, by a young poplar grove, we find the club, the inn and the surgery. At the bottom of an enclosed garden and orchard, at the top of a beautiful alley planted with tall Lombardy poplars, stands the kolkhoz *mikhmankhana*—a small building with an awning and platforms covered with felt rugs and carpets. Here, among the verdure, fruit trees and murmuring irrigation waters, the kolkhoz receives its honoured guests and treats them to various kinds of grapes, peaches, apples and fragrant melons. With the progressive accomplishment of the building project new amenities are emerging in the kolkhoz village, such as a canteen, a public bath-house, a hairdresser's shop, and so forth. All the public buildings of the kolkhoz have been built of clay . . . under the guidance of local craftsmen . . . without recourse to any official architectural standard projects. The sheds for the kolkhoz livestock are on the three cattle farms.

. . . The kolkhoz has three elementary schools working in two shifts. All kolkhoz children from seven to ten are attending school.[1] There are four classes in each school and altogether 203 pupils. Boys and girls are studying together. Children above the age limit of the fourth class are studying in the incomplete secondary school (eight classes) of the neighbouring Kuibyshev kolkhoz, or in the ten-year school of the neighbouring Gorki kolkhoz. There are six teachers, all Karakalpaks, born in the Akhunbabayev kolkhoz and graduates of the Pedagogical School in Chimbai. Moreover, two teachers who have passed the first correspondence course of the Pedagogical Institute in Nukus while continuing to live in their native Akhunbabayev kolkhoz, are teaching Russian, history and geography in the senior classes of the neighbouring incomplete secondary school. Each of the school buildings has three rooms and a storeroom connected by a corridor. Two are classrooms and the third is for the teacher. In one case, the school is combined with a nursery which is attached to it.

The kolkhoz has also a surgery employing a Ukrainian woman doctor who is a graduate of the Tashkent Medical Institute and a Ukrainian nurse who has graduated from the Medical Technicum in Dnepropetrovsk. The surgery serves the population of the three kolkhozy (26 brigades). About 30 patients are treated per day. The

[1] It is implied that, in 1948, even in a model kolkhoz in Karakalpakia seven-year school ('incomplete secondary') education was not yet general.—R.S.

Later Developments in Soviet Nationalities Policies

medical workers also call on patients at home. There are regular inoculations against smallpox and typhoid. The surgery was established in 1939. At first, the population was slow in consulting the doctors, and instead continued to make extensive use of the services of quacks and medicine men. The quacks were treating abscesses by applying dead frogs. In the case of earache, they used to slap the ears of the patient with the lungs of a newly killed sheep. Burns were covered with ground millet. Malaria was being treated by the mullahs by means of charms. The 'cure' of the sick by medicine men (the exorcising of evil spirits) was practised in the presence of a big gathering of people in a tent. All those attending had to wear clean shirts. Both men and women would act as medicine men. No tambourines were used, the ceremony being accompanied by jumping and wild howls. The medicine man announced for whom of the ancestors or sheikhs a funeral repast should be arranged in order to cure the patient.

At present, of course, the picture has radically changed. Both the doctor and the nurse enjoy well-deserved authority among the kolkhoz members and are summoned to patients and to expectant mothers. The medical workers devote much effort to the task of popular enlightenment and never fail to provide patients with drugs. The next task is to establish, at the surgery, a hospital with several beds.

The kolkhoz club is a tall spacious building with an equipped stage. The club, however, is not yet active enough, and most of the cultural and political functions are held irregularly. Yet the kolkhoz has an *aktiv* of cultural workers, a group of young musicians (seven instrumentalists and singers), and a group of propagandists (mostly teachers) who are arranging discussions and lectures in the brigades. This year they held discussions on the international situation, the importance of developing cotton cultivation, on anti-religious subjects and so forth. Several times a year the farm is visited by a mobile cinema and by a mobile kolkhoz theatre. The repertoire of the latter, apart from musical and vocal pieces, includes also recitations by folk-tale narrators from the Karakalpak national epic. The kolkhoz is also visited by artists of the Metropolitan Karakalpak State Dramatic Theatre from Nukus, and by the national ensemble of the Chimbai Philharmonic Orchestra. Recently a good radio set has been installed in the club, and the houses of the kolkhoz members are connected with the radio network. The kolkhoz is linked by telephone with the district centre.

The kolkhoz administration and the schools take several of the Republic's newspapers, one of which is in the Uzbek and another

Everyday Life in a Karakalpak Kolkhoz Aul

in the Karakalpak language. A third is a district paper. Of the Russian papers, the kolkhoz subscribes to *Sovetskaya Karakalpakia* and *Komsomolets Uzbekistana*. Of the central papers, it receives the *Uchitelskaya Gazeta* and the *Pionerskaya Pravda*.[1]

The kolkhoz members have more than 20 gramophones. The selection of records is rather varied. Karakalpak musical works predominate, but there are also many Uzbek, Kazakh and Russian pieces (folk songs and front songs from the period of the Great Patriotic War).

. . . .

. . . The budget of a kolkhoz family is made up of the remuneration for the labour-days of the working members of the family, and of the produce from the private plot and the domestic cattle. The size of the private plot admitted by the law amounts to 0·3 hectares, of which 0·04 hectares are for the house garden and 0·26 hectares for sowings. Among the crops on the private plot, sorghum and millet predominate. The 214 households of the kolkhoz farm have 273 cows (excluding calves), 717 sheep, 658 goats and 134 donkeys in private use. For the pasture of privately owned cattle each brigade has a common shepherd hired from people outside the kolkhoz. The cattle are every day driven to the village. The milking and processing of dairy produce is done by every family at home, and not on the pasture.

In Karakalpakia, not only the public buildings but also the new dwellings of the kolkhoz members illustrate the achievements of the Soviet regime and of the new life. Before the Revolution the population generally had no houses of their own—except for the beys, the village-elders, the clergy and other members of the upper strata of the *aul*, who built for themselves fortress-like country seats. . . . But the remaining population, in summer and winter, lived in tents with occasional small mud huts attached for storing household articles and for keeping the cattle. During the last years before the Revolution, in the economically best developed district in the environs of Chimbai, medium farmers too began to build houses. According to the data for 1912–13, out of 200 households which made up the *aul* population which subsequently joined in the Akhunbabayev kolkhoz 52 had permanent dwelling-houses.

The old-type Karakalpak house, which is becoming a rarity in the kolkhoz *auls* . . ., represented a certain improvement in the life of the Karakalpak peasant family in winter, compared to the crude tent which offered but poor protection against the cold winds and

[1] It appears that central papers—and Russian papers in general—are subscribed to only by the teachers and komsomol organizers.—R.S.

frosts of the season. Yet there were only a few even of these primitive, badly heated and unhygienic winter dwellings, where men and cattle lived together.

At the present time, all the kolkhoz members have warm winter houses with windows and iron stoves. In addition to the house, the tent is a necessary part of the Karakalpak kolkhoz member's household. The living houses that have been constructed in the last few years no longer have the cattle shed under the same roof. The cattle sheds are separated from the house, and are now built nearby.

The typical dwelling of the contemporary kolkhoz farmstead is the clay-made *tan*, a new type of house with two rooms (the main room and the storeroom and kitchen), with several big windows and convenient stoves used for cooking and heating. The house also contains, as before, a storeroom and a big space, taller than the other rooms, for the tent. In the coldest months of the year, the tent stays empty, for the family moves into the living-room. In the spring and autumn they live in the tent inside the house, but in the summer the tent is taken out and placed near the house so that it faces south. Near the tent they erect an awning and hearths. This is where the family spends the summer, and until autumn the house is merely used as a storing place. Thus the tradition of the semi-nomadic life and the national habit of living in a tent are preserved in the everyday life of the Karakalpak kolkhoz members. Among the most cultured families, the interior arrangement of the tent is beginning to depart from tradition. The cooking hearth is transferred to the storeroom. Only the central hearth under the air-hole remains for tea-making and heating in cold weather. The space thus gained is often taken up by a table, chairs, small wardrobes and a sewing-machine. Owing to the removal of the kitchen, greater cleanliness is observed. The tent remains the favourite place for rest, food, sleep and the reception of guests. The national habitation of the Karakalpaks, a product of centuries, provides them in the hottest weather with shade, fresh air and protection against insects. The carpet fabrics, representing the peculiar and rich Karakalpakian folk art, richly ornament the interior.

. . . Side by side with towels, cisterns for drinking water, paraffin lamps, aluminium basins, teapots, saucepans, spoons, washing basins and so forth, the old utensils are still firmly entrenched. Everywhere there are wooden mortars, butter-beaters, vessels of various shapes made of pumpkins, leather bags for flour, groats and dairy products, and cast-iron kettles. Every household has a handmill. Although the new houses and tents have tables, the people by tradition eat on the floor, spreading a tablecloth on the felt rugs and

Everyday Life in a Karakalpak Kolkhoz Aul

carpets. The unhygienic wooden cradle, which has a harmful effect on the physical development of the child, is still very widespread. Invariably also there is, at the entrance to the tent, a suspended bag, affectionately ornamented by the mother with a coloured pattern—appliqué work of scraps—the satchel of the schoolchild, containing his books.

. . . .

The changes have also greatly affected the clothing, especially of the women. Some new forms of national costume have appeared. The red cloth headgears, richly ornamented with embroideries, and also the local variety of the yarmak have either gone out of fashion or are only surviving as a domestic relic. The usual women's attire is a frock of factory-made cotton or silk material (manufactured in the industrial craft artels of Uzbekistan), and a gear in the Uzbek style. . . . Among the men, the old ones—though far more seldom than they do in Uzbekistan—wear the Oriental smocks and the national round sheepskin caps. Generally the men use trousers and jackets of urban cut or short sleeveless waistcoats of dark cloth, and very often quilted jackets or military tunics. Their headgear consists of caps with ear-flaps, peaked caps or embroidered skull-caps.

In the kolkhoz store, as in the markets of Chimbai, there is an abundance of manufactured goods, especially of cotton materials of beautiful bright shades, and ready-made clothing, footwear, galoshes and so forth.

The socialist reconstruction of life and especially the equal participation of women in kolkhoz work and also the equal status granted them by Soviet legislation . . . have produced radical changes in Karakalpak family life in the kolkhoz *aul*. Though patriarchal clan survivals have not yet been quite overcome in this respect, this will no doubt happen in the next few years.

Until the Revolution, the social system of the Karakalpaks . . . was marked by a firm adherence to clan and tribal division. The cumbersome, complicated and stratified structure of tribes, clans and sub-clans, firmly established despite the prevalence of feudal and the penetration of capitalist relationships, had a real significance in social life. It gave rise to the separate settlements of the population, some peculiarities of water and land utilization, and especially the customs of family life. In matrimony, the custom of exogamy—the prohibition of marriages between members of the same clan—was strictly observed. Its violation was punished not only by public censure but also by expulsion of the offenders from the native *aul*.

Marriage was pre-arranged by the parents of the bride and bridegroom, generally at a time when both were still infants, and sometimes even before they were born. The compulsory bride's ransom, polygamy, marriages of young girls with boys under age or old men, and, after marriage, the woman's degrading status of inferiority in the family, the various prohibitions regarding the husband's relatives, the law of the compulsory marriage of a widow to the husband's brother or any of his closest relatives and so forth—these are but a few of the oppressive survivals of ancient customs which enmeshed the whole life of the Karakalpak family, especially as they blended with as many injunctions of the religious laws of Islam. Some of these customs have more or less survived in the kolkhoz *aul*, especially in matrimonial relations. As a rule, clan exogamy is respected. . . .

In the same way they still pay some attention to the question of clan membership in pre-matrimonial relations between young people. Courtship among young men and young girls of one and the same clan is unthinkable. Even playful flirtation is regarded as unseemly, for these young people are considered as brothers and sisters. There are still special traditional relationships—survivals of ancient relationships amongst phratries—whereby not only the families of the husband and wife but the members of the entire *aul* to which they belong still address each other in special terms of kinship.

Although the woman in the family still observes the complicated rules of behaviour towards her husband and his relatives (the taboo on pronouncing their names, the abstention from common meals, especially in the presence of outsiders, and so forth), this is now rather a matter of external etiquette. Actually the role of the woman in the family has changed: her voice is heeded and she is taken into consideration in family affairs. Apart from the fact that the woman herself now earns and contributes her own substantial share—in the form of labour-days—to the farm budget, the new attitude of the Karakalpak kolkhoz family to women is largely due to the honour and respect shown by public opinion to good women workers, their promotion to responsible posts, and the higher degree of literacy, education and culture among the young women—all of which tend to increase woman's independence and personal freedom.

We have heard of many cases illustrating the development of new forms of marriage based upon love and friendship, contracted by the young people themselves. Often a young girl, having fallen in love with a *dzhigit*, leaves with him the home of her parents without their permission, thus paying a kind of token tribute to the ancient customs which are still observed by the old generation. But whilst,

Everyday Life in a Karakalpak Kolkhoz Aul

in the past, in such cases, the girl and the 'kidnapper' were pursued, the parents now generally do not wait more than a year to give their consent and to make their peace with the son-in-law's family.

The traditional bride's ransom is now being replaced by gifts to the parents and close relatives of the bride in the form of clothing, watches, cloth, a cow or sheep, and so forth. The bridegroom is expected to prepare and to present his bride with . . . five garments, namely: (1) footwear . . . good boots of modern make; (2) a big smart kerchief (for outdoor occasions); (3) . . . a gown of Bokhara silk; (4) a black velvet jacket; (5) a coat of European make, often also of black velvet.

We have taken down the details of a contemporary wedding in an intelligent Karakalpak environment. Compared to the old most complicated ritual, all the rites have been simplified and reduced, in most cases, to mutual entertainment and gift-making among the relatives of the bridegroom and the bride. Many of the rites are no longer complied with seriously but in a half-jocular fashion. The festivities are always attended by invited musicians. . . . The basic content of a contemporary wedding is no longer the traditional and archaically strict ceremonial, but jollification.

In order to ascertain the cultural interests of the kolkhoz members we have tried to find out what kind of literature is read by individual families. The domestic 'library' contains mostly the works of the national epic: Karakalpakian variations of the Khiva dastan *Yusup and Akhmet,* the poems *Kobalan, Alpamys, Gor ogly, Sayatkan Kamre, Maspatsha, Yor shora* and others. These works are not in book form but as handwritten excerpts written out in copy-books. There are also handwritten songs and poems of the favourite Karakalpak nineteenth-century national poet Berdak Shair. The book *Berdak,* published in a limited edition by the Karakalpak State Publishing House, is less frequent.

Among the books the works of contemporary Karakalpak writers and poets predominate, for instance the collection of poems by Abbza Dabyolva called *Joy of the Factory,* the poem by Zholmyrzy Aimurzaev, *Yerbai Batyr* (dedicated to a Karakalpak hero of the Patriotic War), the works of the contemporary national poet Sadyk Nurumbetov, *Paluannarym Kiatyr* (dealing with Karakalpak fighters returning from the fronts of the Great Patriotic War) and others. A great favourite enjoying much popularity is the book *Happy Times* —a collection of poems by Nauruz Dzhapakov, poet and chairman of the Council of Ministers of the Karakalpak Autonomous Soviet Socialist Republic. Many Kazakh and Uzbek writers and poets, too, are in vogue. Some families have also Karakalpak translations of

Russian literature (particularly the poems of Nekrasov and others). We find a different selection of books in the families of the kolkhoz intelligentsia. Thus in the home library of a teacher we found very important political literature: a *Short History of the CPSU(B)* and *Problems of Leninism* in the Karakalpak language, the biographies of Lenin and Stalin, the Constitutions of the USSR, the Uzbek SSR and the Karakalpak ASSR, several works by Lenin (in the Karakalpak language), and the *Agitator's Handbook*. Then there were also text-books on the history of the USSR and the history of the Middle Ages, and finally the works of contemporary Karakalpak literature, almanacs, anthologies and so forth. The trend towards the Russian language and literature is very strong. There are a great many translations of Russian classics . . . Pushkin's *The Captain's Daughter* and *Dubrovski*, Lermontov's *Lyrical Poem* and *A Hero of our Time*, Gogol's *Dead Souls*, Griboyedov's *Woe from Wit*, Chekhov's *Cherry Orchard*, and works by Turgenev, Goncharov, Nekrasov and Chernyshevski. Some of these books are in Russian, others in the Karakalpak language. It would be wrong to assume that the study of this wider range of political and artistic literature and acquaintance with the Russian classics is the privilege of the teachers. The secondary school in the neighbouring kolkhoz has a library where all the pupils of senior classes may borrow books. But in view of the immense increase in the cultural requirements of the kolkhoz members, we have noted a shortage of books and an acute need for a library and reading-room at the kolkhoz club.

Until recently, in view of the numerous survivals of ancient beliefs, in particular the cult of trees . . . the practice of medicine men, the ancestral cult in clan cemeteries (a night spent in prayer among the tombs was supposed to help even against serious illness) . . . the influence of the Moslem clergy remained extremely strong during the first years of the kolkhoz. At the present time two mullahs live in the *aul*. Their 'services' to the believers consist mainly in collecting money and produce from their flock. At the time of lent . . . the mullahs manage to collect a fairly considerable sum . . . in the form of one-eighth of a batman of wheat, barley and *dzhugara* from every member of the family, irrespective of his age or of whether he is at home or absent. These collections are, of course, no longer compulsory. People say, 'he who wishes gives, he who will not gives nothing'. A portion of the income collected from the population is surrendered by the mullahs to the official representative of the Moslem church in Chimbai, the Kalimbet-Ishan.

The authority and influence of the two mullahs among the inhabitants of the kolkhoz are declining from year to year. Only the

Everyday Life in a Karakalpak Kolkhoz Aul

old folk are remaining in their flock. The young people have abandoned religion. This is strikingly demonstrated by the fact that the kolkhoz members are, in effect, celebrating two holidays a year, May 1 and November 7, which have become genuine popular holidays, and have almost completely ousted there ligious *mauruz*, *ramazan* and *kurban*. It is an interesting fact that certain forms of the ritual formerly connected with religious holidays, such as the tradition of popular jollification and public repasts, have now been transferred to the revolutionary holidays.

While we were in the Akhunbabayev kolkhoz, the celebrations there began with meetings of the kolkhoz members, with reports made by representatives of the district and by kolkhoz members. This was followed by the award of prizes to Stakhanovites and shockworkers. Then the celebrations were transferred to the individual families and brigades. A custom has already been established whereby each brigade holds a public repast. The sheep for that purpose are collected from the various homes and the wine is bought by pooling money. The young people hold the traditional . . . social with mutual entertainment by young men and girls, whereas the old people and the more mature kolkhoz members sit in the tents conversing sedately, drinking tea and listening to music or folk tales. We have heard that some religious old men do not take part in the common celebrations on the occasion of revolutionary holidays but demonstratively leave at that time for field work: this provokes a great deal of laughter and sarcasm.

. . . .

While, mainly owing to the persistence of the custom of exogamy, the consciousness of membership of a definite tribe and clan still plays a certain part in the family life of the Karakalpak kolkhoz member, this consciousness has been completely overcome in public life, as it has been transformed into national consciousness and the awareness of membership in a given kolkhoz. . . . Our questions as to clan-membership have invariably provoked bewilderment among the kolkhoz members, and sometimes even smiles. . . .

The kolkhoz member is aware that his membership in a given clan is a fact of outdated and secondary importance, without any essential significance in the present state of affairs. He is above all a Karakalpak and a member of the collective of his kolkhoz. He will no longer tell you, as before, that 'this is the land of the Aralbay or Kangly clan' and so forth, but he will say that 'this is the land of our Akhunbabayev kolkhoz, and the neighbouring one is the Maxim Gorki kolkhoz.'[1]

However, the patriotism of the kolkhoz members is not confined to the framework of their own kolkhoz or the frontiers of the Republic. In order to prove this it is sufficient to quote some figures illustrating the part taken by members of the Akhunbabayev kolkhoz in the Great Patriotic War: in 1943 they delivered 220 tons of grain to the state for the organization of a tank column; 155 thousand rubles were given by the kolkhoz members from their personal savings for the purpose of strengthening the might of the Soviet Army. Among the front fighters who have returned there are several officers. . . .

[1] We have come across, this year, an interesting case: a small sub-clan has abandoned its clan name for that of 'Kuibyshev-Yestak' owing to the fact that the clan group lives in the kolkhoz named after Kuibyshev.

INDEX

(In order to avoid an overloading of the Index with references to persons and localities which are mentioned in the text only by way of illustration, names of persons who played no important political part, and of districts and localities mentioned *only* as instances of some more widespread phenomenon, are omitted. As a rule, the Autonomous Republics and Provinces are referred to in catchwords referring also to their predominant nationality. These concepts do not always cover the same field: for example, under the catchword 'Tatars' references not only to the Tatar republic but also to the Tatar minority in neighbouring Bashkiria will be found; these cross-connections, however, may in themselves be of interest for the reader. Apart from avoiding the obvious difficulties of any attempt to separate the references to the nationalities from those to the corresponding territorial units, the method applied also allows for following the references made to some nationality through all the changes in administrative divisions.)

Administrative divisions, 249 ff., 258–9
Adygei, 229
Armenia, *and* Armenians, 6, 23, 70, 216
Army, national units, 67
Artel, 92, 276, 287
Arts, 44; *see also* Literature
Austro-Hungarian Monarchy, *and* socialist movement, 3, 12
Autonomous Republics and Provinces, 8, 36, 114, 249, 258
Autonomy, national, on a personal basis, 12–13; regional, 14–15, 17, 249 ff., 258–9
Azerbaidjan, 6, 105, 124, 131 ff., 140 ff., 215–16

Baku, 134, 222
Balkars, 7; *see also* Kabardino-Balkaria
Baltic states, 262 ff., 268–9, 272
Bashkirs, *and* Bashkiria, 8, 25, 49–50, 65, 189 ff., 204–5, 208, 229, 244, 255
Basmachs, 19, 90, 153
Bauer, O., 13; *see also* Austrian Socialists
Belorussia, 6, 186, 217, 228, 251, 262, 264 ff.
Bessarabia, 267–8
Bokhara, 72–3
Bourgeois nationalists, 5, 10, 19, 27, 75, 80, 107–8, 125–6, 176 ff., 181 ff., 212 ff.
Budget, 20, 82 ff., 160–1; local, 84–5
Bukovina, 268
Bund, 13
Buryat-Mongolia, 4, 174, 204

Cadres, 61 ff., 74, 210 ff., 223 ff., 228 ff.
Caucasus, 7; Northern, 87, 230; *see also* Armenia, Azerbaidjan,

Index

Georgia, Kabardino - Balkaria, Ossetia (Northern and Southern), Transcaucasian Federation
Central Asian Bureau of CP, 98, 257–8
Centralization vs. decentralization, 28, 64, 76
Chokayev, 177
Chubar, 78, 81
Chuvashia *and* Chuvashs, 15, 114, 218, 229
Clans, influence of, *and* clan feuds, 88–9, 116–17, 144 ff., 282, 284, 289–90, 293
Collectivization of Agriculture, *and* collective farms, 24, 27, 92, 105, 145 ff., 152 ff., 172, 243 ff., 264, 272, 275 ff., 282 ff., 293; *see also* Labour Days, Livestock, Peasants
Colonies of Western Powers, analogies, 9
Commerce, 46, 54, 118 ff.; *see also* Co-operatives
Constitutional issues, 4, 68, 73, 75–6, 183–4, 249; *see also* Federation, *and* Secession
Co-operatives, 46, 94, 121, 137, 150
Cotton, 83–4, 103, 105, 171, 284
Courts, criminal, and criminality, 95–6, 118, 140 ff., 146 ff.; *see also* Offences rooted in the traditional way of life
Crimea, *and* Crimean Tatars, 8, 98, 103, 107–8, 125, 174, 245

Daghestan, 43 ff., 103, 108, 125, 206–7
Delegations of the National Republics, 37–8, 42 ff.
Denationalization, 114, 116
Diidigyan, 178
Disfranchisement (under 1918 Constitution), 132–3

Education, general, 21–2, 66, 171, 204 ff., 285; *see also* Literacy, *and* Teachers; higher, 39, 44, 47, 50, 53, 171–2, 219, 224 ff.; for local minorities, 18, 112; *see also* Jews
Elections, Soviet, 24, 86 ff., 92–3, 131 ff., 140 ff., 235 ff.

Famine relief (1921), 54 ff., 57
Federation, 15 ff., 183
Finland, *and* Finns, 4
Fisheries, 121

Georgia *and* Georgians, 6, 23, 70, 179
GOELRO Plan, 253
Gosplan, 254
Great Power (in particular Great Russian) nationalism, 19–20, 75, 122 ff., 196
Great Russians, 3 ff., 6
Grinko, 20, 74, 78, 81

Health services, 113–14, 163, 218, 285–6
Hitler, 19, 25, 186
Housing, 166–7, 193, 196, 238, 287–8

Ikramov, 177
Industrialization, 44, 175, 189 ff., 218, 259–60; *see also* Cadres, GOELRO, Gosplan, *Korenizatsiya*, Labour, Ural-Kuzbas
Intellectuals, 214 ff.

Jews, 13, 14, 113, 173, 180

Index

Kabardino-Balkaria, 229; *see also* Balkars
Kaganovich, 79, 86–7, 182
Kalinin, 242
Kalmyks, 7
Kalym, 117, 122, 145, 280, 291
Karakalpakians, 280 ff.
Kautsky, 12
Kazakhs *and* Kazakhstan, 22, 50 ff., 86, 89 ff., 105, 107, 174, 219, 222, 227
Kazan city, 238–9
Khodzhayev, 20, 82 ff.
Khorezm, 71–2
Khvilevoi, 80
Kindergarten *and* Crèches, 156–7, 195
Kirghiz, *and* Kirghizia, 22, 50 ff., 65–6, 88, 98–9, 102, 106, 158 ff., 245
Kolkhozy, *see* Collective farms
Korenizatsiya, 65, 74, 174–5, 191 ff., 204 ff., 218, 220, 229–30
Koshchi Union, 89 ff.
Kulaks (and beys, etc.), 86, 88, 94 ff., 102, 107–8, 126, 140 ff., 145 ff., 151, 269–70, 273; *see also* Disfranchisement *and* Peasants (social structure)

Labour, industrial, fluctuation, 193; training, 194–5, 208; wages, 195
Labour Day in collective farms, 154 ff., 278
Land, reform, 27, 73, 89 ff., 101 ff., 112, 262 ff.; leasing of, 104, 106–7
Laps, 115
Latinization, *see* Script reform
Law, customary, 117; religious, *see* Shariat
Lenin, 15, 185, 235, 251
Leningrad city, 237

Literacy, 21–2, 70, 133, 156, 173, 205, 229
Literature, nationalist tendencies in, 80, 177–8, 216; supply of, 47, 197 ff., 291–2
Lithuania, 269–70
Livestock, 105–6, 111, 118, 120, 158, 163, 278
Lunacharsky, 22

Mandates, electoral, 87–8, 235 ff.
Manuilski, 76
Mari Province, 245
Marriage age, 117, 137
Marx, 11, 105
Mensheviks, 13
Milli Istiklal, 126, 176 ff., 216
Milli Ittikhad, 176
Minorities, national, 35, 38, 115, 179–80, 209, 229; Russian in the non-Russian Republics and Provinces, 9–10, 26, 79–80; *see also* Ukrainization
Molotov, 99
Mordvins, 113
Moscow city, 236–7
Moslems, 22, 24, 95, 103, 123 ff., 281; *see also* Polygamy, Shariat, Yashmak
Mussavat, 215

Nationalities, definitions in Western Europe and in the USSR, 2 ff., 6 ff., 10 ff.; delimitations in the USSR, 6, 47; of the USSR, 6 ff., 109, 126, 201–3, 226–7; self-determination of, 14 ff., 114
Natural resources, opening of, 43, 57, 189
Nentsi, 112
New Economic Policy, 17 ff., 46, 53–4; *see also* Commerce

Index

Nomads, settlement of, 121, 158 ff., 288
North Ossetia, 144 ff.
Novosibirsk city, 239

Octobrists, 66
Offences rooted in the traditional way of life, 27, 117, 144–5
Otzovists, 62–3

Pan-Islamism, 19
Pan-Turkism, 19, 22; *see also* bourgeois nationalism, *and* Turkey
Party, communist, as centralizing factor in federation, 15–16; educational system, 194, 205; local organizations, 74, 94 ff., 114; purges, 72
Peasants, political attitudes, 17, 21, 24, 67, 86–7, 89 ff., 243 ff., 273, 278–9; social stratification, 104, 106–7; *see also* Kulaks; Collectivization of agriculture
People's Commissariat for Nationalities, 18, 33 ff.
Petrovski, 81
Poland, and Poles, 4, 182, 186, 266–7, 269–70
Polygamy, 117, 136–7
Procurements, 99, 151, 154
Publishing houses, 198 ff.

Rakovsky, 69, 76, 183–4
Red Corners, Red Tea Rooms, etc., 91, 170, 285
Reissner, 16
Religion, and anti-religious propaganda, 13, 94, 113, 133, 137–8, 281, 292–3; *see also* Moslems
Right-wing within CP, 24, 108, 217

Russian settlers (of Tsarist times), 9, 102, 115, 118
Samoyeds, 111, 115
Script reform, 22–3, 123 ff., 133, 197, 207
Secession, right to, 15, 251
Second Chamber, *see* Soviet of Nationalities
Shariat, 103
Shumski, 78 ff., 182
Skrypnik, 69, 74 ff., 182 ff.
Smenovekhovtsi, 20
South Ossetia, 179, 217–18
Soviet of Nationalities, 16, 18, 37, 41–2, 68–9
Soviets, local, 65, 84, 107, 134–5, 138–9, 228 ff.; training of staff, 230 ff.; office of Chairman of Central Executive Committee of, 242 ff.
Specialists, 43, 171; *see also* Cadres, *and* Education, higher
Stalin, 3, 4, 13 ff., 16, 17, 19–20, 61 ff., 78 ff., 152, 218, 223, 228, 252, 256, 259, 278–9
Sultan Galiyev, 19, 125, 213

Tadjiks, *and* Tadjikistan, 229, 252
Tatars, *and* Tataria, 19, 22, 25, 46 ff., 114, 125–6, 152 ff., 175, 178, 194–5, 205, 217–18, 221–2
Teachers, 206, 209 ff., 220–1; *see also* Education
Transcaucasian Federation, 11, 228, 251
Trotsky, 74, 183
Tungusi, 111, 114, 120
Turkestan Soviet Republic, 17, 56 ff., 70–1, 90
Turkey, 22–3, 124–5, 216
Turkmenia, *and* Turkmens, 87, 89, 98, 221, 229, 252

298

Index

Udmurt Province, 244
Ukraine, *and* Ukrainians, 6, 14, 16, 20, 65, 69, 71, 74, 78 ff., 181 ff., 251, 262; industrial development, 71, 79, 260; *see also* Chubar, Grinko, Kaganovich, Khvilevoi, Petrovski, Shumski, *and* Skrypnik
Ukrainization (of Russian minorities), 20, 78 ff., 182
Union Republics, 7, 258
Ural-Kuzbas heavy industrial basis, 204, 255, 257
Uzbeks and Uzbekistan, 7, 22, 83, 89, 98, 105–6, 171, 174 ff., 205, 218, 220, 222, 228, 252; *see also Milli Istiklal, and* Khodzhayev

Vilna, Polish occupation of, 270
Vinnichenko, 181
Voldemaras, 171
Volga Germans, 7, 15

Water supply, 168, 281, 283
Women's emancipation, 24, 88, 135 ff., 141–2, 152 ff., 169, 290–1
World War II, effects of, 26, 294

Yashmak, 133, 137, 142

For Product Safety Concerns and Information please contact our EU representative GPSR@taylorandfrancis.com
Taylor & Francis Verlag GmbH, Kaufingerstraße 24, 80331 München, Germany

www.ingramcontent.com/pod-product-compliance
Lightning Source LLC
Chambersburg PA
CBHW071804300426
44116CB00009B/1201